T0360439

SERIES ON
ECONOMIC DEVELOPMENT
AND GROWTH VOL. 9

INCLUSIVE GROWTH AND DEVELOPMENT IN THE 21ST CENTURY

A STRUCTURAL AND INSTITUTIONAL ANALYSIS OF CHINA AND INDIA

Series on Economic Development and Growth   (ISSN: 1793-3668)

SERIES ON
ECONOMIC DEVELOPMENT
AND GROWTH VOL. 9

INCLUSIVE GROWTH AND DEVELOPMENT IN THE 21ST CENTURY

A STRUCTURAL AND INSTITUTIONAL ANALYSIS OF CHINA AND INDIA

Edited by

Dilip Dutta

University of Sydney, Australia

World Scientific

NEW JERSEY · LONDON · SINGAPORE · BEIJING · SHANGHAI · HONG KONG · TAIPEI · CHENNAI

Published by

World Scientific Publishing Co. Pte. Ltd.

5 Toh Tuck Link, Singapore 596224

USA office: 27 Warren Street, Suite 401-402, Hackensack, NJ 07601

UK office: 57 Shelton Street, Covent Garden, London WC2H 9HE

Library of Congress Cataloging-in-Publication Data
Dutta, Dilip.
  Inclusive growth and development in the 21st century : a structural and institutional analysis of China and India / by Dilip Dutta (University of Sydney, Australia).
    pages cm -- (Series on economic development and growth, ISSN 1793-3668 ; vol. 9)
  Includes bibliographical references and index.
  ISBN 978-9814556880
  1. Economic development--China. 2. Economic development--India. 3. China--Social conditions.
4. China--Economic conditions. 5. India--Social conditions. 6. India--Economic conditions. I. Title.
  HC427.95.D87 2014
  338.951--dc23
                                                                    2013037733

British Library Cataloguing-in-Publication Data
A catalogue record for this book is available from the British Library.

In-house Editors: Sandhya Venkatesh/Dipasri Sardar

Typeset by Stallion Press
Email: enquiries@stallionpress.com

Printed in Singapore

Preface

The School of Economics, in association with South Asian Studies Group and China Studies Centre at the University of Sydney, Australia, had organized an international workshop on *Inclusive Growth in China and India: Role of Institution Building, Entrepreneurship and Management* on 28 October 2011. This book brings together a collection of revised papers presented at the workshop and a few invited/unpublished research papers. Using case studies of both the countries, the book chapters attempt to reinforce the fact that the processes of economic development are *dynamic* and *organic*, in the sense that structural and institutional elements are not only interrelated, but also constantly changing in their patterns of interactions — more so during their transitional period.

PART I Introduction: Structuralism and Institutionalism in Development Economics/Studies

Chapter 1 focuses on the methodology of holistic approaches based specifically on *structuralism/neostructuralism* and *institutionalism/new institutionalism* and notes that it has more relevance for the socio-economic analysis of transitional development processes compared to that of the one propounded by orthodox or neo-classical economists' analytical methods of *reductionism* and *formalism*. Because of their mutual complementarities, the two holistic approaches are being applied for socio-economic analysis of many transitional economies' aggregate/sectoral levels over the past two decades or so. It is argued that a successful development strategy depends on a judicious blend of planning/policy instruments (reflecting effective institution building based on a good understanding of a society's structural rigidities) and market forces as the key to an inclusive and sustainable pattern of growth and development, more so in an increasingly globalized world.

The societal structures of both China and India — the two most populated emerging economies — are dualistic in the sense that two socioeconomic segments: *informal* (i.e., unorganized or traditional) and *formal* (i.e., organized or modern) segments co-exist side by side within their geographic territories. Unlike the formal segment, the informal segment consists mainly of unincorporated household and small-scale enterprises which differ from formal enterprises in terms of level of technological sophistication, economies of scale, use of labor-intensive processes, and accountability with the government. Both China and India have lately been passing through internal segmentation and differentiation not only among different socio-economic interest groups/classes but also between different socio-economic-technological environments. In other words, uneven development has been a common feature of both the societies. As a result, need for appropriate institution building both within and across the two segments has been an urgent challenge for the governments of these societies. In order to translate the globalizing market forces into a successful inclusive growth and development process, complementarity between *structuralist/neostructuralist* and *institutionalist/new institutionalist* views has been explicitly or implicitly reiterated by almost all the authors in this volume.

PART II   Structural and Institutional Analysis of Contemporary China's Growth and Development

In Chapter 2, Limin Wang analyzes the growth experience of China over the past three decades with the objective of reshaping its current policy discourse on economic growth and development. The analysis focuses on the three decades of China's rapid economic growth and its sources, structural transformation, economic reform policies, and its integration into the global economy. Advancement in technology and innovation, poverty reduction, and rising income inequality are discussed in the context of the quality of growth. After assessing rising disparities in social indicators, gender inequality, and environmental and resource degradation associated with the rapid growth, the author critically examines the role of Chinese government. The key message of this chapter is that global policy-makers must not only recognize that the quality of economic growth is critical to sustaining development progress on the planet, but also act on it.

After noting that the economic disparities across three regions (Eastern, Western, and Central) in China have been remarkable since the 'open-door' policy adopted in December 1978, Dilip Dutta and Yibai Yang, in Chapter 3, first identify three major factors for regional disparity of growth in China *viz.*, economy's structural change, its openness to international trade, and receipt of foreign direct investment. They then investigate their effects on economic growth in these regions during 1996–2010. Their study finds that, during this period, the disparity of economic growth (measured in terms of regional gross domestic product) and income growth (measured in terms of regional income per capita) persisted without much divergence between the coastal and the inland regions compared to the earlier period from 1984 to 1993. The policy implication suggests that the regional policy of the Chinese government should improve institutions and infrastructures that favor both foreign direct investment and technology development/ adaptation to stimulate economic growth in the inland regions and therefore to reduce the regional disparity.

Wei Li and Hans Hendrischke in Chapter 4 show the link between inclusive growth as a policy target and China's institutional environment at local level. They argue that inclusive growth in China is not achievable by central government intervention alone, because it depends also on local governments and their support for local enterprise development. They explore this argument by asserting that small and medium enterprises (SMEs) matter for China's inclusive growth. A robust SME sector promotes broad-based and more equitable growth in several ways. These include the creation of employment opportunities (particularly in less developed regions), a critical mass of market participants and transactions leading to improvement in overall resource allocation efficiency, driving economic growth through fixed asset investment and exports, promoting technology assimilation to enhance industrial specialization and differentiation, and generating tax revenue which gives governments leverage to finance key socio-economic programs. This chapter also discusses the current finance challenges faced by China's SMEs. It suggests that policies targeting SME finance should reflect the variation and dynamics within SMEs' finance structure in China. Specifically, an alternative institutional debt-versus-equity finance framework is proposed.

In Chapter 5, Dilip Dutta and Guan Long Ren examine empirically if Baumol's so-called 'cost disease' in terms of lower labor productivity (LP) is prevalent in China's service sector compared to that in its manufacturing sector. They note that, since 1996, there has been a gradual increase in labor productivity growth in both manufacturing and service sectors of China. The growth of labor productivity, particularly in the service sector, has been sustained mainly because the consumption and expenditure levels of people have begun to rise steadily; this trend has prompted growth in demand for consumer services as well. The wide application of information and communication technology (ICT) products in the producer services industry is also partly responsible for growth in service sector's labor productivity. However, their empirical results show that the sustainable growth of LP in China's service sector is predominantly driven by non-ICT capital accumulation. They, therefore, conclude that, at the present stage of China's service sector, non-ICT capital accumulation is still a powerful engine of labor productivity growth; and the influence of ICT and human capital accumulation on labor productivity growth in this sector has its limits and needs to be further explored.

PART III Structural and Institutional Analysis of Contemporary India's Growth and Development

In Chapter 6, Anthony D'Costa starts with India's built-in structural processes that render the notion of 'inclusive' development challenging. This is despite the high rates of economic growth for the last decade and a half and the many recent initiatives launched by the Indian government to share growth. He then delves into the question of why inclusiveness is such an elusive outcome by contextualizing the inclusive development problematic with the framework of compressed capitalism, in which primitive accumulation, a large and expansive petty commodity sector, and a limited advanced capitalist sector coexist and together constrain employment and social mobility for the underprivileged groups in India. In addition to endogenous factors such as the structures of domination mediated by caste, class, and other social attributes primarily work against inclusive development, D'Costa argues that exogenous forces, namely, globalization, also reinforce some of the endogenous mechanisms of inequality and social exclusion. In addition to presenting an overall picture of India's record in inclusive development, D'Costa briefly examines two specific aspects of the Indian economy: role of the information technology and the large unorganized sector. They illustrate the multidimensional aspects of inclusiveness and the difficulties of attaining it under the current global and national structures of capitalism.

Chapter 7 by Dilip Dutta and Supriyo De studies the socio-economic effects of the ICT industry in India. Their analysis reveals that the Indian policy environment contributed significantly to the development trajectory of the Indian ICT industry. The ICT industry development has a dynamic, interdependent relationship with region-specific human resource potential and regional economic development. States endowed with strong human resource potential attract ICT investment and enjoy higher economic growth. However, this process creates disparities between the states that have largely generated and attracted ICT investment and the states that have relatively little such activities/investment. Policy initiatives are suggested to address these imbalances.

In Chapter 8, Elizabeth Hill evaluates the concept of inclusive development from the perspective of women's employment experience in the post-1991 decades of India's high economic growth. She examines the trends in women's labor market participation, access to quality work, and employment status in order to provide the basis for this evaluation. Her examination of the employment dynamics shows that Indian women are not increasing their participation in the labor market, and for most women who do work, employment remains informal, precarious, insecure, poorly paid, and unprotected. She also notes that two industry sectors that have expanded significantly and become highly feminized in the high growth era driven by globalization — information and technology enabled services (ITES) and business process outsourcing (ITES & BPO), and domestic service — highlight informalization and uneven impact of economic growth on women's employment experience in India.

Chapter 9 by Meera Lal examines the nature of inclusive growth in Andhra Pradesh — one of India's 28 states by focusing on its important parameters such as agricultural growth, employment generation, poverty reduction, social sector (health and education) development, and reduction in regional and other disparities (within the state of Andhra Pradesh). Though there has been some increase in the gross state domestic product (GSDP) over the past decade, but its desire to achieve Millennium Development Goals (MDGs) appears, as she argues, to be a distant dream. She notes that Andhra Pradesh may not be in a position to meet MDGs in 10 out of 14 indicators. The progress in MDGs for some regions and socially deprived sections within the state has been slower than the state average. In order to operationalize a plan for achieving inclusive growth in Andhra Pradesh, she suggests an action plan for removing economic and social deprivation for socially disadvantaged sections across all regions within the state.

Contents

About the Editor

Dilip Dutta is Associate Professor at the School of Economics, University of Sydney, Australia. After completing his PhD in Economics from University of California, Berkeley, he was a *Post-Doctoral Fellow* at Research School of Pacific Studies, Australian National University. Apart from his publications in journals such as *Economic Record, Applied Economics, International Journal of Social Economics, Journal of Interdisciplinary Economics, Economic Papers, Indian Economic Review, Journal of Contemporary Asia*, he has contributed a number of chapters to several edited books published by Oxford University Press, Palgrave-Macmillan, Edward Elgar, Emerald Group Publishing Limited, Idea Group Inc., Atlantic Publishers, Orient BlackSwan, etc. His current research interests focus on socio-economic dualism, trade liberalisation, endogenous growth, and role of information and communication technology (ICT) and services on economic growth and development in selected developing countries including China and India. He is also the founding editor of *International Journal of Development Issues* published by Emerald Group Publishing Limited, UK.

About the Authors

Anthony P. D'Costa is Chair and Professor of Contemporary Indian Studies, Australia India Institute and School of Social & Political Sciences, University of Melbourne, Australia.

Supriyo De did his PhD in Economics from the Faculty of Economics and Business, University of Sydney, Australia. He is Officer on Special Duty to the Chief Economic Adviser, Ministry of Finance, Government of India.

Dilip Dutta is Associate Professor at the School of Economics, University of Sydney, Australia. He is also the founding editor of *International Journal of Development Issues* (Emerald Group Publishing Limited, UK).

Hans Hendrischke is Professor of Chinese Business and Management at the Business School, University of Sydney, Australia.

Elizabeth Hill is Senior Lecturer in Political Economy at the School of Social and Political Sciences, University of Sydney, Australia.

Meera Lal is Professor of Economics (Visiting Faculty) at the Birla Institute of Technology & Science, Pilani, Hyderabad Campus, Andhra Pradesh, India.

Wei Li is Postdoctoral Fellow at the Business School, University of Sydney, Australia.

Guan Long Ren did his Bachelor of Economics (Honours) from the School of Economics, University of Sydney, Australia.

Limin Wang is currently a World Bank consultant. She held a position of research officer at London School of Economics, was lecturer at King's college London, and economic adviser for the Department for International Development (DFID) of the UK government.

Yibai Yang did his PhD in Economics from the Business School, University of Sydney, Australia and currently is a lecturer of Economics at the University of Nottingham Ningbo, China.

Part I

Structuralism and Institutionalism
in Development Economics/Studies

1. Convergence of Structuralism and Institutionalism in Development Economics and Studies — Revisited

Dilip Dutta[*]

1. Introduction

With the growth of modern science, two major opposing trends developed in the philosophy of science: *rationalism* and *empiricism*. While 'rationalists' argue that one could know the objective reality through *reason* alone, 'empiricists' believe that it can be known only through *experience*. The two trends together led to the *positivist school* of philosophy of science. The foundation of orthodox mainstream economists' analysis of objective reality is this positivist approach following methods of *reductionism* (i.e., reducing dimensions of *complex* reality into a few constituents)[1] and *formalism* (i.e., emphasizing *form* over *content* of a unit of analysis).[2] To the orthodox mainstream economists, a society is supposed to be *homogeneous* in its character; individual behavior is guided primarily by utilitarian motivation and pecuniary calculation in a so-called *static* equilibrating system of markets; the operating forces behind the market are assumed to be structurally and institutionally given as data (*ceteris paribus* assumption) and hence the process of institutional and structural changes in the face of new scarcities, new technique, new knowledge, new tastes and preferences, new political regimes, new world order, etc., is of no interest. This mechanistic approach to an economy, by separating it from the society as if the society's social, political and cultural forces do not have any bearing on its economic decision making process, is a serious distortion.

---

[*]dilip.dutta@sydney.edu.au
[1]For the concept of *reductionism*, also see Footnote 23.
[2]For an elaborate discussion on *formalism* and its critique, see Rutherford (1994, Ch. 2).

Alternative methodology of *holistic* approaches,[3] particularly based on *structuralism* and *institutionalism*, is often argued by many social scientists to have more relevance for the analysis of development process, more so during the transitional period[4] of an economy in the increasingly globalized world. The usual argument in favor of these alternative approaches[5] is that they help not only to understand the historical processes of growth and development, but also to select a specific *development strategy* reflecting the very structural and institutional constraints of a particular society. In his *Towards a Semi-anthropological Approach* to economic analysis, Higgins (1992) identifies seven major types of society, economy, and behavior patterns,[6] each of which has its own set of leading actors determining the pace and pattern of development process. The implicit idea behind this approach to development theory is that 'behavioral assumptions for each type of society and economy must be derived from prolonged on-the-spot observation.' Alternatively speaking, the construction of a realistic development theory must be based on the in-depth study of the structural composition of various interacting elements and institutional arrangements for socio-economic and technological dynamism in a specific society.

We will first review in Section 2 how some structuralists and institutionalists in the earlier decades from 1950s to 1970s have enriched the

---

[3]*Holistic* approaches are based on 'holism.' *Holism* (from 'holos,' a Greek word meaning all, entire, total) is the idea that all the properties of a given system (biological, chemical, social, economic, mental, linguistic, etc.) cannot be determined or explained by its component parts alone. Instead, the system as a whole determines how the parts behave. The general principle of 'holism' was concisely summarized in Aristotle's *Metaphysics*: "The whole is more than the sum of its parts."

[4]A 'period of transition' can be defined as a particular stage in a society's evolution when it encounters increasing internal and/or external difficulties in reproducing the economic and social relations on which it is based and which give a specific logic to the manner in which it operates and evolves (Godelier, 1987, p. 447).

[5]For a review of the major distinguishing features of the three methodological approaches to analysis of development process, see Appendix A.

[6]The seven major types of society, economy and behavior patterns as identified by Higgins (1992, pp. 412–415) are: the managerial societies of the industrialized capitalist countries (ICCs), societies dominated by owner-managers in ICCs, the modern sectors of newly industrializing countries (NICs), the modern sectors of other less-developed countries (LDCs), capitalist landlords in LDCs, village capitalists in some LDCs, and peasant societies. The peasant societies include four distinct sub-types: societies with scarce land and low productivity, societies with scarce land but high productivity, societies with abundant land but low productivity and societies with abundant land and high productivity.

development economics. The already existing idea of convergence of structuralist and institutionalist views prevalent in development theory during 1980s will then be focused in Section 3 more convincingly by including the views of the 'regulation school.' Section 4 reviews two newer methodologies of *neostructuralism* and *new-institutionalism*, and a renewed idea of their methodological convergence in the context of the need for a pragmatic blend of market force and government intervention during the last decade of the twentieth century. Section 5 makes an attempt to argue that the convergent methodological approach is continuing implicitly or explicitly behind the *diagnostic approach* currently in vogue in both development economics and development studies. Finally, a conclusion is drawn in Section 6.

2. A Review of Earlier Structuralist and Institutionalist Views in Development Economics and Studies from 1950s to 1970s

The focus on economic development literature from 1950s to 1960s was mainly on capital accumulation, technological adoption, and import substitution. Many decolonised states were following development plan/policy[7] for achieving economic self-sufficiency. During the 1970s, macroeconomic policies had been added as a crucial dimension in growth and development process of developing countries.

2.1. *Structuralist view*

The structuralist views[8] on economic development can be traced back to the writings of two groups of development economists/planners during the

---

[7]While 'policy' refers to the state authority's decision-making guideline meant for implementing it in a short period of time (usually one year), 'plan' is a program (or a set of policies) intended to be adopted during a longer period of time (usually more than one year).

[8]According to Arndt (1985), the concept of *structuralism*, in a broader sense than what applies to development economics, originates in the emergence of the doctrine of market failure during the 1930s and 1940s. He (*ibid.*, p. 155) also documents that Kalecki's lectures given in Mexico in 1953 (published in Mexico in 1955) that stressed 'the importance of the rigidity of supply and the degree of monopoly in the economic system' are the source of important intellectual stimulus to the formulation of the Latin American structuralist theory of inflation.

1950s. One group was identified with the 'surface' structuralist outlook that the free market price mechanism is inadequate in less developed countries for the specific rigidities and lags in their economic structures. The other group was associated with the structuralist views of inflation in Latin America, which were developed in Santiago, at the United Nations' Economic Commission for Latin America (ECLA), of which Raul Prebisch was the Executive Secretary, and at the Institute of Economics of the University of Chile. This second group makes an attempt to isolate, what Jameson (1986, p. 227) calls, a 'deep' structure of the international economy and then links it with the 'surface' structure of the domestic economy. The first group includes writers such as Paul Rosenstein-Rodan, Ragnar Nurkse, W. Arthur Lewis and Hans Singer, while the latter group includes writers such as Juan Noyola Vazquez, Osvaldo Sunkel and Raul Prebisch.

According to Chenery (1975, pp. 310–311), who considers the above two groups of structuralist writers together as a single one, the 'methodology of structural analysis has evolved . . . from a set of rather intuitive hypotheses to models of increasing empirical validity and analytical rigor.' He also illustrates this sequence using two basic elements of structuralist systems: the concept of *dualism*[9] and the concept of *complementarity in demand*[10] that underlies theories of *balanced* growth. In fact, many other structural elements of developing economies have been identified by different writers in this tradition. They include the economy's (surface) structural concepts, such as supply inelasticities of various inputs, limited ability of labor absorption, limited price elasticity of demand for exports, indivisibilities of social overhead capital, and effective demand deficiency, to mention a few among many other such constraints.

Raul Prebisch, who postulated the initial ideas on 'center–periphery' relation in his various writings in 1950, is often credited with the

---

[9]'Dualism' is a structural pattern that still exists in many developing countries, especially the labor-surplus ones. The activities, the organizations, and institutions of each of the two segments of a dual economy — *modern* and *traditional* — reflect particular differing modes of socio-economic behaviors, values, and relationships, and also express differing levels of technological sophistication and specialization. Different versions of 'dualism' and a review of major methodologies that could be relevant for socio-economic analysis of dualistic economies can be found in Dutta (1991).

[10]Rosenstein–Rodan's theory of balanced growth lays more emphasis on the complementarity of markets for final goods as an inducement for investment and therefore for further growth. Workers employed in various industries catering for mass consumption become very likely each other's customers and thus provide a market for each other.

development of the structuralist theory of inflation as well. However, the concise proposition of structuralism in this tradition was first made by Sunkel (1958) in a paper[11] published in Spanish. Regarding the chronic inflationary pressures that were persistent in Chile and other parts of Latin America (Argentina, Brazil, Uruguay, etc.) during the 1950s, Sunkel writes:

> These are fundamentally governed by the structural limitations, rigidity or inflexibility of the economic system. In fact, the inelasticity of some productive sectors to adjust to changes in demand — or, in short, the lack of mobility of productive resources and the defective functioning of the price system — are chiefly responsible for structural inflationary disequilibria.[12]

Later on, 'dependency theory'[13] extends the work of the Latin American structuralists by incorporating both moderate (Celso Furtado, Theotonio Dos Santos, etc.) and radical (e.g., Andre Gunder Frank) analyses of 'center-periphery' relationship within a world economic structure.[14] The chief claim to originality of the proponents of this school was, according to Street (1967, p. 53), that 'they were trying to be more accurately descriptive of the economic system in Latin America ...'. As he (*ibid.*, p. 55) further adds:

> Conceptually, the structuralists are best known for their diagnoses of the "structural deficiencies", "bottlenecks", or "internal maladjustments" which they believe account for the lags in Latin American development. Individual members of the school will differ in the relative importance they assign to the respective factors, but all argue that they are basically of two sorts: bottle-necks originating outside the countries concerned, such as the adverse terms of trade and the limited capacity to import; and maladjustments which occur

---

[11] According to Arndt (*op. cit.*, pp. 154–155), the credit for the first formal statement of the Latin American structuralist theory of inflation should go to an article written by a Mexican economist, Juan Noyola Vazquez, and published in a Mexican journal in 1956. 'The intriguing fact is,' as Arndt further explores, 'that both Sunkel and Noyola (to whom Sunkel expressed his indebtedness) cited, as the authority for their statements about structural factors, an article by Kalecki published in Mexico in 1955.'

[12] The quote is taken from Arndt (*op. cit.*, p. 154).

[13] The 'dependency theory' was developed by Latin American neo-Marxists writers, who focused on the state of underdevelopment in countries such as Chile and Brazil. So (1990) suggests that the dependency school formed in Latin America as a response to the failure of both classical Marxisim and the United Nation's ECLA in the early 1960s, and also as a response to the success of the Chinese and Cuban revolutions, which had bypassed some of the "Marxist stages" of development. According to Ficker (2005, p. 149), 'dependency theory' was a more radical offshoot of the structuralist perspective.

[14] Street and James (1982) have a detailed analysis.

internally, such as accelerated population growth, premature urbanization and expansion of the service sectors of employment, lag in agricultural production, the limited size of domestic markets, ineffective tax systems, and politically significant shifts in class structure.

Since the late 1970s, in the wake of increasing activities of international banks in recycling petrodollars into many of the Latin American economies, there has been a resurgence of structuralism, called 'new structuralism'[15] as a vital mode of understanding development problems. Generally speaking, many of the new structuralist writers tend to apply various macroeconomic concepts and theories such as Kaleckian mark-up pricing, exogenously determined investment process, theories of segmented labor markets, disequilibrium macroeconomic theories, etc., in analyzing traditional structuralist issues of both domestic terms-of-trade (between the agricultural and the industrial sectors), and external terms-of-trade (between export and import sectors).

2.2. *Institutionalist view*

The application of 'institutionalist thoughts' for the socio-economic analysis of contemporary underdeveloped countries as such begins a bit late.[16] To the institutionalists as well, the economy is more than just the market mechanism. Although the market itself is a major institution, it, as they argue, comprises a set of other subsidiary institutions and interacts with other institutional complexes in society. The fundamental institutionalist position rests on its primacy of organizational and control networks of the economic system or, more specifically, on the power (rights) structure and technology, in particular.

The primary source for the foundation of the institutionalist development theory goes back to the institutionalist conceptions advanced by the progenitor of economic institutionalism, Thorstein Veblen, during the late 19th and the early 20th centuries. The two cornerstones of

---

[15]There is a short review of the basic elements of 'new structuralism' in Jameson (1986).

[16]In the context of making some introductory remarks on *Institutionalism and Economic Development*, Benjamin Higgins, back in 1960, called for the institutionalists to be prepared to tackle basic policy problems of underdeveloped societies. 'I suggest,' he remarks (1960, p. 20), 'development of underdeveloped countries as a problem for which institutionalist thought is best suited: if institutionalism is good for anything, it should provide guidance for policy in underdeveloped countries.'

this theory are Veblen's 'conceptions of economic activity as an ongoing evolutionary process and his recognition of the dualistic nature of human behaviour as between tool-using and ceremonial activities'.[17] The 'tool-using activities' or 'workman-like pursuits' are assumed to be embodied in scientific-technological process, while 'ceremonial activities,' as character-ized by power and prestige, force and fraud, etc. are embodied in social and cultural institutions. According to the institutionalist theory of eco-nomic development, the utilization of technological (*instrumental*) inven-tion, discovery, and adaptation is the propelling force for economic growth, while the institutional (*ceremonial*) patterns of human behavior present in the culture of many less economically developed countries may inhibit progress.[18]

One of the main contributions to the development theory by the insti-tutionalists, or by CE. Ayres[19] in particular, is their emphasis on the *tech-nological* (instrumental) dimension of the new social structures that are sought for by the structuralists in order to foster socio-economic progress. Ayres related the above 'general conceptions of human behaviour to the long historical progress by which science and technology had come to represent organized human intelligence directed toward the solution of

---

[17]See Street (1987, p. 1865).

[18]Following this dualistic nature of human behavior, two modes of valuation emerge in the institutionalist tradition: *instrumental* and *ceremonial* valuations. While the for-mer one is concerned with conscious (intelligent) selection of future alternative actions (strategies), the latter one is 'laden with instilled emotional influences derived from unthinking, repetitive behavior and the past application of social sanctions.' In fact, these dual valuations are formalized by C. E. Ayres, who provides the institutionalist analysis with a sound philosophical basis of *pragmatism*. By rejecting the conception of a Cartesian dualism between the real and the ideal, the pragmatists interpret all human behavior as culturally determined and therefore governed mainly by social institutions either permitting or hindering technological advance.

[19]Although Clarence Ayres felt the significance of institutionalist thinking to the question of economic development of the 'backward' countries as hinted in his paper: 'Institution-alism and Economic Development' (1960, p. 49), but he elaborates the idea in a new *Forward* to the second edition of his classic work on *The Theory of Economic Progress* (1944). Accordingly, Ayres (1962, pp. xxvi–xxxiii) figures out four basic principles rel-evant for theory of economic development: (i) the process of economic development is indivisible and irresistible, (ii) the technological revolution spreads in inverse proportion to institutional resistance, (iii) importance of raising the educational level of the commu-nity and hence the creation of human capital, and (iv) because the norms and standards imposed by science and technology are, unlike the ceremonial arbitrary values, universal ones, the values engendered in the technological process are universal.

problems and the origination of novel solutions'.[20] Thus, following the instrumental logic of John Dewey (1939), he refined the concept of technology itself to a form of behavior — called *instrumental* behavior, in which both tools and skills were indispensable. As Junker (1983, p. 32) summarizes:

> Instrumental behavior is based on continuum of hypotheses (hunches, leading ideas) involving explanations (confirming or disconfirming the hypotheses) subject to continuous examination and testing, and is the salient feature of the scientific-technological process . . . The scientific-technological process is a moving "joint stock," portions of which are being fused with each other continuously in a "cumulative sequence." This cumulativeness is a function of the principle that all tools (conceptual or physical) are combinations of pre-existing tools and projections of those combinations. Capital equipment, and all tools, as well as human capital are *made possible* in the dynamic sense by previous technology in new combinations, carried out and brought forward by human agents.

The three basic tenets of the institutionalist thought of development as often identified are: (1) the dynamism of technological progress, (2) the resistance of institutions, and (3) the inevitability of change. They are somewhat similar, although in a simpler context of institutional framework, to the Schumpeterian process of (capitalistic) growth: invention (a technological process), innovation (the application of an invention by the enterprises), and the 'creative destruction'.[21]

> What remains to be said, however, is that "creative destruction" or, if one prefers, economic change as a result of the confrontation of the essential dynamism which characterizes technology with the institutional framework which provides at one and the same time both resistance to change and the requisite stability without which no society can function, is a *ceaseless* process.[22]

---

[20]Street (1987, p. 1866).

[21]It should be noted that credit creation is assigned a central role in the capitalist growth process of the Schumpeterian system. Although Schumpeter, in the late 1920s, recognized how the innovating entrepreneurs were being replaced by an institutionalization of the innovation process through changes in the corporate structure, he did not, as Chakravarty (1974, p. 136) argues, go far enough in trying to analyze the social and economic conditions which would tend to make innovations a regular feature of economic life. In fact, in the contemporary developing economies, the direct involvement of the State in the economic matters including both product and process innovations requires more wide than Schumpeterian frame of institutional reference.

[22]Klein (1977, p. 789).

Because the institutionalists are primarily *reformists*, maintaining societal stability within the ideological framework of the prevalent dominant political institutions is regarded as their basic objective. They do not seem to allow any major change that may be required for drastic redesign of the social order, they instead acknowledge the need for some incremental changes in various institutional arrangements that are essentially required either to increase the efficacy of technology or to induce innovation. This is why the development economists/planners, sometimes known as *neoinstitutionalists*, such as Gunnar Myrdal and John Kenneth Galbraith, among others, advocate deliberate State intervention and planning as important instruments for achieving orderly growth and development.

Since the mid-1970s, there has been emergence of a new group of economists such as Oliver Williamson and Douglas North, Robert Thomas, whose works have been given the label of 'new institutional economics' (NIE). Although the new institutional economists accept neoclassical *reductionism*,[23] believing that individual actions alone explain societal phenomena, they also allow for endogenous *institutional changes* arising out of the individual decision making actions. In other words, the 'NIE seeks to explain not only individuals' choices with a given set of institutions but, more important, the way that individuals' beliefs and choices affect the evolution of the institutions themselves'.[24] Thus, NIE believes that the competitive and evolutionary processes lead to socially beneficial (efficient) results as an unintended consequence of individual action.

3. Convergence of Structuralist and Institutionalist Views in Development Economics and Studies During 1980s

In their *holistic* approach toward a general understanding of socio-economic evolutionary processes, both the structuralist and the institutionalist views emerge as attacks on limitations of orthodox economic doctrine or on policies designed from that doctrine. As Street and James (1982, pp. 673–674)

---

[23] Neoclassical *reductionism* allows for 'reduction of the explanatory framework's dimensions' because it is based on the view that a system or a phenomenon can be understood in terms of a knowledge of its isolated parts, rather than of all its constituting parts.
[24] Clague (1997, p. 16).

elaborate, the *holistic* approach embraces two basic conceptions: one relating to the economic system 'as an evolving process rather than an equilibrating mechanism of stable economic relations centering on market activities,' and the other to the nature of 'human behavior as character-ized by habitual patterns resulting from cultural conditioning' rather than by 'utilitarian motivation and pecuniary calculation in a static system of markets.'

Attacks by the heterodox group needed to be more sharpened in their analysis of growth and development processes of contemporary develop-ing and underdeveloped countries with diverse and differentiated socio-economic structures. Specific cultural, political, and economic frameworks of such countries have some inherent structural and institutional biases as the reflection of *unequal* distribution of resources, power, entitlements, and action capabilities among their individuals and groups/classes or *uneven* growth and development across their different parts, regions and seg-ments/sectors. It is often argued that the emergence of institutionalist development theory is essentially to supplement the 'structuralist views.' Some institutionalists even tend to use the term 'structure' interchangeably with 'institution'. As Street (1967, p. 55) argues, '(s)tructures are indeed 'institutions' in some uses of the term, and 'structural maladjustment' is often equivalent to 'cultural lag.' Similarly, Bromley (1985, pp. 779–780) writes:

> I would suggest that the development problem in the newly independent trop-ical countries is one of structure. It is not a problem of low incomes, incorrect prices, badly functioning markets, ... food production falling behind popula-tion growth. These performance indicators are but symptoms of the real devel-opment problem, which is structural in nature. What do I mean by structure? I mean the institutional arrangements that define the choice sets (opportu-nity sets) within which individuals and groups go about the daily business of making a living.

A convergent approach of the two views of structuralism and institutional-ism seems to have been attempted in the formulation of global (capitalist) productive systems by a diverse group of French writers (Michel Aglietta, Alain Lipietz, etc.) known as the 'regulation school.' This school, sprouted during the 1970s and 1980s, is primarily distinguished by its two main stances of:

(i) emphasis on the dynamics and changes of the national dimension and its indigenous factors, and

(ii) reference to the regime of accumulation and mode of regulation.

The regulationists argue that the capitalistic development is not a continual process; they rather see capitalist development as a succession of periods, each period having a specific *regime of accumulation*,[25] i.e., 'a social structure that connects the individual decisions of producers and the socially determined effective demand they must confront'. In order to ensure that a regime of accumulation is stabilized in a crisis-free manner, each such regime has a *mode of regulation* i.e., a regulating network consisting of social norms, habits, law, etc., whether coercive or institutional.

Because the 'regulation school' is useful for explaining diverse (structural) patterns of accumulation and (institutional) mode of regulation in both developed and developing economies, it attempts to analyze growth and development processes of not only then 'newly *de*industrializing' countries (such as Chile and Argentina ruined by inept dictatorships[26]) but also 'newly industrializing' countries (NICs). The critics of the 'dependency theory' argue that it overlooks the indigenous class forces and internal dynamics of a 'peripheral' society *vis-à-vis* the 'center.' The regulation school shows the analytical capability for reconciling these two perspectives. The writers of this school argue that peripheries are dependent on the center, but their potential for partial industrialization should not be overlooked. When the central *Fordism*[27] was, for example, facing the crisis in the 1967 recession, it sought for gaining marketing footholds into the peripheries. However, it needed certain conditions to exist in the peripheries — 'like political regimes autonomous from landed interests and import substitution industrialists, and also regimes not based in the popular masses'.[28] The success of the NICs of East Asia during the 1960s and 1970s is thus linked first to, what the regulationist school calls, 'primitive Taylorism' and then to 'peripheral Fordism.' While 'primitive Taylorism' refers to the transfer of limited branches of production with high rates of exploitation (in terms of wages, length of the working day, and labor intensity) from center to peripheries, the 'peripheral Fordism' refers to the industrialization by the autonomous local capital importing capital goods and skilled assembly products from the center, and exporting unskilled assembly goods to the center.[29]

---

[25]Noel (1987, p. 311).
[26]Noel (1987, p. 329) cites Alain Lipietz who draws the attention to the fact that the share of manufacturing in the GDP in 1982 was equal or below what it was in 1960 in these two countries.
[27]*Fordism* is a system of mass production based on flow-line assembly of products and involving the standardization of products as well as rigid labor laws.
[28]See Peet (1991, p. 156).
[29]*Ibid.*, p. 157.

4. Neostructuralist and New-Institutionalist Views in Development Economics and Studies During 1980s and 1990s

In the 1980s, there was a resurgence of neoclassical free-market decentralized approach toward economic management due to the political ascendancy of conservative governments in North America (the US and Canada), and two major European countries (Britain and West Germany). This greatly influenced economic theory and policy in many of both developed and developing countries. The main argument of this approach is that underdevelopment is a result of inefficient resource allocation due to incorrect pricing policies and too much state intervention by 'overly active developing-nation governments'.[30] Thus 'getting the price right' by eliminating exchange and price controls was the main objective behind the argument. Many developing countries had followed or were forced (by donor countries and/or international institutions like World Bank and International Monetary Fund) to follow the strategy of comprehensive *economic liberalization*[31] and, therefore, various *institutional reforms*,[32] which led to the emergence of the *Washington Consensus*.[33] For much of the 1980s and into 1990s, this so-called 'consensus' on development policy that reflected the free-market approach to development, with total disregard for underdeveloped countries' structural, institutional, and historical legacies

---

[30] Todaro and Smith (2012, p. 127).

[31] *Economic liberalization* involves various policy reforms such as delicensing of industries, elimination of subsidies, privatization of the state-owned enterprises (SOEs), deregulation and internationalization of financial sector, elimination of restrictions on international trade, etc., which, in turn, require either significant restructuring of the existing institutions or completely designing new institutions (Dutta, 2000, p. 3).

[32] While economic liberalization implies a move toward decentralized market mechanisms, institutional reforms allow for required changes in the underlying norms and rules of not only a country's economic system, but also its societal system in general (Dutta, *ibid.*, p. 3).

[33] The *Washington Consensus* is often summarized in 10 policy reforms: (i) Fiscal discipline; (ii) Redirection of public expenditure priorities toward fields offering both high economic returns and the potential to improve income distribution, such as primary health care, primary education, and infrastructure; (iii) tax reform (to lower marginal rates and broaden the tax base); (iv) financial (e.g., interest rate) liberalization; (v) unified and competitive exchange rates; (vi) trade liberalization; (vii) liberalization of (i.e., elimination of barriers to) foreign direct investment (FDI) inflows; (viii) privatization; (ix) deregulation (in the sense of abolishing barriers to entry and exit); and (x) secure property rights.

of their past, had great influence, especially through 'pressures from the international financial agencies in favor of implementing the consensus'.[34]

4.1. *Neostructuralism*

As an alternative to the orthodoxy, neoconservative adjustment and restructuring programs of the 1980s, a theoretical framework of *neostructuralism* emerged.[35] Neostructuralists share the basic structuralist view that the sources of underdevelopment are not primarily due to policy-induced distortions in relative prices, but are rooted in endogenous *structural rigidities* of individual countries/regions. Ramos and Sunkel (1993, p. 7) provide a tangible proof of the neostructuralist view based on three crucial aspects of Latin America's economy in the late 1980s:

(1) An international specialization in products lacking dynamic potential;
(2) The prevalence of an uncoordinated, vulnerable and highly heterogeneous production pattern that tends to concentrate technical progress and is incapable of fully and productively absorbing new entrants into the labor force; and
(3) The persistence of a growth pattern that excludes the vast majority from the fruits of progress, evidencing the system's inability to lower poverty significantly.

The major implication of the above endogenous *structural rigidities*, as elaborated by Ramos and Sunkel (*ibid.*), is that optimal dynamic allocation of resources for growth needs more than free market prices that result in allocative-efficiency models solely based on their efficient allocation in a static neoclassical framework. Furthermore, an active support of the *nation-state* (as a complement to *market*) is necessary to not only provide its classical functions (public goods, macroeconomic stability and equity), but also — within the limits of its administrative capacity — (1) promote or stimulate missing markets (long-term capital markets and future markets in foreign exchange); (2) strengthen incomplete markets (the market for technology); (3) eliminate or correct structural distortions (the heterogeneity of the production structure, the concentration of property, the segmentation of the capital and labor markets) and (4) eradicate or

---

[34]Ficker (2005, p. 153).
[35]Mostly, Latin American and North American economists who are behind this framework include: Alejandro Foxley (1983); Albert Fishlow (1985, 1990); Lance Taylor (1983); Patricio Meller (1991); Osvaldo Sunkel (1993); among others (Ramirez, 1993, p. 1026).

compensate the most significant market imperfections (arising from technology and trade), among others. These tasks are nothing but appropriate designs of *institutional frameworks* after identifying endogenous *structural rigidities*.

Neostructuralists also do critically examine some of the key assumptions of the basic structuralist tradition, especially those pertaining to its excessive reliance on idealized state interventionism; exaggerated pessimism with respect to export possibilities; and insufficient recognition of the importance of timely and operational policies to deal with macroeconomic disequilibria, particularly its underestimation of the importance of monetary and financial aspects. As Lustig (1993, pp. 74–75) notes:

> One of the significant differences between structuralism and neostructuralism is the recognition [in latter] that [policy] recommendations cannot stem from an exclusively long term perspective, without taking into consideration the possible consequences of any structural change process and without having already set up ways to face the problems originated during the transition.

Thus, in neostructuralism, there is an explicit acknowledgement of the shortcomings in making recommendations based solely on long term considerations without paying attention to the short term effects of processes of structural change particularly during the transition.[36]

According to the neostructuralists, *expenditure-switching* policies, such as devaluation (designed to enhance the competitiveness of exports), and *expenditure-reducing* policies, such as indiscriminate cuts in government spending (designed to bring inflation under control), should not be applied simultaneously as has been done in many countries in Latin America.[37] Neostructuralists, instead, recommend for a sequential and gradualist approach in the short to medium run. In the long run, they advocate the implementation of a set of consistent policies designed to change the prevailing pattern of economic growth and development.[38]

4.2. *New institutionalism*

During 1980s and 1990s, various strands of 'institutionalisms' flourished within the social sciences in general and the discipline of economics in particular. They, under the banner of *new institutionalism*, have stimulated

---

[36]Ramos and Sunkel (1993, pp. 7–8).
[37]Ramirez (1993, p. 1028).
[38]*Ibid.*, p. 1030.

'significant discussion not only of formal rules and governance structures, but also of informal norms and social networks, and of the relationships between them. Some of this discussion has reconnected economics with literatures in sociology and political science'.[39] There has also been an increased interest in using such concepts as social capital,[40] trust, community, and civil society across different disciplines. Similarly, aspects of this literature on *new institutionalism* have also served to stimulate attempts to renew the *old institutionalism* by bringing together more recent work in psychology, evolutionary models, and resource- or competence-based theories of the firm, with ideas taken from Thorstein Veblen (1966), John Commons, and other old institutionalists.[41] Over time, the interest in institutions has come from different sources and with different, even opposing, motivations from within social sciences. As Rutherford (2001, p. 190) summarizes:

> Institutional analysis has been used both to explain the failings of unfettered markets and the need for a greater degree of government intervention, and the failings of government interventions and the need for a greater degree of market freedom. But a common theme is that institutions matter a great deal, and that economists need to think hard about the ways in which institutions shape economic behavior and outcomes, and are themselves shaped by economic, political, and ideological factors.

One of the major effects of the revival of new institutionalism has been an explosive growth of literature on NIE. As we have noted towards the end of Section 2, the early literature on NIE started around the mid-1970s, accepting neoclassical *reductionism*, but allowing for *endogenous* institutional changes. Since its revival during the 1980s, there have been several different strands of literature on NIE focusing on economics of transaction cost, imperfect information, property rights, collective action, institutional innovation, and game-theoretic cooperation.[42] The NIE has made 'an attempt to extend the range of neoclassical theory by explaining the

---

[39] Rutherford (2001, pp. 188–189).
[40] The concept of capital has been broadened from 'physical capital' to 'human capital' and then to 'social capital' in the literature on development economics. In some formulations, institutional arrangements, i.e., different sets of institutions at different levels of a society have been called social capitals. They can be organizations or sets of rules and beliefs within organizations, the set of property rights and rules governing market exchanges, or cultural norms of social behavior, patterns of trust and reciprocity, family structure, etc. (Clague, 1997, p. 13; Ostrom, 1995, p. 159).
[41] Rutherford (2001, p. 189).
[42] For more discussion on these strands, see Clague (1997, pp. 18–23) and Bardhan (1989).

institutional factors traditionally taken as givens, such as property rights and governance structures, and, unlike the old institutionalism, not as an attempt to replace the standard theory. ... [Instead,] institutions and institutional change have generally been analyzed as ways of reducing transactions costs, reducing uncertainty, internalizing externalities, and producing collective benefits from coordinated or cooperative behaviour'.[43]

While many developing/emerging countries were engaged in various institutional reforms during the 1980s and 1990s, North (1995, p. 22), a new institutional economist, cautions that a successful development policy must entail 'an understanding of the dynamics of economic change if the policies pursued are to have desired consequences.' To the new institutional economists, economic change is an incremental process that is a consequence of the choices/decisions individuals and entrepreneurs of organizations[44] are making every day within the existing structure of property rights and political rules. When the decisions are not routine and require recontracting or new contracting between individuals and organizations, institutional rules/norms need to be altered/modified or newly designed. Modification of existing institutions or introduction of new institutions occurs because individuals and entrepreneurs perceive that such changes will have the maximum pay-off. The source of this perception is, according to NIE, basically the mental constructs of the players and may be exogenous to the economy — for instance knowledge from foreign sources.

The fundamental source of economic change is, according to NIE, learning by entrepreneurs of organizations, and the rate of learning will determine the intensity of competition amongst organizations. But the kind of learning, being a function of the expected pay-offs of different kinds of knowledge, does 'reflect the mental models of the players and most immediately at the margin, the incentive structure embodied in the institutional matrix' characterized by network externalities, complementarities and economies of scope among the existing organizations.[45] North is, however, very particular in emphasizing that the dominant player, the

---

[43]Rutherford (2001, p. 187).

[44]Note that there is a basic distinction between the two terms — 'institution' and 'organization.' As North (1995, p. 23) distinguishes them, institutions are the rules of the game of a society, or more formally, are the humanly devised constraints that structure human interaction; while organizations are the players: groups of individuals bound by a common purpose to achieve objectives of winning the game or steering the economy to economic development.

[45]North (1995, pp. 23–24).

nation-state, at the top echelon of society 'can never be treated as an exogenous actor in development policy'.[46] 'It is,' as North (1995, p. 25) argues, 'polities that shape economic performance because they define and enforce the economic rules of the game. Therefore the heart of development policy must be the creation of polities that will create and enforce efficient property rights.'

Bearing in mind that institutionalists/neoinstitutionalists are basically reformists operating within the basic ideological framework of the prevalent political and economic institutions, North's (1995, pp. 25–26) following summary of the implications of the above mentioned institutional changes could be applicable in both developed and developing societies alike:

(a) Political institutions will be stable only if they are supported by organizations with an interest in their perpetuation. Therefore an essential part of political/economic reform is the creation of such organizations.

(b) It is essential to change both the institutions and the belief systems for successful reform since it is the mental models of the actors that will shape choices.

(c) Evolving norms of behavior that will support and legitimize new rules is a lengthy process and, in the absence of such reinforcing norms, policies will tend to be unstable.

(d) While economic growth can occur in the short run with autocratic regimes, long-run economic growth entails the development of the rule of law and the protection of civil and political freedoms.

(e) Informal constraints — norms of behavior, conventions, and codes of conduct — are a necessary (but not sufficient) condition for good economic performance. Societies with norms favorable to economic growth can sometimes prosper even with unstable or adverse political rules.

5. Problem Solving Approaches in Development Economics and Studies During 2000s

During the 1990s, institutional changes and active governance had been recognized as the crucial forces for growth enhancement, employment generation and poverty reduction for *sustained* economic development

---

[46]North (1995, p. 23).

across the developing/emerging countries. The East Asian countries have not only realized the importance of institutional change and innovation but also made this realization all the more acute by creating renewed impetus to modernize institutions, including political institutions, particularly after the 1997 crisis. China and India, together accounting for about 40% of the developing world's population, have been relatively successful by moving toward greater reliance on market forces, especially in export markets of merchandize products (China) and services (India).[47] Both China and India are often credited for reforms adopted and institutions built, although within a framework of *partial trade liberalization*.[48] But such successes have not been uniform among the developing/emerging economies across the board mainly because these countries face different binding structural constraints and possess differing level of institutional development. In fact, improving the quality of societal institutions has remained a challenge for many of these countries, and more so after 'accession to the World Trade Organization (WTO) and integration into regional supranational entities such as the European Union and the New Economic Partnership for Africa.[49]

There was also a resurgence of interest in analyzing and measuring inequality during 1990s, fuelled mainly by the neostructuralists' observation that the growth pattern in Latin America persistently excluded a vast majority of people from the fruits of economic growth. This pattern seems to be increasingly visible worldwide, with dire implication for inclusive growth and development strategy. Following a 2004 report 'A Fair Globalization: Creating Opportunities for All,' prepared by the World Commission on the Social Dimensions of Globalization, Stiglitz (2006, p. 8) notes that '59% of the world's people are living in countries with growing inequality, with only 5% in countries with declining inequality.'

---

[47]China, the largest developing economy, has been gradually continuing various reforms it had begun in 1979 after adopting the 'open-door' policy in December 1978. India, the second-largest developing economy, adopted a comprehensive liberalization policy in 1991 by speeding up liberalization started as 'directional changes' in the early 1980s (Dutta, 2004, pp. 170–171).

[48]For details on partial trade liberalization in China and India, see World Bank (2005, pp. 143–144).

[49]World Bank (2005, p. 5).

Below are some of the direct influences of inequality on economic growth and institutional performance, as summarized by World Bank (2005, pp. 5–6):

> A recent body of literature suggests several channels through which inequality affects economic growth. Fairer societies offer their citizens more public goods, more social support, and more social capital. Hence they are more capable of sharing the costs and benefits of improving economic policies, and in turn facilitating consensus building and decision making. ... Fairness also facilitates agreement on the provision of public goods that have strong beneficial side effects on society, such as health services, water supply, or waste disposal. Other channels through which inequality affects growth are market structures and microeconomic incentives. A better distribution of wealth reduces credit constraints, and broader availability of credit is found to have a significant and positive effect on growth rates. If individuals are limited in their borrowing capacity, reallocating capital toward the poorest will increase aggregate productivity.

Recent literature has also made attempts to explore the important links between the distribution of assets in a society and the institutions that emerge (not just the performance of the existing institutions). Following economic research in the 1990s on how institutions emerge and get established in a society, two insights of this process have been documented in World Bank (2005, p. 6):

> First, economic incentives influence what type of institutions emerge and when. The enforcement of property rights to land, for example, will depend on the benefits of enforcement relative to its costs, which for each owner depends on the extent to which other owners enforce their property rights. In an extractive economy, for example if landowners in general do not enforce their property rights, it is uneconomical for one landowner to enforce his: workers will find it attractive to exploit land and appropriate the rents for themselves. Only when this coordination problem is resolved will economic incentives be sufficient for enforcement of property rights.

> Second, concentrated economic and political interests influence institutions. This can be seen from experiences with land distribution in Latin America, and also from the United States in the early 1990s, when the government decided to regulate matters hitherto left to private parties and the courts; the reason for the shift was a perception that judges and the courts, having been corrupted by powerful economic interests, were unable to render fair and equitable judgements.

The above two insights clearly pinpoint the need for quality institutions and good governance as the backbones for ensuring inclusive growth and development in a society. In the face of the socio-economic problems that developing/emerging countries face in the globalizing world with increasing inequalities both within and between nations, people have been demanding for inclusive growth directly or indirectly since the late 1990s, and the demand is getting intensified, especially through various action groups and networks mediated by information and communication technology (ICT).[50]

Amidst popular demand for inclusive growth and development during 2000s, the individual nation-states, particularly in developing/emerging countries, find it increasingly difficult to manage all socio-economic and political issues simultaneously. There has been 'a shift in attention from a sole focus on reform *contents* (what should be done) toward reform *context* (where it is to be done) and *process* (how the problem is to be agreed on and a solution developed or reform sequenced)'.[51] Hausmann, Rodrik, and Velasco's (HRV) (2005) *growth diagnostics* approach is one such framework that emphasises on reform *context* and *process*, rather than on a sole focus on reform *contents*.

5.1. *Growth diagnostics approach*

HRV (2006, pp. 1–2) note that their *growth diagnostics* approach is motivated by three considerations:

> First, while development is a broad concept entailing the raising of human capabilities in general, increasing economic growth rates is the central challenge that developing nations face. Higher standards of living are the most direct route to improvements in social and human indicators. Reform strategies should be principally targeted at raising rates of growth — that is, they should be growth strategies.
>
> Second, trying to come up with an identical growth strategy for all countries, regardless of their circumstances, is unlikely to prove productive. Growth strategies are likely to differ according to domestic opportunities and constraints. There are, of course, general, abstract principles — such as property rights, the rule of law, market-oriented incentives, sound money, and sustainable public finances — that are desirable everywhere. But turning these general principles into operational policies requires considerable knowledge of local specificities.
>
> Third, it is seldom helpful to provide governments with a long list of reforms, many of which may not be targeted at the most binding constraints on economic

---

[50]For example, the *Global Knowledge Partnership Foundation* (GKPF) is one such organization that networks with public, civil society, and commercial organizations and is committed to harnessing the potential of ICT for sustainable and equitable development (http://www.gkpfoundation.org). *info*Dev is another global partnership program with mission 'to enable innovative entrepreneurship for sustainable, inclusive growth and employment in developing countries' (http://www.infodev.org).
[51]Blum, Manning and Srivastava (2012, p. 5).

growth. Governments face administrative and political limitations, and their policymaking capital is better deployed in alleviating binding constraints than in going after too many targets all at once. So growth strategies require a sense of priorities.

As has been further clarified by HRV (2006), they are mainly concerned with short-run constraints, and, therefore, their approach is meant to 'help clarify the options available to policymakers for responding to political constraints.' They propose a decision tree methodology in order to help identify the relevant binding constraints for each country. Their 'focus is on igniting growth and constraints that inevitably emerge as an economy expands, not on anticipating tomorrow's constraints on growth.' In response to a number of critiques[52] of HRV's growth diagnostics approach, Hausmann, Klinger and Wagner (HKW, 2008) further elaborate on the strategies and methods of this 'top-down approach as a natural complement to cost-benefit analysis' in search for better policy alternatives. One of the main criticisms against this approach is that growth diagnostics require in-depth knowledge of the economy under analysis.[53] Consequently, its analysis of reform *context* and *process* is likely to be shallow.

5.2.   An approach of thorough diagnostic, agility and experimentation

In a recent analysis of a problem-solving approach to public sector management reform, Blum, Manning and Srivastava (2012, pp. 5–7) highlight three broad principles that can help bridge the gap between what is known about such reform and how it is conducted. 'These principles call for designing reforms based on thorough diagnostics, agility and experimentation in implementing reforms, and continuous learning from reform experiences...' They argue that these three principles, bolstering *tacit* knowledge that likely to work in a particular context, along with more *codified* scientific knowledge[54] about what works in general, could help to develop practical reform strategies. The approach is basically in line with the methodology

---

[52]See the responses to these critiques by HKW (2008).
[53]Leipziger and Zagha (2006).
[54]The difference between *tacit* and *codified* knowledges, as summarized in Dutta (2009, p. 294), is: 'The former is specific, experimental and heavily influenced by user needs, and hence less amenable to replication and transmission. The latter is generic and easy to transfer among the firms in an industry or among the industries in a sector.'

of new institutionalism in the forefront, and that of neostructuralism in the background, although terminologies used here are borrowed from the principal–agent theoretic literature that deals with motivating one party, the agent or stakeholder (such as the government/politicians), to act in the best interest of another, the principal (such as the people/voters), instead of in its own interest (at least in short run).

Following Blum, Manning and Srivastava (2012, pp. 5–7), a summary of these three principles is given below:

Principle 1: *Designing solutions based on rigorous diagnostics*

Diagnostic approaches are a key in countering 'strong priors about the nature of the problem and the appropriate fixes'[55] and in discovering outside-the box solutions. Good diagnostics can take many forms, but recent discussion emphasizes a few basic steps:

- Using the available empirical evidence and the accepted theory, diagnostics could determine the most promising entry points for reform by identifying the major root cause (or *binding constraint*) of a problem in a specific context.
- For narrowing down the most plausible cause of a performance problem, diagnostic analyses can draw on comparative indicators, if available somewhere else, or country-specific data on a specific constraint and those agrees with this constraint.
- In order to solve a performance problem, diagnostics define a problem in terms of the *functions* that the institutions/public agents are meant to serve, rather than in terms of the absence of particular institutional *forms*.[56]
- Diagnostics engage stakeholders in the problem-solving process because it is considered crucial for building agreement around a feasible, context-tailored solution — and for building solutions from local insights into the problem, rather than from imported ideas about best practice.[57]

---

[55]Quoted in Blum, Manning and Srivastava (2012, p. 5) from Rodrik (2008).

[56]For example, a functional problem might be that the public sector achieves low value for money in public road construction projects or that teachers are often absent — not the absence of a particular procurement process or pay policy for teachers (Blum, Manning and Srivastava, 2012, p. 5).

[57]Diagnostics often allow processes to navigate politically sensitive issues for the interest of stakeholders because they may help surface underlying conflicts that have prevented

Principle 2: *Implement with agility*

The conventional emphasis on a well-defined but rigid project design is challenged by the growing evidence that implementation processes are crucial for success (e.g., in building public sector institutions). If experimentation and learning by doing are increasingly seen as the keys to success, the traditional distinction between design and implementation in reform projects can be a constraint. Process matters in part because knowing what works to achieve an intended result may be hard to know at the design stage — it may only emerge during project implementation through stakeholder engagement and experimentation.

The rapid dissolution of ICT brings promising new opportunities to engage more easily with stakeholders for gathering their subjective views on how well a project's implementation is progressing

Principle 3: *Learn as we go*

Practitioner's experience is of course an invaluable source of knowledge for reform design — many senior administrators and advisors can sense that a reform is implausibly ambitious or excessively modest. However, by itself, tacit knowledge held by experts is insufficient — constant empirical testing of what works in reform is still needed.

The above three principles essentially call on the policy makers to be ready to adapt on the basis of evidence — to adapt reform designs to clients' specific problems and context and to adapt solutions to what is learnt from experimentation along the way. They are ultimately about a move toward a more scientific method combining *new institutionalism* with *neostructuralism* than the orthodox mainstream economists' so-called analysis of objective reality based on methods of *reductionism* and *formalism*.

6. Conclusion

Most of the less developed societies not only are internally segmented and differentiated by different socio-economic-technological environments but also have various socio-economic groups/classes competing each other to achieve their economic and non-economic objectives. Being deeply embedded in their history and structural constraints, and now directly or

---

the problem from being solved in the past. Thus diagnostics use political economy analysis prospectively (Blum, Manning and Srivastava, 2012, p. 5).

indirectly integrated into the globalized world, their policy makers need to design development strategies very carefully. Selection of an appropriate development strategy by studying the socio-economic structure of such a society is as important as to gear up its behavioral and motivational patterns in terms of appropriate institutions. A successful development strategy will essentially depend on a judicious blend of market forces and strategic planning/policy, which is also the key to a sustainable pattern of growth and development in developing societies. Picking up either 'market forces' or 'government intervention' as the villain in the case of failure is now hardly justifiable. This is why remarks such as 'governments may not have wrongly intervened, but they may have intervened wrongly' or 'the market has not wrongly freed, but freed wrongly' are noteworthy.[58] Both these remarks suggest nothing other than the need for a theory of optimal blend of market forces and strategic planning/policy (reflecting effective institution building based on a good understanding of a society's structural rigidities).

Generally speaking, the complementarity between the structuralist/neostructuralist and the institutionalist/new-institutionalist views reinforces the fact that the processes of development and underdevelopment are dynamic and organic in the sense that structural and institutional elements are not only interrelated but also constantly change their interaction patterns — more so during the transitional period in a developing society. An inclusive growth and development strategy is expected to adopt a redistributive income policy through land distribution, employment generation programs, subsidies for small- and medium-scale industries and promotion of broad access to credit, infrastructure and social sector particularly health and education. The success of this policy largely depends on the effectiveness of the related institutions for the greater impact of, for example, 'public spending on equity, both in a static sense (incidence of public spending) and a dynamic sense (changes in individuals' earnings potential).[59] It is also noteworthy that a 'foundational level of institutional quality in relation to property rights and the rule of law appear to be necessary for sustained economic growth . . . , but beyond that, it could be that institutions are an outcome of economic development as richer societies demand better governance structures'.[60]

---

[58]Savoie and Higgins (1992).
[59]World Bank (2005, p. 6).
[60]Blum, Manning and Srivastava (2012, p. 8).

References

Arndt, H. W. (1985). "The Origins of Structuralism," *World Development*, Vol. 13, No. 2, pp. 151–159.

Ayres, C. E. (1960). "Institutionalism and Economic Development," *Southwestern Social Science Quarterly*, Vol. 41, No. 1, pp. 45–62.

Ayers, C. E. (1962). *The Theory of Economic Progress: A Study of the Fundamentals of Economic Development and Cultural Change*, 2nd edn., New York: Schocken Books.

Blum, J., N. Manning, and V. Srivastava (2012). "Public Sector Management Reform: Toward a Problem-Solving Approach," *Economic Premise*, No. 100 (December).

Bromley, D. W. (1985). "Resources and Economic Development: An Institutionalist Perspective," *Journal of Economic Issues*, Vol. 19, No. 3, pp. 779–796.

Chakravarty, S. (1974). *Reflections on the Growth Process in the Indian Economy* (Hyderabad: Administrative Staff College, 1974). Reprinted in C. D. Wadhva (1977) (ed.), *Some Problems of India's Economic Policy*, 2nd edn., New Delhi: Tata McGraw-Hill.

Chenery, H. B. (1975). "The Structuralist Approach to Development Theory," *American Economic Review*, Vol. 65, No. 2, pp. 310–316.

Clague, C. (ed.) (1997). *Institutions and Economic Development: Growth and Governance in Less-Developed and Post-Socialist Countries*, Baltimore & London: The Johns Hopkins University Press.

Dutta, D. (1991). "Socio-Economic Analysis of Dualistic Economies: A Review of Methodological Alternatives," *Journal of Interdisciplinary Economics*, Vol. 3, No. 4, pp. 255–273.

Dutta, D. (ed.) (2000). *Economic Liberalisation and Institutional Reforms in South Asia*, New Delhi: Atlantic Publishers and Distributors.

Dutta, D. (2004). "Effects of Globalisation on Employment and Poverty in Dualistic Economies: The Case of India," in *Economic Globalisation — Social Conflicts, Labour and Environmental Issues*, C. Tisdell and R. K. Sen (eds.), Cheltenham, UK & Massachusetts, USA: Edward Elgar.

Dutta, D. (2009). "Social Shaping of India's Computer Software Technology Sector: A Methodological Analysis in terms of Actors and Networks," in *Post-Reform Development in Asia — Essays for Amiya Kumar Bagchi*, M. Sanyal, M. Sanyal and S. Amin (eds.), Hyderabad, India: Orient Blackswan Private Limited.

Dewey, J. (1939). *Theory of Valuation*, Chicago: The University of Chicago Press.

Ficker, S. K. (2005). "From Structuralism to the New Institutional Economics: The Impact of Theory on the Study of Foreign Trade in Latin America," *Latin American Research Review*, Vol. 40, No. 3, pp. 145–162.

Fishlow, A. (1985). "The State of Latin American Economics," in *Inter-American Development Bank: Economic and Social Progress in Latin America*, Washington, DC: IDB.

Fishlow, A. (1990). "The Latin American State," *The Journal of Economic Perspectives*, 4(3), pp. 61–74.

Foxley, A. (1983). *Latin American Experiments in Neoconservative Economics*, Berkeley: University of California.

Godelier, M. (1987). "Introduction: The Analysis of Transition Processes," *International Social Science Journal*, Vol. 114, November, pp. 447–458.

Harriss, J., J. Hunter, and C. Lewis (eds.) (1995). *The New Institutional Economics and Third World Development*, London & New York: Routledge.

Hausmann, R., D. Rodrik, and A. Velasco (2005). "Growth diagnostics," John F. Kennedy School of Government, Harvard University (Cambridge, Massachusetts). Available at: http://www.hks.harvard.edu/fs/drodrik/Research%20papers/barcelonafinalmch2005.pdf. [Published in D. Rodrik (2007). *One Economics, Many Recipes: Globalization, Institutions, and Economic Growth*, Ch. 2, Princeton, N.J.: Princeton University Press.]

Hausmann, R., D. Rodrik, and A. Velasco (2006). "Getting the Diagnosis Right," *Finance and Development*, Vol. 43, No. 1.

Hausmann, R., B. Klinger, and R. Wagner (2008). "Doing Growth Diagnostics in Practice: A 'Mindbook'," Center for International Development at Harvard University Working Paper No. 177, September.

Higgins, B. (1960). "Some Introductory Remarks to Institutionalism and Economic Development," *Southwestern Social Science Quarterly*, Vol. 41, No. 1, pp. 15–21.

Higgins, B. (1992). "Towards a New Paradigm?" in *Equity and Efficiency in Economic Development — Essays in Honour of Benjamin Higgins*, D. Savoie and I. Brecher (eds.), Montreal: McGill-Queen's University Press.

Jameson, K. P. (1986). "Latin American Structuralism: A Methodological Perspective," *World Development*, Vol. 14, No. 2, pp. 223–232.

Junker, L. (1983). "Institutionalism and the Criteria of Development," *Economic Forum*, Vol. 14, No. 1, pp. 27–56.

Kalecki, M. (1955). "El problema del financiamento del desarollo economico," *El Trimestre Economico*, Vol. 21, No. 4. [English version, in M. Kalecki (1976), *Essays in Developing Economies*, London: Harvester Press.]

Klein, P. A. (1977). "An Institutionalist View of Development Economics," *Journal of Economic Issues*, Vol. 11, No. 4, pp. 785–807.

Leipziger, D. and R. Zagha (2006). "Getting Out of the Rut," *Finance and Development*, Vol. 43, No. 1.

Lustig, N. (1993). "Equity and Development," in *Development from Within: Toward a Neostructuralist Approach for Latin America*, O. Sunkel (ed.), Boulder & London: Lynne Rienner Publishers.

Meller, P. (1991). *The Latin American Development Debate*, San Francisco: Westview Press.

Noel, A. (1987). "Accumulation, regulation, and Social Change: An Essay on French Political Economy," *International Organization*, Vol. 41, No. 2, pp. 303–333.

North, D. (1995). "The New Institutional Economics and Third World Development," in *The New Institutional Economics and Third World Development*, J. Harriss, J. Hunter, and C. M. Lewis (eds.), London & New York: Routledge.

Ostrom, E. (1995). "Investing in capital, Institutions, and Incentives," in *The New Institutional Economics and Third World Development*, J. Harriss, J. Hunter, and C. M. Lewis (eds.), London & New York: Routledge.

Peet, R. (1991). *Global Capitalism: Theories of Societal Development*, London & New York: Routledge.

Prebisch, R. (1950). *The Economic Development of Latin America and Its Principal Problems*, New York: United Nations.

Ramirez, M. D. (1993). "Stabilization and Adjustment in Latin America: A Neostructuralist Perspective," *Journal of Economic Issues*, Vol. 27, No. 4, pp. 1015–1040.

Ramos, J. and O. Sunkel (1993). "Toward a Neostructuralist Synthesis," in *Development from Within: Toward a Neostructuralist Approach for Latin America*, O. Sunkel (ed.), Boulder & London: Lynne Rienner Publishers.

Rodrik, D. (2008). *The New Development Economics: We Shall Experiment, But How Shall We Learn?* Cambridge, MA: John F. Kennedy School of Government, Harvard University.

Rutherford, M. (1994). *Institutions in Economics: The Old and the New Institutionalism*, New York and Melbourne: Cambridge University Press.

Rutherford, M. (2001). "Institutional Economics: Then and Now," *Journal of Economic Perspectives*, Vol. 15, No. 3, pp. 173–190.

Savoie, D. J. and B. Higgins (1992). "Towards a New Paradigm? Two Views," in *Equity and Efficiency in Economic Development — Essays in Honour of Benjamin Higgins*, D. Savoie and I. Brecher (eds.), Montreal: McGill-Queen's University Press.

So, A. Y. (1990). *Social Change and Development Modernisation, Dependency and World System Theories*, London: Sage Publications.

Stiglitz, J. (2006). *Making Globalization Work*, W. W. Norton & Company.

Street, J. H. (1967). "The Latin American 'Structuralists' and the Institutionalists: Convergence in Development Theory," *Journal of Economic Issues*, Vol. 1, Nos. 1 & 2, pp. 44–62.

Street, J. H. (1987). "The Institutionalist Theory of Economic Development," *Journal of Economic Issues*, Vol. 21, No. 4, pp. 1861–1887.

Street, J. H. and D. D. James (1982). "Institutionalism, Structuralism, and Dependency in Latin America," *Journal of Economic Issues*, Vol. 16, No. 3, pp. 673–689.

Sunkel, O. (1958), "La inflacion chilena: Un enfoque heterodoxo," *El Trimestre Economical*, Vol. 25, No. 4. (English translation in *International Economic Papers*, No. 10, London, 1960).

Sunkel, O. (ed.) (1993). *Development from Within: Toward a Neostructuralist Approach for Latin America*, Boulder & London: Lynne Rienner Publishers.

Taylor, L. (1983). *Structuralist Macroeconomics*, New York: Basic Books, Inc.

Todaro M. and S. Smith (2012). *Economic Development*, 11th edn., Boston: Addison-Wesley.

Veblen, T. (1966, first pub. 1919). *The Place of Science in Modern Civilization*, New York: Atheneum.

World Bank (2005). *Economic Growth in the 1990s: Learning from a Decade of Reform*, Washington, DC.

Appendix A: Three major methodologies for socio-economic analysis.

Mainstream (Orthodox) economists' Atomistic Competitive Market Approach	Systemic Approach of Structuralism & Functionalism	Strategic Approach of Economic Institutionalism
i. Individual households and firms are the basic units of analysis. In this approach, the operating forces behind the market are assumed to be institutionally given as data. However, the markets can only reflect a prior underlying structure of entitlements that indicate who has rights, duties, privileges, power and liability. Society is considered a universe of commodity relations.	i. Interest groups/classes are the basic elements. The essential behavior of a system is determined by the totality of the laws governing it, i.e., by its structure or the set of necessary and essential relations, not just commodity relations. It includes socio-economic, politico-legal and cultural-religious relations as well (which are all functionally regulated from within).	i. Different institutions — formal or informal — are the basic units of analysis. Like structuralism, this approach emphasizes the influences of the societal environment on individuals' economic behaviors. Institutions are not just buildings or group of people, an institution is instead a group of people with some common behavioral patterns or norms. Its members have an awareness of the institutional groupings.
ii. On the basis of the economic rationality principle of individual behaviors in markets, the *static* equilibrating analytical tool is used. Economic rationalism is the theory that (economic) reason is the foundation of certainty in (socio-economic) knowledge. Individual behavior is guided primarily by utilitarian motivation and pecuniary calculation. Process of institutional changes in the face of new scarcities, new techniques, new knowledge, new tastes and preferences, etc., here is of no interest.	ii. Societal transformation studied *dynamically* in the process of change, as tendencies, not as (static) states. Societal transformation takes place due to the existence of differentiation of social status, inequality in distribution of economic wealth and concentration of political power among a few groups/classes or sectors/segments.	ii. Focus is on institutionalized behavior norms or folkways of various institutions. Certain individual behaviors are encouraged, while certain others are discouraged (as under tribute system, share cropping, tenancy, labor-tying production arrangement). Individuals' choices, attitudes, and behaviors thus vary across the segments/sectors of society. Indeed, if one starts from institutions, only a minimal set of assumptions about individuals is required for societal analysis.

(Continued)

Appendix A: (*Continued*)

Mainstream (Orthodox) economists' Atomistic Competitive Market Approach	Systemic Approach of Structuralism & Functionalism	Strategic Approach of Economic Institutionalism
iii. Conflict and competition are assumed inherent in human nature, but no conflict in socio-economic system is acknowledged. The mainstream or orthodox economics grew out of the 18th-century English society, supposedly homogeneous in its character. Economic individualism was allowed to operate and flourish in the society.	iii. Empirical relations among socio-economic elements are explained by postulating some deep or hidden structures. Karl Marx's assertion of the surplus value of unpaid labor as the source of capitalist profit may be considered an example of discovering a hidden structure. Similarly, in the non-Marxian tradition, e.g., in Max Weberian analysis, monopolistic/oligopolistic market share (or capacity) is an example of a hidden structure behind the corporate profit.	iii. Emphasis on dynamism involved in ongoing technological changes in both material tools and mental skill. In overcoming obstacles to the continuity of human life, not only 'instruments and means over ends' are stressed, but also ideals are viewed as 'instruments of action.'
iv. The conviction among the adherents of this tradition is that Adam Smith's *invisible hand* not only works well through self-interest. Markets are considered fully monetized and organized so that 'gains-from-trade' can be guaranteed through voluntary exchanges.	iv. The societal structures have their laws of composition and functionally regulated from within the society. All kinds of conflicts, complementarity, and compatibility in the behavior of individuals, groups/classes, and institutions are in fact influenced by the mode of functioning of society as an entity.	iv. *Institutionalism* is often regarded as 'economics of control' within the basic ideological framework. According to institutional economics, an economic problem is frequently institutional rather than logical. The basic problem is to form a consensus as to what one wants to do and then effecting the institutional changes appropriate to that consensus. Institutionalists are basically reformists operating within the basic ideological framework of the prevalent dominant institutions.

(*Continued*)

Appendix A: (*Continued*)

Mainstream (Orthodox) economists' Atomistic Competitive Market Approach	Systemic Approach of Structuralism & Functionalism	Strategic Approach of Economic Institutionalism
v. The 'worm's-eye-view' of actor-centered socio-economic analysis is noted in this approach.	v. The 'bird's-eye-view' of any systemic (societal or sub-societal) analysis is prevalent in this tradition.	v. The strategic actor's planned or interventionist view is reflected here.
vi. *Idealism* is the philosophical basis in this tradition because of the inherent belief that no material objects or external realities exist apart from one's subjective knowledge or consciousness of them. This leads to the mental conception of economic world as rational, homogeneous, and perfectly competitive in this approach.	vi. *Realism*, which holds that material objects exist not only externally to human beings but also independently of their sense experience, is the philosophical basis in this tradition. Basic changes in all levels of society and their organizations are, therefore, incorporated in analyzing the dynamic behaviors of its systemic structural components.	vi. *Pragmatism*, which rejects the dualism between the real and ideal realities is the philosophical basis of this approach. It holds the view that all human behaviors are culturally determined and, therefore, are institutionalized behaviors (norms or folkways). They can always be related to some particular consequence in society's future practical experience (whether passive or active) within tool development or knowledge generation (as the basis for *instrumental value theory*).

Part II

Structural and Institutional Analysis of Contemporary China's Growth and Development

2. Shifting the Discourse on China's Growth and Development: It is the Quality Not the Speed of Growth That Matters

*Limin Wang**

1. Introduction

The growth experience from a large number of countries over the past several decades reaffirms that it is the "quality" of growth that advances development and well-being. In addition to the growth rate, the notion of the "quality" of growth is intended to capture other important aspects of development, including poverty reduction, equity and environment and resource sustainability (Thomas, Lopez and Wang, 2000). While the rapid growth of the past three decades was instrumental in lifting millions of people out of poverty, growth in itself does not guarantee achieving desirable development outcomes, as illustrated in China's growth experience from 1978 until now. The goal of development, as Sen (1999) outlines, lies in expanding capability through improvement in health and education, and promoting equity and equality of opportunities — ultimately providing freedoms and rights to people to participate in economic and social life.

Three decades of rapid economic growth has transformed China from an egalitarian society into one of high inequality, with the disparity surpassing all the countries in Europe and approaching the level of Latin American countries by 2008. Along with rising income inequality, disparities in social indicators, including health and education outcomes, are also on the rise. Gender equality, one of China's major pre-reform era achievements, has even reversed. Much of China's recent increase in income inequality has been a result of unequal opportunities — excluding the disadvantaged population from the new employment opportunities that are more skill-based

---

*99limin@gmail.com

(Riskin, 2010). The potential threat to political and social stability posed by growing inequality has now been widely regarded as the major issue in China.

Environmental sustainability, a critical aspect of the quality growth, has largely been sidelined, in growth-focused policy discourse on China. This is particularly reflected in the large and growing body of studies that is overwhelmingly devoted to China's growth miracle and its rising power in the global economy, while omitting the issue of environment degradation and depletion of natural capital that is associated with its recent energy intensive-pattern of growth.

This chapter aims to provide compelling evidence based on the most recent data sources to reshape current policy thinking on China's future economic growth and development. Section 2 presents China's economic miracle over the past three decades. Section 3 explains how China has achieved such a miracle. In Section 4, the source of growth is analyzed, while Section 5 assesses the quality of growth. Disparity in social indicators is the focus of Section 6. Section 7 discusses the environmental and resource cost of three decades' economic growth. A conclusion follows in Section 8.

2.   China's Economic Miracle

Within a span of three decades, China has transformed itself from one of the poorest and most isolated countries in the world to a well-established, middle-income country, producing about one fifth of global manufacturing output. At the same time, industrialization and urbanization are taking place at an unprecedented rate in its history. This section presents the impressive achievement that China has made since 1978 when it started its transition from a centrally controlled system to a market economy.

2.1.   *The sustained high rate of growth*

China's fast economic growth is widely heralded as a growth miracle. From 1978 to 2010, China has experienced a sustained economic growth at an average annual GDP growth rate of about 10%, with per capita GDP increased by over 16 times, from a level of about US$150 (in 2000 constant US$) in the 1970s to about US$2423 in 2010. After the global financial crisis in 2008, while many countries experienced an economic downturn, China remains resilient to the economic shocks by maintaining a growth

Figure 1: GDP growth rate.

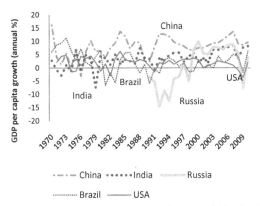

Source: Author's own construction based on China Statistical Yearbooks.

rate at about 10% in 2010. Based on National Bureau of Statistics, China became the world's second largest economy after the US in 2011.

China's growth record is most striking from an international perspective. Both the duration and the rate of growth have outperformed the four large economies (India, Brazil, Russia and the US) as shown in Figure 1. China's growth also surpasses that of the East-Asian miracles of Taiwan, Hong Kong, Singapore and Korea in the 1980s and 1990s which grew at a rate of about 7–8% for less than two decades. A comparison between China and India (Figure 2) — two countries comparable in terms of population size and stage of development — is particularly interesting. In the early 1980s, both countries were at the same level of income, but three decades later, per capita income in China was nearly three times that of India in 2009.

2.2. *Rapid structural transformation and urbanization*

The three decades' rapid economic growth has been accompanied by fundamental transformation of China's economic structure. The Chinese economy has transformed from a low-productive, agriculture-based economy to one that is dominated by industry and service sectors, as shown in Figure 3(a). The GDP share of the value added by agriculture, industry and services have changed from 30%, 42% and 28% in 1978 to 10%, 47% and 43%, respectively, in 2010.

Figure 2: GDP per capita.

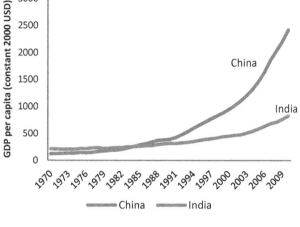

Figure 3: Sectoral share of GDP and labor force: 1978–2010.

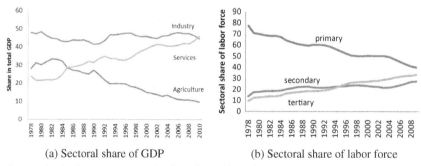

| (a) Sectoral share of GDP | (b) Sectoral share of labor force |

Source: Author's own construction based on *China Statistical Yearbooks.*

At the same time, a large-scale population relocation also took place across sectors and between urban and rural areas. The share of employment in agriculture dropped from 78% in 1978 to 40% in 2010 (Figure 3(b)), releasing a large amount of surplus labor force that made it possible for rapid expansion of industrial and service sectors. China experienced the fastest urbanization among all developing countries, with urban population increased by almost three-fold with the share of urban to total population rising from 17% in 1970 to over 45% in 2010.

China's structural transformation, in many respects, resembles the process of industrialization that took place in Europe in the 18th and 19th centuries, in the US in the early 20th century, and in the Newly Industrial

Economies in East Asia in the 1970s and 1980s. However, it took much less time for China, a country with nearly a quarter of the world population, to complete its transformation from an agriculture-based economy to one dominated by industry and service sectors.

2.3. *Leading world trader and major FDI destination*

In the 1970s, China was a much closed economy — total value of China's import and export was only US$20.6 billion, ranking 32nd in world trade and accounting for less than 1% of the world's total trade. Within three decades, China became the world's largest exporter and second-largest importer. In 2010, the total value of China's import and export reached US$2.974 trillion, 144 times as much as that in 1978, with the total volumes of China's export and import accounting for 10.4% and 9.1% of the world's total, respectively.

More importantly, the commodity structure of export had significantly upgraded since the early 1990s. There has been a sharp decline in the share of agriculture and low-skilled manufacturing products, such as textiles and apparel, while the share of manufacturing products, such as consumer electronics, appliances and computers, increased substantially.[1] The share of high-technology export in manufacturing increased from 6% in 1992 to 31% in 2009, as a result of rapid production upgrading in the industrial sector. The average productivity in manufacturing was only 5.6% of that in the US in 1995, but in less than a decade it increased to 15.8% by 2004, and the production in coastal provinces has closed the technological gap with the international frontier (Deng and Jefferson, 2011).

China also became a major destination of foreign direct investment (FDI). According to official statistics, FDI was near zero in the late 1970s and rose to about only US$2.3 billion in 1984–1989. Since the early 1990s, China had become the largest FDI recipient among developing countries, with FDI inflow to China reached US$95 billion, accounting for about 19.9% of total FDI in developing countries, and 8.5% of total global FDI in 2009 according to UNCADT data sources http://stats.uncatad.org/lsci).

---

[1]Some argue that a large component of this export growth in machinery is attributed to growth in processing trade, i.e., assembling duty free intermediate inputs of high skill content from developed economies such as the US and Japan using low-cost Chinese labor (Dean, Fung and Wang, 2007; Amiti and Freund, 2008).

2.4.   *The emerging industries*

China is now embarking on a new stage of production upgrading. The development of strategic emerging industries (SEIs) is the key focus of the 12th Five-Year Plan (2010–2015), which includes biotechnology, new energy, high-end equipment manufacturing, energy generation and environmental protection, clean energy vehicles, new materials and new generation information technology (IT).

China has started to shift investment toward clean technology. In 2009, overtaking the US, China became the largest investor in clean energy technology; its investment of US\$34.6 billion accounted for about 21% of global total investment in clean energy. At the same time, it surpassed countries such as Denmark, Germany, Spain and the US in 2009 to become the world's largest maker of wind turbines and solar panels.

3.   How has China Made Such Miracle?

China's economic miracle has attracted global attention and spurred a proliferation of studies that attempt to identify factors underlying its unprecedented growth.[2] Five factors are broadly considered to be the key determinants of China's phenomenal growth performance.

3.1.   *Economic reform policies*

China's economic reform policies have been the key impetus behind the country's sustained growth. Since the early 1980s, China's highly distorted and inefficient centrally planned economy has been gradually transformed into an economic system that depends, to a great extent, on market forces to allocate resources, enforce private property rights and operate within a set of relatively developed regulatory institutions.

The reform process started in the early 1980s in the agricultural sector through the introduction of household responsibility system and development of Town and Village enterprises, replacing the inefficient rural collective system. The decision of the 14th Party Congress in 1993 to establish a "socialist market economy" paved the way for the next stage of reforms

---

[2]See Dollar and Wei (2007); Keefer (2007); Lin, Cai and Zhou (2003); Lin and Liu (2000); Naughton (2006); OECD (2005); El-Erian and Spence (2008); Knight, Yang and Yueh (2011); and Wang, Yan and Yao (2003).

in state-owned enterprises (SOEs) and the financial sector. The reform of SOEs involved devolution of management and control from the central government to managers of local enterprises, and privatization of the majority of SOEs through the transfer of ownership of state assets. As SOEs reform deepened, the private sector had become an increasingly dominant force in the economy, with the private sector share of total industrial output rising from 6% in 1998 to about 52% in 2009 (*China Statistical Yearbook*, 2010).

Another important structural reform involved fiscal and administrative decentralization from the central government to local tiers of institutions. Decentralization also created competition among local governments and improved efficiency through better decision-making based on local conditions and better information flows. These reforms unleashed enormous creativity and incentives of individuals, firms and local governments that strived to maximize economic returns, by seeking out opportunities, both domestically and globally.

3.2. Government commitment and the Chinese-style reform

History shows that growth entails much more than just economics. It requires the leadership of governments that are committed, credible and capable. China's reform experience is a case in point. The Chinese government has evidently demonstrated its strong commitment and leadership to transform China from a poverty-ridden country to a prosperous nation by implementing a wide range of long-term economic reform programs, while recognizing the challenges and political risks associated with these reforms.

China's approach to pursuing these reforms is unique. Chinese policymakers understood the enormous uncertainties brought about by economic reforms on such a scale. Following the principle developed by Deng Xiaoping "to cross the river by feeling for the stones," the Chinese government adopted a gradual, experimental and pragmatic approach to reform, scaling up successful reforms over time and across regions based on the principle of learning-by-doing (Hofman and Wu, 2009). The Chinese approach reduced the risks associated with the Big Bang reform approach that was adopted by many Eastern European countries, where many reforms were brought to a halt or even redundant due to political constrains.

3.3.   *Strong emphasis on public investment in social services and rural development*

The third factor lies in China's long-term commitment to public invest-ment in infrastructure, education and health and basic services, in partic-ular, before and during the early period of economic reforms. Although the centrally planned system had severely distorted resource allocation and hindered economic growth, progressive policies in promoting public invest-ment in health, education and access to basic services such as electricity, safe water and sanitation had laid the foundation for China's economic success once distortions and constraints were removed through economic reform.

Public investment prior to China's economic reform focused on expand-ing the population's access to basic health and education services in both urban and rural areas. Promoting gender equality was also one of the devel-opment priorities. These development policies resulted in China's impres-sive human development outcomes despite its low per capita income. As shown in Table 1, in the early 1980s, per capita income in China was much lower than India, Brazil and Indonesia, and even lower than Tanzania, but the social indicators, measured by child mortality, life expectancy and adult female literacy rate, were far superior to these countries.

China's agricultural productivity growth since the early 1980s was largely attributed to the government-led investment in rural infrastructure,

Table 1: Human development indicators during the 1980s: A cross-country comparison.

	Per capita income			Adult female	Improved water source	Agricultural irrigated land
	Constant US\$	Child mortality	Life expectancy	literacy rate	% of population with access, 1989	% share in arable land, 1979–1981
China	194	62	67	51 (1981)	67	46.6
India	238	143	56	26 (1980)	72	23.57
Brazil	3303	87	63	73 (1979)	88	3.54
Russia	2693 (1988)	33	67	96.8 (1988)	93	3.7 (1999–2001)
Indonesia	412	118	58	57.7 (1979)	71	23.38
Tanzania	292 (1987)	165	51	48.1 (1987)	55	4.02

Source: The World Bank database.

including electricity access, rural roads and irrigation. The superior rural infrastructure in China compared with many developing countries (see Table 1) made it possible to achieve a faster growth in the agricultural sector when the constraints of the collective farming system were removed.

Essentially, prior to the transition to a relatively open economy, China had built a literate and healthy labor force, and developed an infrastructure base thanks to strong government-led investment in social services. When a conducive business climate was created by economic reform, the majority of the Chinese population had the capabilities to participate fully in the expanded economic opportunities brought by the reform policies, raising national income at a rapid pace.

3.4. *Integration into the global economy*

China's economic growth was further strengthened by its integration into the rest of the world. Indeed, the growth experience from 13 countries since the early 1970s,[3] all of which experienced an annual growth of 7% or more over 25 years, highlights the importance of integration into the global economy for sustaining growth. Before 1950, sustained growth at a level of about 7% was not conceivable. It was feasible only because the world economy became more open and integrated since the early 1970s (World Bank, 2008). The global economy offers China a nearly unlimited market for its export of goods and services, while allowing it to improve efficiency and productivity by exploring its comparative advantage in low-cost labor and economies of scale.

The integration into the world economy also provides China with the opportunity to import technology and ideas, know-how and modern management skills that are embodied in FDI and joint ventures. By opening up its economy through trade and FDI, growth in the export sector also played a key role in stimulating technology upgrading.

Another important channel of knowledge transfer is through various exchange programs. Along with openness of trade and foreign investment, Chinese policy makers paid special attention to foreign education through

---

[3]These include Botswana, Brazil, China, Hong Kong, Indonesia, Japan, the Republic of Korea, Malaysia, Malta, Oman, Singapore, Taiwan and Thailand (see Commissions on Growth and Development, 2008).

exchange. The Chinese government invited a stream of foreign experts to help them learn about the functioning and features of a market economic system while at the same time sending many waves of Chinese students and government officials to be trained in US and European universities. Many prominent Chinese reformers were selected from the pool of western trained technocrats to be placed in key positions in China's economic reform policy think tanks, playing an important role in reshaping China's reform policy-making.

4. What are the Sources of Growth?

While China has maintained a high growth rate over three decades, the sources of economic growth had changed over time. Numerous empirical studies[4] that attempt to identify the sources of growth in China have concluded that its record growth rate over the first two decades (1978–2000) was sustained largely through growth in labor productivity, but economic growth in the third decade (2000–2010) was largely driven by investment in fixed assets (real estate investment, in particular) and growth in energy-intensive industries.

4.1. *The first two decades (1978 to the early 2000s)*

Table 2 summarizes the sectoral decomposition of growth accounting equation[5] from 1978 to 2004. During the period from 1978 to 1993, all three sectors were growing at a high but comparable pace, ranging from 4.3% for agriculture, 4.7% for services and 4.8% for the industrial sector. As structural transformation accelerated, the industrial and service sectors[6] overtook the agricultural sector during 1993–2004, with labor productivity growth in industry and services reaching 9.8% and 5.1%, respectively, compared with that of 4.3% in the agricultural sector.

---

[4]These include Bosworth and Collins (2008), Chow and Li (2002); Chow (1993); Dekle and Vandenbroucke (2006); Fan and Zhang (2002); Hu and Khan (1997), Holz (2006b); International Monetary Fund (2006); Kuijs and Wang (2006); Kwan (2006); and Riedel, Jing and Gao (2007).

[5]See Appendix A for an explanation on growth accounting equation.

[6]These two sectors contributed about 59% and 20% of total growth during 1993–2004, while the agricultural sector accounted for only 8% (Bosworth and Collin, 2008).

Table 2: Sources of growth by sector: 1978–2004.

	Total growth	Agriculture (1)	Industry (2)	Services (3)	Reallocation (4)
1978–1993					
Sectoral contribution to growth (%)	6.4	1.2	2.4	1.1	1.7
Output/per worker (annual growth rate %)	6.4	4.3	4.8	4.7	
1993–2004					
Sectoral contribution to growth (%)	8.5	0.7	5	1.7	1.2
Output/per worker (annual growth rate %)	8.5	4.3	9.8	5.1	

Source: Bosworth and Collins (2008).

More importantly, the declining importance of agriculture in the economy was accompanied by sustained productivity improvement in the agricultural sector. The annual average growth of labor productivity in the agricultural sector increased steadily: from 4.8% during 1991–2000 to 5.9% during 2001–2005, and to 7.2% during 2006–2009.

The firm-level evidence also confirms the improved productivity in industrial sector, which further sustained China's overall economic growth. The study based on firm-level data by Li *et al.* (2011) shows that productivity among Chinese firms is much higher than that of Indian firms, mainly because of the availability of more skilled labor, higher returns to skills, better local infrastructure and, in particular, the greater reliability of power supply that is critical for continued production operation[7] and greater labor market flexibility.

The productivity growth was also reinforced by the reallocation of resources between sectors. The shift of resources from a low-productivity agricultural sector to industry and services sectors was responsible for a large part of the efficiency gain in the Chinese economy. Based on estimates from several studies (Bosworth and Collins, 2008; Heiesh and Klenow,

---

[7]The average proportion of annual sale lost due to power outages for Chinese firms is 2% compared to 9% for Indian firms as recorded in Li *et al.* (2011), based on firm-level data.

Table 3: Sources of growth: Comparison of China, India and East Asia* (1978–2004).[a]

		1978–2004	1978–1993	1993–2004
China	GDP per worker (annual growth rate %)	7.3	6.4	8.5
	Contribution from			
	(1) growth in capital per worker	3.2	2.4	4.2
	(2) growth in years of schooling	0.3	0.4	0.3
	(3) growth in total factor productivity	**3.6**	**3.5**	**3.9**
India	GDP per worker (annual growth rate %)	3.3	2.4	4.6
	Contribution from			
	(1) growth in capital per worker	1.3	0.9	1.8
	(2) growth in years of schooling	0.4	0.3	0.4
	(3) growth in total factor productivity	**1.6**	**1.1**	**2.3**
		1980–2003	1980–1993	1993–2003
East Asia	GDP per worker (annual growth rate %)	3.7	6.4	2.5
	Contribution from			
	(1) growth in capital per worker	2.2	2.6	1.8
	(2) growth in years of schooling	0.5	0.6	0.5
	(3) growth in total factor productivity	**0.9**	**1.4**	**0.3**

[a]East Asia also includes Indonesia, South Korea, Malaysia, Philippines, Singapore, Taiwan and Thailand.
Source: Bosworth and Collins (2008).

2009), the reallocation effect explained about 25% of total labor productivity growth during 1978–1993, and about 15% in the following period of 1993–2004 (see Table 3).

The growth in total factor productivity[8] (TFP), a measure of overall productivity of the economy, sets China's growth performance. Annual TFP growth in China increased from 1.1% during 1953–1978, to 3.5% during 1978–1993, again up to 3.9% during 1993–2004 (Hu and Khan, 1997). This is in sharp contrast with other countries: India experienced

---

[8]See Appendix A for the definition of total factor productivity (TFP).

a TFP growth rate of 1.6% during 1978–2004, 0.9% in East Asia during 1980–2003, and 0.4% in the US during its fast growth period of 1960–1990.

The Chinese economy has been in a virtuous cycle with sustaining feedback effects: high investment produced rapid economic growth, and rapid growth in turn boosted expectations, which then encouraged high investment. The positive interaction between investment and efficiency gained from both technological progress and resource reallocation is in line with what the endogenous growth theory predicts (Knight and Ding, 2010). In short, China's fast and sustained economic growth was largely driven by a combination of efficient usage of factors of production and technological progress as reflected in the increase of labor productivity and TFP during the first two decades.

4.2. The third decade (2000–2010)

Since the early 2000s, the sources of growth have changed, and growth has largely been driven by investment in fixed asset (e.g., real estate investment), capital-intensive industries and export sectors. In 2008, fixed asset investment accounted for about 40% of GDP, higher than all other large economies, including Japan (22%), Germany (19%), US (14%), Brazil (18%) and India (39%) — the world average was 21% in 2008.

The growth pattern during this period was particularly energy intensive. The fast-growing industries were those producing energy-intensive products, such as steel, aluminum and cement, to meet China's massive domestic demand for housing construction, transportation and infrastructure development, as well as to export to international markets. China accounted for 48% of global cement production, 49% of flat glass production, 35% of steel production, 28% of aluminum production and 11% of passenger cars production in 2006.

The government also aimed at driving economic growth through developing the automobile industry.[9] Between 2002 and 2007, China's national automobile market grew by an average 21%, or one million new vehicles year-on-year. In 2009, 13.79 million motor vehicles were manufactured in

---

[9]Recent initiatives include tax incentives through reduced purchase tax on small-engine cars below 1.6 L and a 5 billion RMB direct-subsidy for farmers purchasing minivans and light trucks. This has had the effect of dramatically stimulating the production and sale of domestic small-engine cars.

China, surpassing the US as the world's largest automobile producer by volume (Hong and Mu, 2010).

While empirical studies analyzing China's sources of growth during the 2000s are scarce, many indicators suggest that productivity growth and efficiency gain from resource reallocation between sectors became less important sources in driving China's overall growth during this period (Eberhardt, Helmers and Yu, 2011). The growth pattern during the decade of 2000s is, as put bluntly by the then Chinese Premier Wen Jiabao (in 2009), "unstable, unbalanced, uncoordinated and unsustainable."

5.   Assessing the Quality of Growth

This section assesses three aspects of the quality of growth involving technology advancement, poverty impact and income inequality. Technological upgrading and innovation are fundamental to a sustained growth. A pertinent question rises as to how China can sustain its growth when overreliance on capital accumulation and export becomes a binding constraint, while the efficiency gain from resource allocation between sectors and the comparative advantage of low-cost labor diminish. More importantly, what is the impact of the past three decades of rapid growth on poverty and inequality?

5.1.   *Technology advancement*

As improvement in productivity from resource relocation between sectors diminishes, and the pressure of resource constraints increases, sustaining growth and competitiveness in China requires the development of technology-based industries and the knowledge-based service sector, together with a highly educated labor force. Recognizing investment in R&D is the driving force of productivity, and many OECD countries set their target at 3% of GDP devoted to R&D in order to develop knowledge and technology-based economies. In contrast, the R&D share of GDP in China, although steadily rising, was only about 1.5% by 2007 (Figure 4).

Although China became the second largest economy in the world, the share of knowledge- and technology-intensive output had remained relatively small over the past two decades. Figure 5(a) shows China's knowledge-intensive and high-technology industries' share of GDP

Figure 4: R&D expenditures as percent of GDP: 1996–2007.

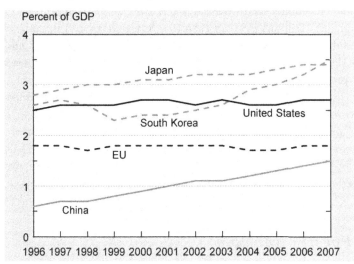

Source: Organization for Economic Co-operation and Development, Main Science and Technology Indicators (2009/1 and previous years).

Figure 5: Value added of knowledge-intensive and high-technology industries and services: 1995–2007.

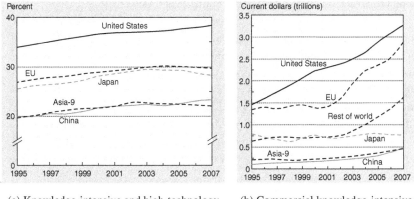

(a) Knowledge-intensive and high-technology industries as share of GDP

(b) Commercial knowledge-intensive services

Source: IHS Global Insight, World Industry Service database, Science and Engineering Indicators 2010.

increased moderately, from about 20% in 1995 to 23% in 2007, compared with 38% in the US, 30% in the EU and 27% in Japan in 2007. The total value added in commercial knowledge-intensive services also rose slowly, from about 0.1 (trillions US$) in 1995 to 0.5 (trillions US$) in 2007, while the US and EU increased from 1.5 and 1.4 (trillions US$) to 3.2 and 2.8 (trillions US$), respectively during the same period as shown in Figure 5(b).

The production upgrading of many Chinese companies that was made possible through FDI and joint ventures during the first two decades was mainly through assembling and processing operations, rather than technological progress and innovation. In the decade of 2000s, however, the majority of Chinese companies did not catch up with their counterparts in the developed economies in technology development and innovation, despite their rapid expansion of production driven by a large domestic market and export.

5.2. *Poverty reduction*

Since the beginning of economic reform in 1978, China had created two miracles in modern history. First, China has transformed itself from one of the poorest countries in the world to a middle-income country within a span of three decades through sustained economic growth at a record pace. In the 1980s and 1990s, China was a major aid recipient among developing countries. From the beginning of the 21st century, it had become a major donor to Africa, Latin America and South East Asia.[10]

The second miracle is poverty reduction. China has made the largest contribution to the reduction of global poverty by lifting over a fifth of the world's poor people out of poverty. Based on the World Bank international poverty line of US$1.25 per person per day, the number of poor people dropped from 842 million to 166 million in China — more than 600 million people had moved out of poverty.[11] This is equivalent to lifting more than half of the population of the entire African continent out of poverty.

In a comparative study of three large emerging economies, China, Brazil and India, Ravallion and Chen (2007) provide important insights into the

---

[10]In 2007, China provided about US$1.4 billion Overseas Development Aid (ODA) to Africa (Bräutigam, 2008) whereas ODA to Africa from the US amounted to US$7.6 billion and from the EU, US$6 billion.

[11]According to World Bank estimates, the people below the poverty line of US$1.25 per person per day in consumption accounted for 12.6% of the total population in 2008.

Table 4: Comparison of China, India and Brazil.

	GDP per capita (US$ ppp per year)			Inequality (Gini index %)			Poverty headcount index (poverty line US$1.25)		
	China	India	Brazil	China	India	Brazil	China	India	Brazil
1981	543	901	7072	29.1	35.1	57.5	84	59.8	17.1
1993	1505	1274	7241	35.5	30.8	59.7	53.7	49.4	13
2005	4076	2233	8471	41.5	33.4	57.6	16.3	41.6	7.8
1981– 2005 Change %	8.8	3.9	0.8				−80.6	−30.4	−54.4

Source: Ravallion and Chen (2007).

key factors that are associated with each country's success in reducing poverty. During the period of 1981–2005, the three large economies experienced a starkly different growth rate, with China achieving 8.8% GDP per capita growth, while Brazil and India maintained 0.8% and 3.9%, respectively (see Table 4).

In the case of Brazil, despite the relatively slow growth and high level of inequality, it managed to reduce poverty (measured by poverty headcount index) by 54% between 1981 and 2005 while preventing increase in inequality. Social security systems reforms and the introduction of large-scale social assistance transfer programs, including various conditional transfer programs that covered over one quarter of the population, played key roles in poverty reduction. In addition, maintaining macroeconomic stability by controlling inflation and promoting services sector growth have also been instrumental in reducing the number of poor people in Brazil.

The growth in India was largely driven by the service sector in IT, software and financial services, which require high skills and educational qualifications. Such a growth pattern had brought moderate reduction in poverty, about 30% reduction between 1981 and 2005, largely due to its high inequality in human capital, which excludes the poor segment of population from participating in the rapid growth of the highskilled sectors. In a striking contrast to China, a large number of people in India's rural areas continued to be trapped in poverty due to slow growth in the agricultural sector, a direct consequence of underdeveloped rural infrastructure as shown in Table 1 and the deep rooted unequal distribution of land ownership.

Figure 6: Inclusive growth: growth incidence curve.

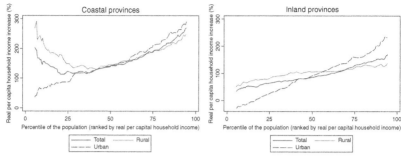

Source: Luo and Zhu (2008).

In contrast, China experienced the highest growth and the largest reduction in poverty (by 81% measured by the headcount index), while it also saw the largest rise in inequality. Indeed, it was the rapid economic growth in the first two decades of reform, equal access to land among rural residents and low inequality in human capital, which provided the foundation for China's success in both generating growth and reducing poverty on a massive scale during the 1980s and 1990s.

Indeed, the impact of growth on poverty in China shows clearly that the growth process, particularly during the first two decades of the reform, was inclusive in that it had enabled the majority of Chinese to participate in the expanded employment opportunities brought about by economic growth. The evidence from a large-scale household survey covering eight provinces, including three coastal provinces (Jiangsu, Shandon and Liaoning) and five inland provinces (Henan, Hubei, Hunan, Guangxi and Guizhou) also confirms the inclusiveness of China's economic growth.

This study also shows that in the coastal regions, where the economic growth was faster than the inland regions, the entire rural population experienced a large increase in income between 1989 and 2004. In particular, the poorest and richest segments of the rural population registered the largest increase in household income, as reflected in the U-shaped growth incidence curve shown in Figure 6. However, the slow poverty reduction and rising inequality during the decade of 2000s is attributable to a combination of investment bias in capital-intensive sectors and slow growth of the service sector.

5.3. *Income inequality*

The three decades of rapid growth has transformed China from an egalitarian society into one of alarmingly high inequality, approaching the level of many Latin American countries. Five decades ago, Lewis made it clear "development must be inegalitarian because it does not start in every part of the economy at the same time." As China was deepening its economic and structural transformation, rising income inequality was, therefore, inevitable.

The relationship between growth and income inequality, although remaining controversial,[12] has occupied a central place in economic policy debates for over 50 years since the pioneering work of Kuznets (1955). The central message of the Kuznets curve is that income inequality dynamics and growth are intimately connected when countries are undergoing a structural transformation, typically from agricultural-based economy to one dominated by the industrial sector. The rising income inequality in China should be examined in the context of a wider process of economic development.

Inequality in China has risen sharply since the beginning of the economic reform in 1978. This rising trend of income inequality is confirmed using various measures and data sources. Figure 7(a) shows that the Gini index increased steadily from the early 1980s to 2005. Compared with other large developing economies and OECD countries, China experienced the largest increase in inequality between the 1990s and 2000s (Figure 7(b)).

The overall inequality in China, as summarized in Figure 8, is a reflection of both the regional disparity and rural–urban divide. The regional development gap is most evident between coastal and inland regions. The coastal to inland GDP per capita ratio rose from 1.7 in the late 1980s to 2.4 in 2004 (Huang and Luo, 2008), reaching the highest level in a half-century (Kanbur and Zhang, 2005).[13] The growing concern about the spatial dimension of inequality is not unique to China. In Russia, India, Mexico and South Africa, as well as in most other developing and transition economies, various measures show that regional disparities in economic activity, incomes and

---

[12] As reviewed by Lundberg and Squire (2003), the empirical literature has evolved in one of two directions. One line of research follows in the tradition of Kuznets and focuses on the question of whether more inequality enhances or inhibits the growth rate (Anand and Kanbur, 1993; Alesina and Rodrik, 1994; Persson and Tabellini, 1994; Perotti, 1996; Li and Zou, 1998; Forbes, 2000). The second approach involves examining the determinants of growth and inequality as essentially independent processes (Lundberg and Squire, 2003). Deininger and Lynsquire (1997) conclude that the fear that economic growth on its own will have a systematic negative effect on the distribution of income is unfounded.

[13] For a more detailed analysis on regional disparity in China during 1996–2010, see the chapter by Dutta and Yang in this publication.

Figure 7: Trends of inequality: 1975–2006.

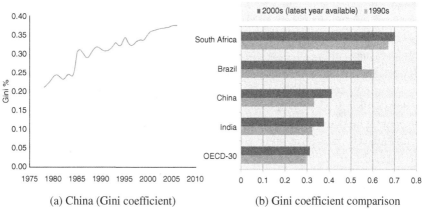

(a) China (Gini coefficient)   (b) Gini coefficient comparison

Source: National submissions for Brazil, India and South Africa. WDI for China and OECD-30.

Figure 8: Inequality decomposition.

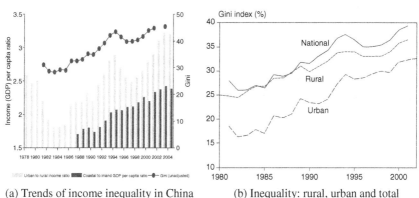

(a) Trends of income inequality in China   (b) Inequality: rural, urban and total

Source: Figure 8(a) is from Huang and Luo (2008) and Figure 8(b) is from Ravallion and Chen (2007).

social indicators, are on the rise. In China, regional inequality has become a concern as it is considered a potential source of ethnic tensions that cause social instability.

In recent years, the rapidly rising inequality in urban areas has become a major public concern. Inequality in urban areas has been fast catching up with that in rural areas since the late 1990s (see Figure 7(b)). Urban inequality, being a major contributor to the overall inequality in China, accounted for about 36% of overall inequality in 2004, rising from 20% in 1989 (Luo and Zhu, 2008). The rising urban inequality warrants special policy attention for two reasons. First, the significant political stake that the urban population commands in Chinese society means a sharp rising inequality in urban areas can potentially lead to social unrest. Second, the continuous massive inflow of rural migrants into urban areas is likely to further aggravate inequalities and urban poverty if policy measures were not put in place to reverse such trends.

Many studies most likely have underestimated urban poverty and inequality because of the exclusion of rural migrants in the sample on urban residents, even though many of them reside in urban areas almost permanently. Evidence based on targeted surveys shows that the average income of migrants is much lower than that of urban residents — the average hourly wage for migrants was about 9.8 (RMB), compared with 13.5 (RMB) for urban residents in 2010 (Cai, Yang and Wang, 2011). In addition, income inequality among migrants is much higher, with the Gini coefficient of hourly income at 0.42 for migrants, compared with 0.38 for their urban counterparts (Zhang, 2011). This suggests that urban inequality is likely to be much higher when taking into account migrant populations.

5.4. *What is driving China's rising income inequality?*

The rising spatial income disparity, in particular, between the coastal and inland regions, is likely attributable to a combination of differential geographical conditions and government preferential industrial policies. The coastal provinces enjoyed geographical advantages in terms of proximity to ports and the closer trade links with the rest of the world. In addition, the labor force in coastal regions is relatively more educated.[14] The Chinese Government's industrial policy in terms of providing subsidies and preferential tax treatment for investment in the special economic zones designed to open up coastal regions to international trade and attract FDI, also played a key role in widening regional inequality.

The second source of China's rising income inequality lies in the significant increase in returns to education. The increasing dominance of the

---

[14]The average years of formal education of the working-age population was 5.9 in coastal rural areas, compared with 5.2 in inland in 1989, although disparity in education attainment among the urban population was negligible (Lou and Zou, 2008).

private sector in China's overall economy, together with the restructuring of SOEs, intensifies competition among firms. In order to maintain competitiveness, firms strive to continuously improve efficiency, upgrade production through new investment and employ more educated and skilled workers.

The economic reform has created a labor market where wage-returns to education have been substantially increased. For example, the wage-return to one additional year of schooling increased from 4% in 1988 to 11% in 2003 (Zhang *et al.*, 2005). Similarly, the salary premium of more skilled occupations has increased substantially, with 'white-collar' jobs (e.g., professional/technical personnel, factory managers and administrators), earning sustainably higher salaries than unskilled, 'blue-collar' workers. In 1989, the average wage of 'white-collar' workers was 10% higher than their blue-collar counterparts, but by 2004, the wage gap increased to 55%.

In many respects, the growing income inequality in China reflects the rising importance of the middle class which did not exist before the early 1980s (Figure 9). The per capita income share of the middle 60% of the population increased sharply during the past two decades. By 2008, the middle 60% population accounted for about 55% of total income, while the top quintile (20%) accounted for 40%, which is similar to class distribution observed in the OECD countries in the mid-2000s.

The rising inequality in education and health services in recent years in China, a subject to be discussed in the following section, indicates that the disadvantaged populations, including the less educated and rural populations, were most likely excluded disproportionally from the growth process, which may have exacerbated income inequality in recent years.

6. Disparity in Social Indicators and Opportunities

In *Development as Freedom*, Sen (1999) emphasizes that development must be focused on individual entitlements, capabilities, freedom and rights, and that economic growth is the means to these ends and equity must be central to economic development. The notion of equity includes both income and human capabilities, such as health and education outcomes, equality of opportunities and gender equality. However, judged by the notion of development advocated by Sen, China's economic growth process in recent years, in many aspects, falls short of what constitutes development.

Figure 9: Per capita income shares by quintile (%).

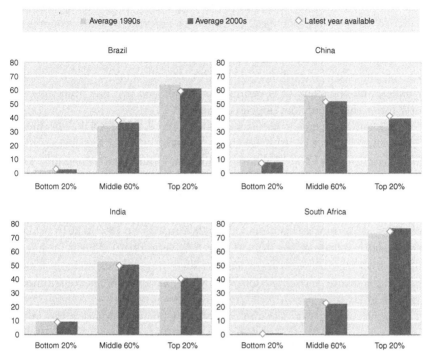

Source: National submissions based on PNAD for Brazil, NSS for India and SALDRU 1993, IES 2000 and NIDS 2008 for South Africa. For China, data came from the Milanovic database.

China was able to achieve impressive health and education outcomes, with a very low level of income, as illustrated in Table 1. But as its economic status elevates to the rank of the middle-income countries in recent years, its social indicators are becoming stagnant, while disparities in health and education, both in terms of access and outcomes, are also widening. The impressive achievements in gender equality before the early 1980s have reversed in the recent years, as highlighted in the 2008 UNDP Millennium Development Goal Progress Report.

6.1.   *The shrinking role of government*

In achieving development and equity, history shows that public policies, rather than market forces, are the important sources of social insurance.

This is particularly true when countries are undergoing major economic transformation and experiencing faster economic growth with rising income inequality, as has been the case in China. In contrast to many countries that were burdened with large government budget deficit and slow growth, China's fiscal capacity increased by over 22 times between 1980 and 2010. However, the role of government in the provision of social services has been shrinking, and the share of government's social spending has been significantly lower than many developed economies.

In China, government social spending as a share of GDP, although increased from 17.7% in 1995 to 20.8% in 2008, is much lower than the OECD average of 44.5%. Public spending on health and education, for example, amounted to the equivalent of 3% of GDP in 2008, which was much lower compared with the OECD level of over 30% in the same year (OECD, Statextracts). The government's contribution to health care financing also declined sharply during this period, from 28% in 1980 to 18% in 2010, while private health spending rose from 16% to 52% (Figure 10). This is in sharp contrast with OECD countries, where the share of public spending in total health expenditure accounted for 76% while private sources contributed only 24% in 2010.

Before the mid-1980s, the majority of the Chinese population was able to have access to basic health care at an affordable cost (Gu and Tang, 1995). The Cooperative Medical Scheme covered over 90% of the rural population in China (Liu *et al.*, 1998), while the Government Insurance Scheme and Labour Insurance Scheme provided almost free health care to the majority employees in the public sector and SOEs in urban areas. The

Figure 10: Health spending by source: 1980 versus 2010.

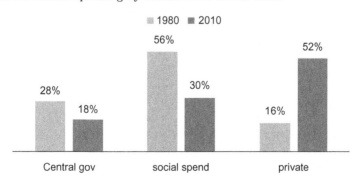

Source: Author's construction based on *China Statistical Yearbooks*.

reform eroded the widespread provision of basic social services that was achieved during the pre-reform era. The newly established health insurance scheme has been designed with a strong emphasis on profit-making, partially in response to the declining role of government in health care financing, thus, leading to a rapid escalation in health care costs in the past decade.[15] Together with the lack of health insurance, hospital care has become unaffordable to a majority of rural residents. The average patient has to pay 60% of the cost of a hospital visit out-of-pocket, compared with 25% in Mexico, 10% in Turkey and a much lower amount in most developed countries (Dollar, 2008).

China's highly decentralized fiscal system further aggravates social disparities. With local governments responsible for funding local services, those in poor regions were not able to provide quality social services, and poor households could not afford the high private costs of health and education services. Consequently, rising income inequality reinforces inequality in social indicators.

6.2. *Disparity in health and education*

While China had made great strides in improving population health outcomes over the past two decades, the progress was uneven across regions. First, improvement in life expectancy has been much slower in poor provinces than in rich ones. In Shanghai, the richest city in China, the life expectancy was 78 years in 2008, but in the poorest provinces, it was 65 years — a gap of 13 years is striking in comparison with the US and the UK. In 2001–2003, the gap in life expectancy between the US states with the highest (Minnesota) and lowest (District of Columbia) life expectancy was 6.5 years.[16] In the UK, among the 12 regions and counties, the average life expectancy gap in 2004–2006 was about 2.6 years.[17]

Second, the gap in mortality rates between rural and urban areas is also widening. A recent study by UNICEF shows that maternal and child mortality rates in poor rural areas are 4 to 6 times higher than those in

---

[15]The health sector reform distorted the incentives of health care providers, encouraging hospitals to recover costs through high fees on drugs and undertaking expensive medical procedures while reducing the supply of preventive care services.

[16]US Census Bureau Population Division, *Interim State Population Projections*, Washington DC: US Census Bureau, 2005.

[17]Office for National Statistics, Life expectancy at birth and at age 65 by local areas in the United Kingdom.

urban areas, with poor rural areas accounting for 70–75% of all maternal and child deaths in 2004. The majority of maternal and child deaths in these areas are caused by a few preventable conditions,[18] suggesting a lack of access to basic health care services being the major factor underlying the disparity in mortality rates between rural and urban areas.

The trend in education disparities is also similar to that in health. While significant progress has been made in raising overall education attainment since the early 1980s, disparity in education outcomes is increasing. Up through the 1990s, there was little difference in school attainment rate across provinces, but by 2008, a strong positive association between the school attainment rate and income across provinces emerges (see Figure 11). Children from rich provinces are more likely to progress up to middle school level than their counterparts from poor provinces, with the average middle school enrolment rate being about 12% among poor provinces, but over 25% among the rich ones in 2008.

The rapid increase in income, together with the reduced role of government in educational financing, also spurs the development of private sector education. Increasingly, betteroff households send their children to private schools which are equipped with better facilities and higher quality teaching staff, while many public schools, in particular in poor areas, were struggling with recruiting qualified teachers. For example, in 2007, substitute or part-time teachers with less qualification accounted for more than 94% total teaching staff in rural and township schools (China Human

Figure 11: Education and income correlation.

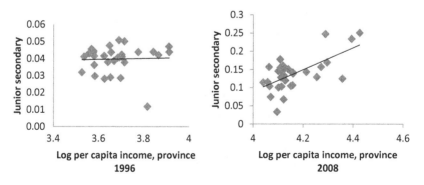

---

[18]The leading causes of death include postpartum hemorrhage, hypertension and embolism for maternal deaths, and neonatal trauma, preterm delivery and low birth weight for child deaths.

Development Report, 2005). The sharp increase in returns to education, one of the positive developments in China's economic transition, creates strong incentives for families to invest in their children's education. However, if only the better-off households can invest on their children's education, then privileged and high-income groups maintain a permanent advantage over the poor segment of the population, which will reinforce income inequality and inequality in opportunities, limiting intergenerational (or social) mobility.[19]

Despite the lack of official statistics, high social mobility was evident and widely considered as one of China's major social achievements before the 1990s. For example, a significant proportion of university students came from poor and rural areas in the 1980s and 1990s, thanks to government-supported rural education system and the availability of university scholarships. This trend has reversed in recent years. Figure 12 shows that, compared with a large pool of countries, China stands out as a country

Figure 12: Intergenerational mobility and inequality.

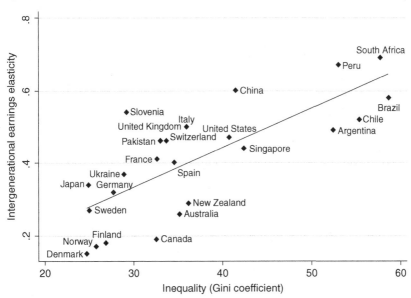

Source: Miles Corak (2011).

---

[19]The intergenerational (or social) mobility is commonly measured by intergenerational earnings elasticity — elasticity of earnings between parents and their children (the higher the number, the lower the intergenerational earnings mobility).

of much lower social mobility (measured by intergenerational earning elasticity) and higher income inequality. The comparison between China and the US is particularly informative. While income inequality is at the similar level in both countries, the Chinese children from low-income families have much limited opportunities to climb up the income ladder than their American counterparts. In contrast, countries, including the Nordic countries, Canada, France, New Zealand and Australia, that have a tradition of equity-focused public policies and strong government involvement in the provision of basic social services, see much higher intergenerational mobility (low elasticity) and low income inequality.

In many respects, recent economic growth, together with the reduced role of government in basic services provision, has heightened the population's insecurity, and widened inequality as well as inequality of opportunities. China is in danger of embarking on a course of a self-reinforcing spiral of inequality. While high-income groups will benefit from the rising returns to education and skills through investment in human capital of their children, disadvantaged groups with low education attainment will be trapped in the low-income low-return economic activities.

6.3. *Gender inequality*

The famous phrase that 'Chinese women were holding half of the sky,' symbolizes the equal role of women in China as a result of progressive gender-focused development since the early 1970s. However, the impressive achievements in gender equality before the early 1980s have reversed in recent years, as reflected in excess female infant mortality and a widening gender gap in human capital accumulation and employment opportunities. The excess female infant mortality rate was a result of the deeply rooted preference for sons in China, which manifests in discrimination against girls at birth and deprives access to preventive and curative health care in early childhood (Li, Zhu and Feldman, 2004). According to the World Bank's World Development Report 2012, excess female deaths have risen since 1990, from 890,000 to 1.1 million in 2009. Over a quarter of all excess female deaths in China occur at birth.[20]

---

[20]These are the numbers of "missing girls" if the normal sex ratio at birth of 105 boys to 100 girls had prevailed in China (the observed sex ratio in China was almost 120 boys born for every 100 girls in 2009). This problem of "missing girls" was exacerbated in recent decades by the practice of sex-specific abortions (Banister, 2004).

Gender disparity in human capital[21] is also on the rise in recent years. While the human capital for both females and males increased, the gender disparity widened. The female per capita human capital was 22% lower in 2007 than their male counterpart, but it was only 13% lower in 1985 (Li *et al.*, 2009). The increase in gender differential in human capital gap was a consequence of both lower returns to schooling and less working years of females than males. For example, the mandatory retirement regulations now force women to retire at the age of 50 while men can work until the age of 60. Men and women also face differential employment opportunities because the labor market became more segregated by gender. The 2000 census shows that 95% of females were in low-paid jobs, compared with 90% of males, despite female average schooling (12 years) being higher than that of males (11 years). Not only have women been affected disproportionately by the layoffs of SOEs restructuring, they also have faced more discrimination in getting subsequent job offers than men have.

7. The Environmental Cost of Growth

One important aspect of the quality of growth is the environment and resource sustainability. China's economic growth in the past few decades has come at a heavy environmental cost, resulting in severe environmental and resource degradation, and a surge in greenhouse gas emissions. In 2007, China surpassed the US to become the largest greenhouse gas emitter, although carbon-dioxide (CO_2) emission per capita remains relatively low — about a quarter of that in the US. According to the Netherland's Environmental Assessment Agency, the soaring demand for coal to generate electricity and a surge in cement production have caused China's record greenhouse gas emission.

The severity of air and water pollution, heavy-metal pollution in soil and an acute water shortage have all reached alarming levels. This is a direct consequence of rapid expansion of energy-intensive heavy industries with predominantly coal-based energy use that has fueled the GDP growth in the past few decades. However, inadequate policy measures to safeguard the

---

[21]The human capital indicator captures all three components: (1) the level of education attainment, (2) return to schooling and work experience and (3) the total years of working life available that is related to the mandatory retirement age.

environment and weak enforcement of environment regulations, in particular, the mindset of 'grow first and clean afterward' at all levels of government in China have also played an important role in the current environmental crisis.

7.1. *Water shortages and air pollution*

The World Bank has warned that water scarcity will become an increasingly pressing issue in China. From 2000 to 2009, China's total water reserves fell by 1.5% annually, about 35 billion cubic meters of water a year according to the Ministry of Water Resources. Among the 600 large cities, 400 suffer from water shortages according to the 2007 OECD Environmental Performance Reviews of China. The deterioration of water quality from widespread pollution further aggravates water shortages in China. According to the OECD report, about 30% of the rivers monitored are classified as worse than grade V (i.e., highly polluted), three quarters of China's major lakes are also considered to be highly polluted (grade V or above) and a quarter of China's coastal waters are very polluted too (grade IV or above). Water pollution in China is caused primarily by chemical fertilizers and pesticides, industrial waste and raw sewage. China's first pollution census, published in 2010, reveals that fertilizer use is a bigger source of water contamination than factory effluents. The intensive use of both chemical fertilizers and pesticides is three to four times higher than the OECD average.[22] Factor reallocation and poor selection of plant locations have exacerbated water contamination. In 2006, as many as 81% of total 7,555 chemical and petrochemical construction plants were located in and around environmentally sensitive areas, such as densely populated localities, rivers, and lakes, while 45% of those were the sources of high-risk pollution (SEPA, 2010a).

Water scarcity has become a limiting factor in sustaining the scale of China's agricultural production. In Northern China, water shortages have also forced farmers to use waste-water for the irrigation of about 40,000 square km of agricultural land, resulting in contamination of food by heavy metals. Water scarcity is also constraining the capacity of natural

---

[22] About 11.7 million pounds of organic pollutants are emitted into Chinese waters very day, compared to 5.5 million in the US, 3.4 million in Japan, 2.3 million in Germany, 3.2 million in India and 0.6 million in South Africa.

bodies of water to serve their ecological functions. The excessive surface water withdrawals have made it impossible to sustain a minimum level of environmental and ecological flows for major rivers in North China. Water shortages have also led to over exploitation of groundwater, and consequently, the lowering of water tables, drying up of lakes and wetlands and land subsidence are frequent in many cities (World Bank, 2008).

Air pollination in urban area has become a serious public health threat. According to a World Bank study among the world's 20 most polluted cities, 16 are in China; and only 1% of the China's 560 million city dwellers breath air considered safe by European Union standards. About a third of 113 cities surveyed in 2009 failed to meet national air quality standards based on Chinese official data, despite the fact that air pollution levels set by China's national air quality standards are four to five times higher than the OECD standards. The main sources of outdoor air pollution in China are coal combustion, motor vehicle exhaust and the massive scale of urban construction, generating particles of soot, organic hazardous material, heavy metals, acid aerosols and dust, in addition to emissions of sulfur dioxide (SO_2) and nitrogen dioxide (NO_2). The particulate matter that is less than 10 microns (PM_{10}) poses the biggest health threat. In China, PM_{10} accounts for about 72%, SO_2 8% and NO_2 0.3% of primary pollutants of concern during the period of 2000–2007 (Andrews, 2011). Coal, the number one source of air pollution in China, is also the principal source of energy. Figure 13 shows that about 80% of electricity and 70% of total energy in China are produced from coal (much of it of high sulfur coal), compared with only 45% in the US.

Figure 13: Energy source of electricity production: China and USA.

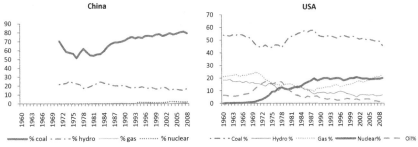

Source: Author's construction based on the World Bank database.

7.2.   *Uncontrolled growth of motorization*

China has by far the highest growth rate of vehicle ownership, 10.6% annually, followed by India (7%) and Indonesia (6.5%). The rapid growth of motorization in cities has led to rising congestion levels, increased air pollution and a high traffic fatality rate. Unfortunately, this adverse impact has been largely overlooked by all level of governments during the expansion of the automobile industry in the past decade.

According to a 2010 study by of 20 large cities, Beijing and Mexico City have the worst traffic in the world. Unfortunately, to date, no study has fully investigated the total economic costs of congestion, in terms of time and productivity loss. The constraints imposed by very high population densities and the limited amount of land available for residential and commercial development show that Chinese cities cannot physically expand at the current rate of motorization. However, the policy incentives designed to stimulate economic growth through a rapid increase in private car ownership have led many city governments to respond to motor vehicle congestion by expanding existing lanes and more infrastructure construction. A study of six large Chinese cities from 2000 and 2006 shows that although the amount of road space per capita has increased in major Chinese cities, road space per private car has dropped significantly (Table 5). In comparison to three of the most populated cities in the world, London, Tokyo and New York City, all of the Chinese major cities under study have less road length and road length per capita.

Emissions from vehicles make up a high and rising proportion of total urban air pollution. Shows that 45–60% of NO_x[23] emissions and 85% of carbon monoxide (CO) emissions are from mobile sources in most Chinese cities. Estimated that vehicular emissions would produce 75% of total NO_x emissions, 94% of total CO emissions, and 98% of total hydrocarbon (HC) emissions in Shanghai by 2010. Even with stricter emission controls and cleaner fuel, mobile-source pollution is likely to continue rising due to increased use of individual vehicles and longer trip length, and, therefore, increasing population's exposure to vehicle emissions through direct inhalatio.

The environmental risk factors, particularly air-, water-, and industrial waste-related pollution, are a major source of morbidity and mortality in China. Despite the frequent references to China's environmental risks in

---

[23]NO_x is a generic term for mono-nitrogen oxides of NO and NO_2.

Table 5: Private cars and road space in Chinese cities: 2000 and 2006.

City	Year	Private car (million)	Road length (km)	Paved road (m^2 per cap)	Road space (m^2 per car)
Beijing	2000	0.49	3624	3.7	85
	2006	1.81	5866	7.4	54
Tianjin	2000	0.21	3608	6.1	200
	2006	0.55	5991	13.8	145
Shanghai	2000	0.05	6641	7.2	1607
	2006	0.51	14619	11.8	422
Chongqing	2000	0.06	2693	2.4	438
	2006	0.28	4011	8.1	243
Guangzhou	2000	0.22	2053	8.2	125
	2006	0.62	5208	13.9	140
Xi'an	2000	0.07	975	5.14	134
	2006	0.26	1480	8.6	125
Average	2000	—	—	5.5	431
	2006	—	—	10.6	188

global policy discussion, comprehensive analyses of environmental indicators and health outcomes through scientific publications and popular media are surprisingly scarce. The overall cost of health damage is estimated to be between 1.8% and 4.8% of GDP (World Bank, 2007; Millman, Tang and Perera, 2008), and projected to reach 13% of GDP by 2020. Evidently, the quality of life of the Chinese population, in terms of environment, is at a serious risk when the quality of growth is overlooked by a blind pursuit of the pace of growth.

7.3. *Energy-intensive growth*

China's growth pattern in the 2000s is largely energy intensive. Although China made a rapid improvement in energy efficiency (measured by energy use per unity of GDP) from 1978 to 2000,[24] the total energy consumption increased twofold between 2000 and 2008, while energy import rose from 1% of total energy consumption in 1990 to 13% in 2008. Energy use in industry and households increased by three and two times, respectively, between

---

[24]Energy efficiency is measured by energy use per unity of GDP. On average the energy use of one unit of GDP was estimated to be eight times less in 2000 than in 1980.

Table 6: China's overall energy balance sheet.

	1990	1995	2000	2005	2008
Energy dependency					
Total Energy Available for Consumption	96138	129535	142605	232225	287011
Total Energy Consumption	98703	131176	145531	235997	291448
Imports	1310	5456	14334	26952	36764
(import as % energy use)	1	4	10	11	13
Energy use by sector					
Industry	67578	96191	103774	168724	209302
(as % energy use)	68	73	71	71	72
Construction	1213	1335	2179	3403	3813
(as % energy use)	1	1	1	1	1
Transport, Storage and Post	4541	5863	11242	18391	22917
(as % energy use)	5	4	8	8	8
Household Consumption	15799	15745	15614	25305	31898
(as % energy use)	16	12	11	11	11

Source: Author's construction based on *China Statistical Yearbooks.*

1990 and 2008 (Table 6). China now ranks with middle-income countries, and energy-intensive consumer goods, like air conditioners and automobiles, are within reach of many Chinese households, as reflected in the rapid of increase of private car ownership. Clearly, China is on a development path that features unsustainable production and consumption patterns because of both resource constraints and environmental degradation. Based on current energy consumption, the IEA has raised their China 2030 forecast by 1.2 billion tons of oil equivalent, a 63% upward revision (Figure 14). Under this scenario, China will account for 20% of global energy demand, more than Europe and Japan combined, and easily surpass the US as the world's largest energy consumer within the next decade.

The heightened resource scarcity and degradation not only poses a significant health risk to the Chinese population today and in decades to come, but also will act as a constraint on economic growth. The costs of cleaning up can be significant, and the increasingly fierce competition between energy and water will bring China to the chocking point, limiting its future development prospect.

The rising environmental and resource degradation has also become a major social issue, fueling instability and protests. According to the Ministry of Environment website, one environmental accident occurs every two

Figure 14: Energy consumption and forecast.

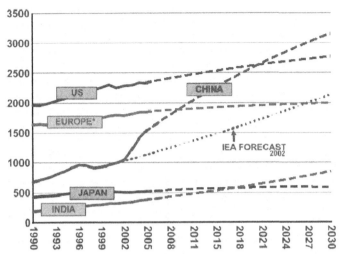

Source: IEA, World Energy Outlook (2006).

days, and there were 600,000 environment related complaints in 2006. Perhaps, the voice of ordinary people in China can best convey the key messages of their concerns about environmental problems and discontent with the current pattern of growth in China:

> We are surrounded by black and smelly waterways, breathing the foul air every day and paying the price at the cost of our health. If we can't breathe clean air or drink clean water, high economic growth is meaningless.

8. Conclusion

The Chinese growth experience, as presented in this chapter with some global perspective, evidently shows that economic growth can be a powerful force to reduce poverty when it is combined with targeted public investment that emphasizes equal access to health and education services, and rural development. But growth in itself does not guarantee for achieving desirable development outcomes as measured by improvement in health and education, equity and equality of opportunities. Nor does it ensure environmental and resource sustainability. The role of government is critical in key areas, such as human capital accumulation, natural capital conservation and mitigation of negative production externalities.

China's first two decades of growth is marked by its first-stage transformation from an agriculture-based economy to one dominated by industry and services sectors and elevation to becoming a middle-income country. Economic growth was largely driven by productivity growth, through improvement in resource allocation efficiency as the centrally planned system was gradually replaced by market forces. The rapid growth in the agricultural productivity made it possible to achieve the expansion of industrial and service sectors through the release of surplus rural labor and rural–urban migration.

During the third decade between 2000 and 2010, China's economic growth has, however, been driven largely by excessive capital accumulation, and growth in energy intensive industries. Although China has become the second largest economy in the world, it lags behind in its development of knowledge-intensity and high-technology industries and services, compared with the OECD and major Asian economies. During this period, China has also been experiencing fast rising inequality and disparities in social indicators as well as reduced social mobility.

One important aspect of the quality growth — the environment and resource sustainability — has largely been overlooked by China during its rapid growth process. China's growth experience shows that a blind pursuit of rapid growth will eventually bring a country to the brink of an environmental catastrophe, limiting the prospect of future economic growth and harming the welfare of its population.

The message that it is the quality of growth that can achieve the goal of development and improved well-being is *not* new. Over the past few decades, policy-makers have been reminded repeatedly that economic growth, poverty reduction, equity and environmental and resource sustainability must all be integrated into their national development strategies. In reality, however, as illustrated in the case of China, the single most important national policy of pursuing fast growth at all costs overrides other development objectives and social concerns. The underlying reason for the adoption of such a one-sided national policy can very well be analyzed in a political economic framework since policy-making is intrinsically a political process, and is determined by as much political factors as economic ones. This is, however, beyond the scope of this chapter.

References

Alesina, A. and D. Rodrik (1994). "Distributive Politics and Economic Growth," *Quarterly Journal of Economics*, Vol. 109, pp. 465–490.

Amiti, M. and C. Freund (2008). "An Anatomy of China's Export Growth," Prepared for 2008 NBER Conference.

Anand, S. and R. Kanbur (1993). "The Kuznets Process and the Inequality-Development Relationship," *Journal of Development Economics*, Vol. 40, pp. 25–52.

Andrews, S. Q. (2011). "Beijing's hazardous blue sky." Available at: http://www.chinadialogue.net/.

Banister, J. (2004). "Shortage of Girls in China Today," *Journal of Population Research*, Vol. 21, No. 1, pp. 19–45.

Bosworth, B. and S. Collins (2008). "Accounting For Growth: Comparing China and India," *Journal of Economics Perspectives*, Vol. 22, No. 1, pp. 45–66.

Brautigam, D. (2008). "China's African Aid: Transatlantic Challenges," German Marshall Fund of the United States, Washington, DC.

Fang, C., D. Yang, and M. Y. Wang (2009). "Migration and Labour Mobility in China," UNDP Human Development Report Research Paper.

Cai, F., D. Yang, and M. Y. Wang (2011). "Rural Labour Migration and Poverty Reduction in China," IPRCC Working Paper Series No 7.

Chow, G. C. (1993). "Capital Formation and Economic Growth in China," *Quarterly Journal of Economics*, August, Vol. 108, No. 3, pp. 809–842.

Chow, G. C. and K. W. Li (2002). "China's Economic Growth: 1952–2010," *Economic Development and Cultural Change*, Vol. 51, No. 1, pp. 247–256.

Commissions on Growth and Development (2008). The Growth Report: Strategies for Sustained Growth and Inclusive Development.

Corak, M. (2012). "Inequality from Generation to Generation: The United States in Comparison," in *The Economics of Inequality, Poverty, and Discrimination in the 21st Century*, R. Rycroft (ed.), ABC-CLIO.

Dean, J. K., C. Fung, and Z. Wang (2007). "Measuring the Vertical Specialization on Chinese Trade," unpublished mimeo.

Deininger, K. and L. Squire (1996). "Measuring Income Inequality: A New Data Base," *The World Bank Economic Review*, Vol. 10, pp. 565–591.

Dekle, R. and G. Vandenbroucke (2006). "A Quantitative Analysis of China's Structural Transformation." Available at: http://www.frbsf.org/public ations/economics/papers/2006/wp06-37bk. pdf

Deng, P. D. and G. H. Jefferson (2011). "Explaining Spatial Convergence of China's Industrial Productivity," *Economic Growth in China: Productivity and Policy*, Vol. 73, No. 6, pp. 818–832.

Dollar, D. (2007). "Poverty, Inequality and Social Disparities during China's Economic Reform," World Bank Working Paper.

Dollar, D. and S. J. Wei (2007). "Das (Wasted) Kapital: Firm Ownership and Investment Efficiency in China," IMF Working Paper.

Eberhardt, M., C. Helmers, and Z. Yu (2011). "Is the Dragon Learning to Fly? An Analysis of the Chinese Patent Explosion," The University of Nottingham Research Paper No. 2011/16.

El-Erian, M. A. and M. Spence (2008). "Growth Strategies and Dynamics: Insight from Country Experiences," Commission on Growth and Development Working Paper No. 6.

Fan, S. G. and X. B. Zhang (2002). "Production and Productivity Growth in Chinese Agriculture: New National and Regional Measures," *Economic Development and Cultural Change*, Vol. 50, No. 4, pp. 819–838.

Forbes, K. (2000). "A Reassessment of the Relationship between Inequality and Growth," *American Economic Review*, Vol. 90, pp. 869–887.

Gu, X. and S. Tang (1995). "Reform of the Chinese Health Care Financing System," *Health Policy*, Vol. 32, pp. 181–191.

Hofman, B. and J. Wu (2008). "Explaining China's Development and Reforms," Commission on Growth and Development Working Paper No 50.

Holz, C. A. (2006). "China's Reform Period Economic Growth: How Reliable Are Angus Maddison's Estimates?" *Review of Income and Wealth*, March, Vol. 52, No. 1, pp. 85–119.

Hsieh, C.-T. and P. J. Klenow (2007). "Misallocation and Manufacturing TFP in China and India," NBER Working Paper No. 13290.

Hu, Z. and M. Khan (1997). "Why is China Growing So Fast?" IMF Economic Issues.

Huang, Y. and X. Luo (2008). "Reshaping Economic Geography: The China Experience," in *Reshaping Economic Geography in East Asia*, Y. Huang and A. Magnoli Bocchi (eds.), forthcoming.

IEA (2006). World Energy Outlook. Available at: http://www.iea.org/publicat ions/freepublications/publication/name,31287,en.html.

Kanbur, R. and X. Zhang (1999). "Which regional inequality? The evolution of rural-urban and inland-coastal inequality in China, 1983–1995," *Journal of Comparative Economics*, Vol. 27, pp. 686–701.

Keefer, P. (2007). "Governance and Economic Growth," in *Dancing with Giants*, L. A. Winters and S. Yusuf (eds.), Washington, D. C. and Singapore: World Bank and Institute for Policy Studies.

Knight, J. and S. Ding (2011). "Why has China Grown So Fast? The Role of Physical and Human Capital Formation," *Oxford Bulletin of Economics and Statistics*, Vol. 73, No. 2, pp. 141–174.

Knight, J., Y. Yang, and L. Yueh (2011). "Economic Growth in China: Productivity and Policy," *Oxford Bulletin of Economics and Statistics*, Vol. 73, No. 6, pp. 719–721.

Kuijs, L. and T. Wang (2006). "China's Pattern of Growth: Moving to Sustainability and Reducing Inequality," *China and the World Economy*, January–February, Vol. 14, No. 1, pp. 1–14.

Kuznet, S. (1955). "Economic Growth and Income Inequality," *American Economic Review*, Vol. 65, pp. 1–28.

Kwan, C. H. (2006). "Improving Investment Efficiency in China through Privatization and Financial Reform," *Nomura Capital Market Review*, Vol. 9, No. 2, pp. 33–43.

Li, H. Y. and H. F. Zou (1998). "Income Inequality is not Harmful to Growth: Theory and Evidence," *Review of Development Economics*, Vol. 2, pp. 318–334.

Li, H. Z., B. M. Fraumeni, Z. Q. Kui, and X. J. Wang (2009). "Human Capital in China," NBER Working Paper 15500, National Bureau of Economic Research, Cambridge, MA.

Li, S., C. Zhu, and M. Feldman (2004). "Gender Differences in Child Survival in Contemporary Rural China: A County Study," *Journal of Biosocial Science*, Vol. 36, pp. 83–109.

Lin, Y. F. (2010). "The China Miracle Demystified," Paper prepared for the Panel on Perspectives on Chinese Economic Growth at the Econometric Society World Congress, Shanghai, 19 August.

Lin, Y. F., F. Cai, and Z. Li (2003). *The China Miracle: Development Strategy and Economic Reform*, Hong Kong, China: The Chinese University Press.

Lin, J. Y. and Z. Liu (1998). "Fiscal Decentralization and Economic Growth in China," Conference Paper No. D01, 4th Annual International Conference on Transition Economics.

Liu, Y., K. Rao and J. Fei (1998). "Economic Transition and Health Transition: Comparing China and Russia," *Health Policy*, Vol. 44, pp. 103–122.

Lundberg, R. and L. Squire (2003). "The Simultaneous Evolution of Growth and Inequality," *The Economic Journal*, Vol. 113, No. 487, pp. 326–344.

Luo, X. and N. Zhu (2008). "Rising Income Inequality in China: A Race to the Top," The World Bank Policy Research Working Paper 4700.

Millman, A., D. Tang, and F. P. Perera (2008). "Air Pollution Threatens the Health of Children in China," *Pediatrics*, Vol. 122, No. 3, pp. 620–628.

Naughton, B. (2007). *The Chinese Economy: Transitions and Growth*, Cambridge: MIT Press.

Perotti, R. (1996). "Growth, Income Distribution, and Democracy: What the Data Say," *Journal of Economic Growth*, Vol. 1, pp. 149–187.

Persson, T. and G. Tabellini (1994). "Is Inequality Harmful for Growth?" *American Economic Review*, Vol. 84, pp. 600–621.

Ravallion, M. (2009). "A Comparative Perspective on Poverty Reduction in Brazil, China and India," World Bank Policy Research Working Paper No. 5080.

Ravallion, M. and S. Chen (2007). "China's (Uneven) Progress Against Poverty," *Journal of Development Economics*, Vol. 82, No. 1, pp. 1–42.

Riedel, J., J. Jing and J. Gao (2007). *How China Grows: Investment, Finance and Reform*, Princeton: Princeton University Press.

Riskin, C. (2010). "Inequality and Economic Crisis in China," in *Development, Equity and Poverty*, L. Banerjee, A. Dasgupta, and R. Islam (eds.), India: Macmillan Publishers India Ltd.

Sen, A. (1999). *Development as Freedom*, Oxford: Oxford University Press.

SEPA (2010). Environmental Risk Survey of the Chemical and Petrochmical Project in China. Available at: http://env.people.com.cn

SEPA (2010). *State of the Environment Report.* Beijing: State Environmental Protection Administration.

Thomas, V., M. Dailami, A. Dhareshwar, R. E. López, D. Kaufmann, A. Kishor, and Y. Wang (2000). *The Quality of Growth*, New York: Oxford University Press.

Thomas, V., R. E. López, and Y. Wang (2008). "Fiscal Policies for the Quality of Growth," IEG Briefing 9, The World Bank.

UNDP (2005). China Human Development Report.

UNDP (2008). Millennium Development Goals Progress.

Walsh, M. P. (2005). "Emerging Air Pollution Trends in China," in *Urbanization, Energy, and Air Pollution in China*, Proceedings of a Symposium, National Academies Press.

Wang, X. L., L. M. Wang, and Y. Wang (2012). *The Quality of Growth and Poverty Reduction in China*, Beijing: Social Science Academic Press.

Wang, Yan and Yao, Yudong (1999). "Sources of China's Economic Growth, 1952–1999: Incorporating Human Capital Accumulation," World Bank Policy Research Working Paper No. 2650. Available at: SSRN: http://ssrn.com/abstract=632718.

World Bank (2007). Cost of Pollution in China: Economic Estimates of Physical Damages. Available at: http://siteresources.worldbank.org/INTEA PREGTOPENVIRONMENT/Resources/China_Cost_of_Pollution.pdf.

World Bank (2008). "The Growth Report: Strategies for Sustained Growth and Inclusive Development," Report.

Hong, Y. and Y. Mu (2010). China's Automobile Industry: An Update, EAI Brief No. 500.

Zhang, J., Y. Zhao, A. Parl, and X. Song (2005). "Economic Returns to Schooling in Urban China, 1988–2001," *Journal of Comparative Economics*, Vol. 33, pp. 730–752.

Zhang, L. W. (2011). "Income Inequality in Urban China: A Comparative Analysis between Urban Residents and Rural–Urban Migrants," The Sanford School of Public Policy, Duke University Working Paper.

Zhu, N., X. B. Luo, and C. Z. Zhang (2007). "Growth, Inequality and Poverty Reduction: A Case Study of Eight Provinces in China," CERDI-IDREC, University of Auvergne Working Paper.

Appendix A: Growth Accounting Analysis

Growth accounting approach provides an analytical framework for attributing changes in a country's GDP into contributions from changes in its factor inputs — capital and labor, plus a residual, typically named total factor productivity (TFP). TFP is interpreted as a measure of efficiency gains from factor input usages due to technology upgrading, and improvement in management and business climate in general. The Cobb–Douglass production function is widely used for estimating TFP: $Y = AK^\alpha(LH)^{1-\alpha}$, where Y, A, K and α are measures of output, total factor productivity, physical capital services and capital's share of income, respectively. The capital share (α) is usually assumed equal to 0.4–0.5. L and H are labor input, and educational attainment (e.g., average years of schooling of the labor force). The product of L and H is the adjusted labor input, taking account of improvements in the level of skills. The growth per worker $\Delta\ln(Y/L)$ can be decomposed into growth in capital per worker $\Delta\ln(K/L)$, education per worker $\Delta\ln(H)$, and a residual measure of the contribution of improvements in TFP, $\Delta\ln(A)$, i.e., $\Delta\ln(Y/L) = \alpha[\Delta\ln(K/L)] + (1-\alpha)\Delta\ln H + \Delta\ln A$. In interpreting the results from growth accounting decomposition, caution should be taken because TFP captures anything unmeasured in the production function, except capital and labor input, ranging from technical progress, the effects of other determinants of the efficiency of factor usage, such as government policy, political region and weather shocks.

3. Major Factors Behind Regional Disparity of Economic Growth in China During 1996–2010

Dilip Dutta* and Yibai Yang

1. Introduction

As noted in the previous chapter, China has been experiencing a dramatic economic growth since it opened up its economy in 1979 after the "open-door" policy gained political approval in December 1978. By 2010, China's gross domestic product (GDP) increased to 14.5 times that of 1980, with an average annual growth rate of 10.58%.[1] In particular, during 1996–2010, the GDP increased by about 6.7 times, and the annual growth rate reached 14.5%. However, regional disparities in economic and income growth between the coastal and the two inland regions were evident. For example, the growth rate in the Eastern region was 14.45% on average, while it was 13.95% and 13.78% in the Western and the Central regions respectively.[2] Despite the Chinese government's efforts to balance the economic growth across the three regions by reducing income disparity, thereby leading to some growth convergence between these regions, in 2010, the income per capita in the Eastern region was still 1.96 and 1.65 times that of the Western and Central regions, respectively. There are many factors

---

*Corresponding author: dilip.dutta@sydney.edu.au.
[1]In 1979, the GDP of China was US$263,190 million, and it grew to US$5,951,462 million in 2010. See United Nation National Accounts Main Aggregates Database 2012 for the sources.
[2]For this chapter, the *Eastern* region includes the provinces of Guangdong, Fujian, Jiangsu, Zhejiang, Shanghai, Shandong, Hebei, Beijing, Tianjin, Liaoning and Hainan; the Western region includes the provinces of Shaanxi, Chongqing, Sichuan, Gansu, Qinghai, Xinjiang, Ningxia, Guizhou, Yuannan and Tibet; while the *Central* region includes the provinces of Shanxi, Inner Mongolia, Jilin, Heilongjiang, Anhui, Jiangxi, Henan, Hubei, Hunan and Guangxi.

that are responsible for these regional per capita income disparity in China; but the major factors include favorable economic policies toward the Eastern provinces, a coast-oriented policy to adopt technology and thereby an attraction of foreign investment to the Eastern/coastal region.

There are different strands of literature that analyze different aspects of China's regional disparity. One group of authors (e.g., Fujita and Hu, 2001; Lee *et al.*, 2012) examines the influence of globalization and economic liberalization on regional economic/financial disparity, while another strand of literature (e.g., Sun, 2002; Zhang and Felmingham, 2002; Özyurt and Mitze, 2012) focuses on the impact of foreign direct investment (FDI) and trade on China's regional economic development. In addition, Sun and Dutta (1997) had studied the regional disparities of development and income mainly between Eastern (coastal) and Western (far inland) regions in China during 1984–1993 (the earlier post-reform era).[3] They found that the dualistic growth patterns of the two regions stemmed from the structural characteristics of their own. Three such characteristics as had been identified by them are: economic structure, openness of the economy, and investment structure.

This chapter extends the research done in Sun and Dutta (1997) by including the central region of China and provides a thorough up-to-date study of the regional growth patterns of the Chinese economy and the factors that have important bearing on the continuity of still uneven development between the three regions (Eastern, Western and Central). The rest of this chapter is organized as follows: Section 2 briefly describes the regional growth patterns and the income disparity prevailed in the contemporary China. Section 3 would examine if the three structural characteristics identified in Sun and Dutta (1997) as responsible for China's regional dualism could still account for growth disparity across its three regions. Finally, a conclusion and some policy implications will follow in Section 4.

2.   Regional Growth Patterns in China

This section first shows the nature of the Chinese economy's growth pattern during the period of 1996–2010 and then conducts a comparative analysis of the difference of the growth processes in the three regions. It is well

---

[3]Sun and Dutta (1997, p. 850, Table 4) have, however, provided a regional distribution of FDI between three regions of Coastal (East), Central Inland and Western Inland.

Figure 1: Regional GDPs.

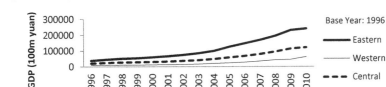

Source: Various issues of *Statistical Yearbook of China* over the period of 1997–2011.

known that income growth measured in GDP is one of the good indicators for aggregate economic growth. As can be seen from Figure 1, all the three regions have maintained an increasing trend in their regional GDPs throughout the 15 years, from 1996 to 2010, although the Eastern region's level of GDP has dominated over the Central region, as the Central region has done the same over the Western region. As a result, divergence in the regional GDP levels has drastically widened during the same period. One of the common indicators to examine regional economic growth is the variation in income per capita among the regions. It is evident from Table 1 that all the three regions in China have experienced a dramatic uniform average per capita income growth rate (also in real terms, i.e., measured in terms 1996 prices).[4] The average per capita income growth rates during this period in the Eastern, Western and Central regions are 11.75%, 11.62% and 11.27%, respectively (Table 1), although yearly per capita incomes are very different among the three regions. In fact, real income per capita in the Eastern region rose from 3,584 Yuan in 1996 to 16,973 Yuan in 2010, while the same in the Western region increased from 1,849 Yuan to 8,621 Yuan, and in the Central region from 2,302 Yuan to 10,265 Yuan (Table 1). Generally speaking, these results demonstrate that China's "open-door" policy has been successful at least in terms of raising average real income per capita in all the three regions during 1996–2010, although underlying divergence between yearly regional GDPs and yearly per capita incomes have persisted.

In 1996, the real income per capita in the Eastern region was 1.938 times as much as in the Western region, while it was 1.557 times as much as in the Central region. Then in 2010, the ratio of income per capita

---

[4]See Fan and Sun (2008) for a similar observation of non-divergent regional economic growth.

Table 1: Income per capita and population in Eastern and Western regions.

	Income per capita (Yuan in 1996 prices)					Population (Millions)		
	Eastern	Western	Central	E/W	E/C	Eastern	Western	Central
1996	3584	1849	2302	1.938	1.557	446.9	273.9	474.7
1997	4109	2148	2663	1.912	1.543	450.4	276.3	479.1
1998	4461	2365	3769	1.886	1.183	453.7	280.0	482.6
1999	4755	2515	3024	1.890	1.572	457.7	280.9	486.4
2000	4966	2608	3071	1.904	1.617	462.7	284.4	490.0
2001	5357	2783	3288	1.925	1.629	465.3	286.2	492.9
2002	6195	3134	3714	1.977	1.668	467.9	288.3	496.1
2003	6962	3344	3945	2.082	1.765	470.6	290.7	499.1
2004	7668	3665	4407	2.092	1.740	473.8	293.5	503.2
2005	8870	4164	5042	2.130	1.759	477.1	295.8	505.5
2006	10,065	4626	5674	2.176	1.774	481.9	298.9	512.4
2007	11,185	5212	6428	2.146	1.740	486.3	308.9	518.8
2008	14,583	7261	8740	2.008	1.668	522.8	292.9	492.6
2009	17,244	8692	10,383	2.054	1.661	527.6	294.5	494.5
2010	16,973	8621	10,265	1.969	1.653	553.3	309.6	521.7
1996–2010 growth %	11.75	11.62	11.27	1.001	1.004	1.54	0.88	0.68

Note: The population in each region consists of both urban and rural populations.
Sources: Various issues of *Statistical Yearbook of China* over the period of 1997–2011.

between the Eastern and Western regions increased slightly to 1.969, and that between the Eastern and Central regions rose to 1.653. The income ratio between the Eastern region and the Western region ranged between 2.0 and 2.2, while this measure between the Eastern region and the Central region was relatively less in magnitude, ranging between 1.2 and 1.8. Therefore, economic disparity between the Eastern region and the inland regions still persists, and a "convergent" growth phenomenon is unlikely to be observed in near future.

The main contribution to the income inequality among the regions is the differential of economic growth rates. During 1996–2010, the GDP growth rate in the Eastern region was 0.51% and 0.68% higher than the Western and the Central region, respectively. Nevertheless, the regional disparity in the GDP growth rates in this period was not as significant as reported in Sun and Dutta (1997).[5] The direct reasons could be several.

---

[5] According to Sun and Dutta (1997, p. 845), the real income per capita in the Eastern region was 2.5 times higher than that in the Western region during 1984–1993.

Figure 2: Regional Incomes per capita.

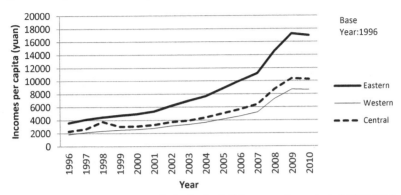

Source: Various issues of *Statistical Yearbook of China* over the period of 1997–2011.

First, the population in the Eastern region grew slightly faster than in the other two regions (see Table 1), which could reduce the differential in income per capita (Figure 2). Second, the growth in the domestic investment and foreign direct investment (FDI) was lower in the Eastern region than in the Western and Central regions. This could also attenuate the contribution of economic growth to income per capita. Third, the economy in the Eastern region has been more open than the ones in the inland regions, and it is more affected by the volatility of the international market, especially during the financial crisis in 2008. Hence, the following section will follow Sun and Dutta (1997) to examine the structural factors that have been responsible for the resulting differential patterns of growth process among the three regions.

3. Structural Characteristics

This section focuses on three structural characteristics (*sectoral transformation*,[6] *openness of the economy*, and *investment structure*) that have been identified in earlier literature as crucial for resulting differential in economic growth pattern and income disparity between the regions in China.

---

[6]National Bureau of Statistics of China computes GDP from three sectors: primary industry (agricultural, forestry, animal husbandry and fishery), secondary industry (mining; manufacturing; production and supply of electricity, gas and water; and construction) and tertiary *industry* (all services).

3.1. Sectoral transformation

In the early stage of development, an economy is usually less industrialized and uses less sophisticated technology. Thus, a large proportion of GDP and employment is attributed by the primary sector. However, as the economy becomes more developed and accumulates more technology, and with the improvement of its productivity, labor force is increasingly reallocated to the secondary and tertiary sectors, which, in turn, tend to account for a larger share of GDP and employment.

During 1996–2010, all the three regions in China have experienced continuous sectoral changes, although they are not uniform. As can be seen from Table 2, the share of tertiary sector in regional GDP increased in the Eastern region from 35.6% in 1996 to 43.8% in 2010, compared to that in the Western region, from 31.7% to 37.3%, and in the Central region, from 28.3% to 35.1%. In addition, the secondary sector in the Eastern region produced only 0.6% of its GDP more in 2010 than that in 1996, while this sector in both the Western and Central regions experienced a remarkable boom in the share of their GDPs (i.e., from 41.3% to 49.6% in the Western region and from 45.1% to 52% in the Central region). All the three regions had a considerable decline of their primary sectors' contribution to their GDPs by more than 50% over only 15 years. These changes in economic structure for the three regions are illustrated in Figures 3–5. The pattern is consistent with the usual process of economic development for a less industrialized economy. This shows that the Chinese economy is becoming industrialized at a faster rate with more and more resources reallocated to the secondary and tertiary industries.

It is, however, noteworthy that the sectoral growth rates in all the three regions were not significantly different during 1996–2010. For instance, the GDP in the *primary* sector grew approximately 7.6% in the Eastern region, 8.3% in the Western region and 8.1% in the Central region, while the GDP in the secondary sector of the three regions had uniformly higher growth rates of 14.6% for the Eastern, 15.4% for the Western and 14.9% for the Central regions. Finally, for the tertiary sector, the Eastern region experienced a slightly higher growth (16.2%) in contrast to that in the Western (15.3%) and the Central (15.5%) regions. Although the sectoral growth rates in all the three regions were more or less similar, the different sectoral contributions (in terms of their percentage share of regional GDPs) in the three regions may have played a significant role in contributing to the regional economic disparity. The share of GDP contributed by the secondary and

Table 2: Sectoral contributions of Eastern, Western and Central regions (% of regional GDP).

	Eastern region			Western region			Central region		
	Primary sector	Secondary sector	Tertiary sector	Primary sector	Secondary sector	Tertiary sector	Primary sector	Secondary sector	Tertiary sector
1996	15.4	49.1	35.6	27.0	41.3	31.7	26.6	45.1	28.3
1997	14.2	43.4	42.4	25.5	41.7	32.8	24.7	45.0	30.4
1998	13.4	48.8	37.7	24.3	42.0	33.7	23.4	44.7	32.0
1999	12.6	48.7	38.7	22.7	41.9	35.4	21.7	44.5	33.9
2000	11.5	49.2	39.4	21.3	42.5	36.2	20.0	45.2	34.9
2001	11.0	48.8	40.4	20.1	41.6	38.3	19.2	45.2	35.7
2002	10.2	48.9	40.9	19.2	42.2	38.6	18.4	45.7	36.0
2003	9.2	51.2	39.6	18.7	43.5	37.8	17.0	47.1	35.9
2004	9.1	52.9	38.0	18.8	44.6	36.6	17.7	48.4	33.9
2005	8.1	51.4	40.5	17.3	43.3	39.4	16.6	46.5	36.9
2006	7.5	51.9	40.6	15.8	45.7	38.5	15.3	48.1	36.6
2007	7.1	51.6	41.3	15.8	46.3	37.9	14.8	49.0	36.2
2008	7.0	52.0	41.0	15.5	47.8	36.7	14.6	50.5	34.8
2009	6.7	49.5	43.7	13.8	47.1	39.2	13.6	49.7	36.7
2010	6.5	49.7	43.8	13.2	49.6	37.3	12.9	52.0	35.1

Source: Various issues for *Statistical Yearbook of China* over the period 1997–2011.

Figure 3: Eastern region.

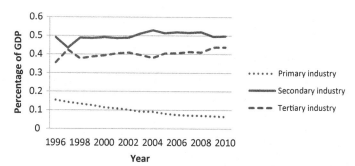

Source: Various issues of *Statistical Yearbook of China* over the period of 1997–2011.

Figure 4: Western region.

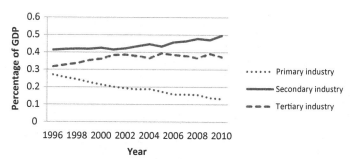

Source: Various issues of *Statistical Yearbook of China* over the period of 1997–2011.

Figure 5: Central region.

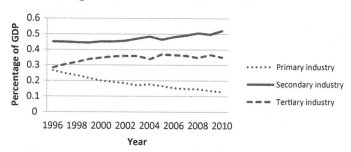

Source: Various issues of *Statistical Yearbook of China* over the period of 1997–2011.

tertiary industries together in the Eastern region reached about 94% by 2010, which was typically larger than the ones in the Western (86.8%) and Central (87.1%) regions. The Eastern region's dominance is also worth mentioning, in terms of relatively high percentage of its GDP contribution from the secondary and tertiary sectors has been continuing from the earlier period of 1984–1993, when the corresponding figure was 84% compared to 74% of the Western region.[7]

Generally speaking, in the case of China, the secondary and tertiary industries have increasingly become technologically sophisticated compared to the primary industry, which, in turn, has created better economic and technological institutional frameworks particularly for the Eastern region to stimulate its economic growth. Both the above facts could partially explain the continued economic disparity among the regions, although uniform sectoral growth rates across all the three regions may have prevented this disparity to significantly diverge.

3.2. *Openness of the economy*

This subsection focuses on another crucial structural characteristic of *openness of the economy* and its degree among the regions in China, which seems to have some implication for the regional economic disparity. The adoption of the 'open door' policy in 1979 has been the main factor behind China's rapid economic boom. Openness of an economy has many advantages in promoting economic growth, such as specialization and comparative advantage in production, better resource allocations and especially the ability to adopt new technology for improving the efficiencies of social infrastructure (including organization and management).[8]

This characteristic is usually measured by the sum of exports and imports values as a ratio of GDP. Because of the historical and geographical reasons, in the last three decades, the Chinese government has implemented an obviously biased and favorable policy to increase the degree of *openness of the regional economy* (ORE) in the coastal provinces (i.e., the Eastern region), leading to a significant difference of exports and imports volumes[9] between the coastal region and the inland regions. The trend of ORE in

---

[7]Sun and Dutta (1997, pp. 846–847).
[8]See Sun and Dutta (1997) for more analysis of the effects of openness of economy on economic growth.
[9]Exports and imports volumes are computed by location of importers/exporters in different provinces.

Figure 6: Openness of regional economies.

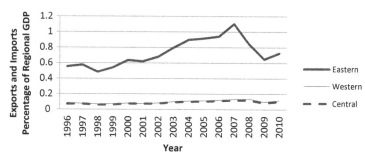

Source: Various issues of *Statistical Yearbook of China* over the period of 1997–2011.

the regions over the last 15 years can be seen in Figure 6. It is very obvious that the degree of ORE in the Eastern region was significantly higher than the counterparts in the inland regions, while there is virtually no difference between the Western and Central regions over the entire period of 1996–2010.

This very fact of biased openness of the economy continued and became more considerable during 1996–2010. Specifically, as shown in Table 3, ORE in the Eastern region was about 55% in 1996, and this went up to 73% in 2010. In the earlier period, this degree of openness increased from 15% to 36% over the period of 1984–1993 in the Eastern region, while the corresponding figures for the Western region changed from 2% to 10%.[10] The Central region also had similarly slow rise in the share of ORE, from 7% in 1996 to 11% in 2010.

As could be seen from Table 3, the figures for ORE in the three regions once reached a high level in the period 2007–2008 and then started to decline (e.g., the Eastern region used to have 110% of ORE in 2007). This may be due to the global financial crisis that occurred during 2008–2009, which significantly influenced the purchasing power in the international market and thus dampened the demand for goods and services, thereby affecting both exports and imports worldwide.

Moreover, although the average growth in exports was highest in the Western region (18.8%), followed by the Eastern (18.3%) and the Central regions (16.8%), the per capita exports in the Eastern region (i.e., US$302 in 1996 and US$2569 in 2010) were significantly much higher than the

---

[10]Sun and Dutta (1997, p. 848).

Table 3: Openness of the Eastern, Western, and Central regions.

	Eastern Region (ER)			Western Region (WR)			Central Region (CR)		
	Exports (X) (US$ mill.)	Imports (M) (US$ mill.)	(X+M)/ GDP	Exports (X) (US$ mill.)	Imports (M) (US$ mill.)	(X+M)/ GDP	Exports (X) (US$ mill.)	Imports (M) (US$ mill.)	(X+M)/ GDP
1996	134,904	117,447	0.55	5277	4443	0.08	11,064	5947	0.07
1997	162,978	132,143	0.58	6106	3534	0.07	13,613	6683	0.07
1998	166,363	129,645	0.48	5835	4073	0.07	11,559	6449	0.06
1999	177,892	152,993	0.54	5937	4717	0.07	11,101	7989	0.06
2000	226,878	209,942	0.64	7468	5043	0.08	14,857	10,108	0.07
2001	243,987	226,138	0.62	7187	5824	0.07	14,980	11,651	0.07
2002	192,260	381,628	0.68	9468	6275	0.08	17,248	13,887	0.08
2003	402,307	384,153	0.79	13,117	8797	0.10	22,803	19,810	0.09
2004	546,715	522,608	0.90	16,846	11,857	0.11	29,765	26,764	0.10
2005	703,242	615,928	0.92	21,106	13,969	0.11	37,606	30,055	0.10
2006	890,670	797,913	0.94	28,383	16,656	0.12	49,883	37,492	0.11
2007	1,110,773	882,469	1.10	38,980	22,613	0.13	68,022	50,928	0.12
2008	1,284,585	1,036,550	0.84	54,406	30,168	0.14	91,702	65,845	0.12
2009	1,094,457	915,531	0.65	41,348	29,295	0.10	65,807	61,097	0.08
2010	1,421,523	1,264,838	0.73	59,077	42,840	0.11	97,153	88,565	0.10

Note: The sum of exports and imports as a share of GDP = [The sum of exports and imports converted into the Chinese currency/ GDP]. The exchange rates used are annual official exchange rates between Chinese Yuan and US$. The values of GDP are in current prices.

Source: Various issues of *Statistical Yearbook of China* over the period of 1997–2011.

corresponding figures for the Western (i.e., US$19 in 1996 and US$191 in 2010) and the Central (i.e., US$23 in 1996 and US$186 in 2010) regions.[11]

Overall, the different degrees of ORE across regions could be another important factor that has contributed to the regional disparity of economic and income growth. Nevertheless, in the recent years, the decline in the degree of ORE for the Eastern region due to the impact of the volatility of the international market could be another reason that avoided the regional income disparity between the coastal region and the inland regions to diverge.

3.3. *Foreign investment and capital formation*

As FDI started to flow into China since the adoption of the 'open-door' policy, it became an important component of capital formation and a 'trigger-out' factor for accelerating economic growth.[12] This observation was especially obvious in the Eastern region because, as aforementioned, the coastal provinces had a tradition of building better institutions for designing preferential trade policy and legal system, as well as creating trade facilitating infrastructure including transportation and communication, all of which attract foreign investors to invest mainly in this region. This subsection analyzes the use of FDI and regional capital formation during the period 1996–2010, as well as their potential impacts on the disparity of economic and income growth across the regions.

Figure 7 yields a clear summary of the regional distribution of FDI in the three regions of China, which shows the FDI flows are still unevenly biased to a great extent towards the Eastern region during 1996–2010. As shown in Table A.1 (in Appendix A), during the period 1996–2010, about 79% of FDI that flowed into China was invested in the Eastern region, with 15.7% in the Central region and only 5% in the Western region. However, during the earlier post-reform era (e.g., 1983–1993), about 89.7% of FDI was located in the Eastern region, and the rest was shared between the two with 6.9% in the Central region, and 3.4% in the Western region.[13]

When the recent distribution is compared with that during the earlier period studied by Sun and Dutta (1997), one can see that there has

---

[11]See *Statistical Yearbook of China 1997–2011*, National Bureau of Statistics of China, for the details on exports and population in each province.

[12]See Sun and Dutta (1997) for a summary on China's early policies during 1984–1993 that favored FDI and its effect on economic growth and development in the regions.

[13]See footnote 3 for the source of these figures.

Figure 7: Regional distribution of FDI (US$100 million).

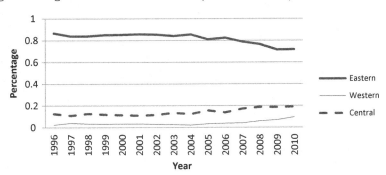

Source: Various issues of *Statistical Yearbook of China* over the period of 1997–2011.

been a constant spread of FDI from the coastal to the inland regions over the last 15 years. In 1996, the Eastern region took up approximately 86.7% of FDI realized in China as a whole, while the West and the Central had 2.4% and 10.9%, respectively. Due to the continual policy reform that improved the economic environment in the inland provinces, by 2010, the percentage of FDI utilization in the Western and Central regions increased steadily to 9.5% and 18.9%, respectively, and the counterpart in the East declined to 71.7%. This trend can be seen from Figure 7. This result was mainly contributed by the percentage change of recipients in the Eastern region. For example, Guangdong province in the Eastern region had received US$117.5 million in 1996 (27.5% of the total national FDI). Its spatial proximity to Hong Kong was the most important factor for flowing in this high percentage of FDI into this province. By 2010, Guangdong's receipt of FDI, although increased to US$210.3 million, but with a reduction to 11.4% of the total national FDI. A similar change can also be observed in other provinces of the Eastern region, such as Fujian, whose FDI distribution declined rapidly from 11.7% in 1996 to 4.3% in 2010.

The decline of the FDI share, particularly in Guangdong province, may have been caused by an increasing labor cost resulting in foreign investment being diverted to other coastal provinces within the Eastern region or to other regions for cheaper labor costs in production, or for better investment environment created by the local governments in terms better policy and financial support. Gradually, FDI began moving to mainly the Changjiang (Yangtze River) Delta and the two inland regions. The representative successful province was Jiangsu province of the Eastern region.

In 1996, its FDI share was only 12.2% of the national total and 44.3% of that in Guangdong province. However, in 2010, Jiangsu province became the single largest recipient of foreign investment in China, with US$287 million (15.6% of the national total). Although the two inland regions increased their FDI share substantially during 1996–2010, the FDI attracted by these two regions together is still only 26% of the FDI amount attracted by the Eastern region. Hence, the regional distribution of FDI in China maintains considerably uneven distribution.

Next, because of the uneven regional distribution of FDI, its share in total capital formation was also significantly different across regions. Although there has been a convergence in the trends of this share for Central and Western regions, there has been a rapid decline in the trends of this share for the coastal provinces, and therefore for the Eastern region as a whole. This can be shown in Figure 8. For instance, in 1996, the ratio of FDI over the total capital in the Eastern region was 19.6%, which was much larger than those in the Western (2.5%) and Central (5.6%) regions. In that year, some provinces in the coastal region had a huge FDI share of total capital, such as Guangdong (41%), Fujian (41.6%) and Tianjin (34.1%). In contrast, by 2010, the FDI contribution to total capital dropped quickly in the Eastern region to 7.9%. The shares in Guangdong and Fujian provinces, in particular, achieved only less than 20% of those figures achieved in 1996. However, during the same period of 1996–2010, this share in the Central region also reduced to 2.9%, while that in the Western region rose to 3.1%. These changes are obviously, to a greater extent, contrary to what happened during the period of 1984–1993, when the FDI share of total capital formation in the coastal provinces experienced a huge growth. This remarkable change might be due to three reasons.

Figure 8: FDI's share of regional capital formation.

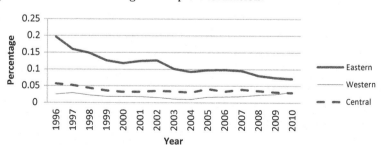

Source: Various issues of *Statistical Yearbook of China* over the period of 1997–2011.

Figure 9: Regional capital formation (% of regional GDP).

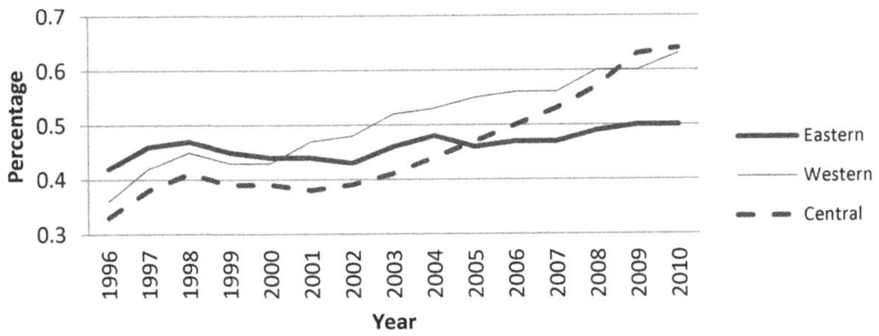

Source: Various issues of *Statistical Yearbook of China* over the period of 1997–2011.

First, as mentioned earlier, the economic environment for attracting foreign capital has been improving in the inland regions over the past decade because of the Chinese government's further strengthening of its policy reform. Second, owing to increase of production cost in terms of labor wage in the Eastern provinces, foreign capital had widely been spread over the country. Finally, the 'Chinese Economic Stimulus Program,' adopted in 2008 to minimize impact of the global financial crisis, boosted capital investment in infrastructure in all the regions by US$586 billion. Its effect can be seen from Figure 9. This substantial increase in domestic investment across all the regions diluted the contribution of FDI in total capital formation.

Nevertheless, FDI as one of the most important elements in China's capital formation which could affect the regional disparity of economic growth cannot be neglected, because as shown in Table B.1 in Appendix B, the FDI share over total capital in the Eastern region has been constantly ahead of that in the inland regions in any single year during 1996–2010. It is worthwhile to note that, unlike the situation in the earlier post-reform era, when the ratio of FDI to capital investment in the Eastern region was higher than those in the Western and Central regions together, this share in the inland regions has reversed since the early 2000s.

Let us now turn our attention to the share of fixed capital as a share of GDP (Table C.1 under Appendix C). In 1996, the share of fixed capital over GDP in the Eastern region was 0.42, while this share in the Western and Central regions was 0.36 and 0.33, respectively. Although all the regions had a growth in this share in 2010, the share in the Eastern region was 0.50, which is lower than the ones in the Western and Central regions, which were 0.63 and 0.64, respectively. Given that the average rate of economic growth in the Eastern region is still ahead of those in the Western and Central regions, the above evidence may suggest the possibility of interregional capital flows, and, more importantly, the existing regional disparities in various institutional supports for the development of infrastructure and technology. Thus, despite the existence of a higher rate of capital formation as a percentage of regional GDP in the Western and Central regions together compared to that in the Eastern region in the recent years, their rates of economic growth need to be substantially higher for a possibility for convergence.

4. Conclusion and Policy Implications

Since the economic reform adopted in 1979, the Chinese economy has been experiencing a remarkable economic growth, which has obviously resulted in interregional economic disparities between the coastal and inland provinces. This chapter presents a comparative analysis of the growth pattern across the Chinese provinces. It is found that, during the period 1996–2010, regional income and economic disparities persisted, but did not diverge. The factors responsible for this state of economy have been explored by focusing on the structural characteristics of the three economic sectors, openness of the economy, and FDI. It has been noted that FDI is still a crucial contributor to the economic growth differential between the regions, but its impact has reduced. Instead, factors such as domestic investment, reallocation of labor force across economic sectors and, especially, technology adoption and development have been playing a more important role in maintaining the growth differentials between the three regions.

The continuing non-divergent interregional economic disparities could be caused by the initial coastal-oriented reform policy and factor endowment. Because of the geography and history, the coastal region has been the main region heralding economic growth in China. In the early stage of development after the reform was initiated, the Chinese government established a special economic policy to improve the trade facilitating economic institutions, legal system and infrastructure in this region. Consequently, this exacerbated the regionally comparative advantage across the provinces. Although the growth and contribution of FDI in the Eastern region in the recent years have been much lower than it was in the early reform era, better economic institutions and infrastructural facilities in this region still enabled it to attract more domestic investment and labor, and adopt more sophisticated technology, than the inland provinces. Generally speaking, economic and income disparities still exist across the regions, and reallocation of labor force from the primary sector to secondary and tertiary sectors has made technology become labor-augmenting.[14]

There are some policy implications that stem from China's economic disparities. First, the Chinese government should continue promoting the 'open-door' policy in both coastal and, particularly, inland regions. This policy has been vital for China's rapid growth over the last three decades. The Chinese government should also help the inland provinces to adjust their regulatory systems in order to participate in international market and further remove barriers to entry, both of which can help the regions absorb more foreign investment and adopt appropriate technology.

Second, strengthening of interregional transport and information networks is also essential for eliminating the economic disparities. Using the advantage of having already a success story of high economic growth in the Eastern region, the government may help the inland provinces by providing additional resources (e.g., fiscal revenue and human capital) in order to replicate some already-tested programs with necessary adjustments if required for their feasibility. However, to achieve this, the Western and Central provinces should also be prepared for improving their financial and working environments for this linkage (re-)allocation to be effective.

Finally, as we have pointed out earlier, the domestic capital growth has been the main contributor to economic growth for all the three regions in the recent period of 1996–2010. Nevertheless, the government should also focus on other engines of economic growth as well. This is because capital is subject to diminishing returns, and without technological innovation or adoption, it may not sustain growth in the long run. Given that technology is another major engine that can help sustain long-run growth, the government should implement policies and provide subsidies to facilitate innovation and adoption of technology that augment the relatively abundant factors of production (including labor) in these regions. As a precautionary note, the achievement of a sustained and regionally inclusive economic growth will depend not only on the success of capital formation and

---

[14]Acemoglu (2002, 2003) provides both theoretical and empirical discussion on directed technological change and labor-augmenting technology. In developed countries over the last three decades, a strong evidence supports the fact that technology becomes biased toward the factor that is abundant. In the case of China with abundant labor, it is not surprising that technology has become labor-augmenting.

technological development but also on the supporting institutional framework developed at both national and regional levels of the Chinese society.

References

Acemoglu, D. (2002). "Directed Technical Change," *Review of Economic Studies*, Vol. 69, No. 4, pp. 781–809.

Acemoglu, D. (2003). "Labor- and Capital-Augmenting Technical Change," *Journal of the European Economic Association*, Vol. 1, No. 1, pp. 1–37.

Fan, C. C. and M. Sun (2008). "Regional Inequality in China, 1978–2006," *Eurasian Geography and Economics*, Vol. 49, No. 1, pp. 1–20.

Fujita, M. and D. Hu (2001). "Regional Disparity in China 1985–1994: The Effects of Globalization and Economic Liberalization," *Annuals of Regional Science*, Vol. 35, No. 1, pp. 3–37.

Lee, B., J. Peng, G. Li, and J. He (2012). "Regional Economic Disparity, Financial Disparity and National Economic Growth: Evidence from China," *Review of Development Economics*, Vol. 16, No. 2, pp. 342–358.

Özyurt, S. and T. Mitze (2012). "The Spatial Dimension of Trade- and FDI-Driven Productivity Growth in Chinese Provinces: A Global Cointegration Approach," *Ruhr Economic Paper*, No. 308.

National Statistical Bureau of China (Various Years). *Statistical Yearbook of China (SYOC)*, 1995–2011; *Ministry of Commerce and China Economic Information Network 2004–2011*, Beijing: the Statistical Publishing House.

Sun, H. (2002). "Foreign Direct Investment and Regional Export Performance in China," *Journal of Regional Science*, Vol. 41, No. 2, pp. 317–336.

Sun, H. and D. Dutta (1997). "China's Economic Growth During 1984–93: A Case of Regional Dualism," *Third World Quarterly*, Vol. 118, No. 5, pp. 843–864.

Zhang, Q. and B. Felmingham (2002). "The Role of FDI, Exports and Spillover Effects in the Regional Development of China," *Journal of Development Studies*, Vol. 38, No. 4, pp. 157–178.

Appendix A

Table A.1: Distribution of total FDI (utilized) in the Eastern region during 1996–2010 (100 mil. US$).

Regions/Provinces	1996		1997		1998		1999		2000		2001		2002		2003	
	Value	%	Value	%	Value	%	Value	%	Value	%	Value	%	Value	%	Value	%
All Regions	427.8	100	449.0	100	416.8	100	371.0	100	371.7	100	420.8	100	482.0	100	474.7	100
Coastal (East) Region	371.1	86.7	376.8	83.9	350.0	84.0	315.8	85.1	317.3	85.3	360.5	85.7	411.9	85.4	399.2	84.1
Guangdong	117.5	27.5	117.1	26.1	120.2	28.8	116.6	31.4	112.8	30.3	119.3	28.4	113.3	23.5	78.2	16.5
Fujian	49.8	11.7	42.0	9.3	42.1	10.1	40.2	10.8	34.3	9.2	39.2	9.3	38.4	8.0	26.0	5.5
Guangxi	6.6	1.6	8.8	2.0	8.9	2.1	6.4	1.7	5.2	1.4	3.8	0.9	4.2	0.9	4.2	0.9
Zhejiang	15.2	3.6	15.0	3.3	13.2	3.2	12.3	3.3	16.1	4.3	22.1	5.3	30.8	6.4	49.8	10.5
Jiangsu	52.1	12.2	54.4	12.1	66.3	15.9	60.8	16.4	64.3	17.3	69.1	16.4	101.9	21.1	105.6	22.3
Shanghai	39.4	9.2	42.3	9.4	36.0	8.6	28.4	7.6	31.6	8.5	42.9	10.2	42.7	8.9	54.7	11.5
Shandong	26.3	6.2	24.9	5.6	22.0	5.3	22.6	6.1	29.7	8.0	35.2	8.4	47.3	9.8	60.2	12.7
Beijing	15.5	3.6	15.9	3.5	21.7	5.2	19.8	5.3	16.8	4.5	17.7	4.2	17.2	3.6	21.9	4.6
Tianjin	21.5	5.0	25.1	5.6	21.1	5.1	17.6	4.8	11.7	3.1	21.3	5.1	15.8	3.3	15.3	3.2
Hebei	8.3	1.9	11.0	2.5	14.3	3.4	10.4	2.8	6.8	1.8	6.7	1.6	7.8	1.6	9.6	2.0
Liaoning	17.4	4.1	22.0	4.9	21.9	5.3	10.6	2.9	20.4	5.5	25.2	6.0	34.1	7.1	28.2	5.9
Hainan	7.9	1.8	7.1	1.6	7.2	1.7	4.8	1.3	4.3	1.2	4.7	1.1	5.1	1.1	4.2	0.9

(Continued)

Table A.1: (*Continued*)

Regions/Provinces	2004 Value	%	2005 Value	%	2006 Value	%	2007 Value	%	2008 Value	%	2009 Value	%	2010 Value	%	1996–2010 Value	%
All Regions	609.3	100.0	811.0	100.0	960.6	100.0	1210.1	100.0	1419.0	100.0	1597.9	100.0	1845.1	100.0	11866.8	100.0
Coastal (East) Region	521.0	85.5	657.3	81.0	792.0	82.5	953.5	78.8	1085.4	76.5	1142.0	71.5	1322.3	71.7	9375.9	79.0
Guangdong	100.1	16.4	123.6	15.2	145.1	15.1	171.3	14.2	191.7	13.5	195.3	12.2	210.3	11.4	2032.5	17.1
Fujian	19.2	3.2	26.1	3.2	32.2	3.4	40.6	3.4	56.7	4.0	57.4	3.6	78.95	4.3	623.2	5.3
Guangxi	3.0	0.5	3.8	0.5	4.5	0.5	6.8	0.6	9.7	0.7	10.4	0.6	9.12	0.5	95.3	0.8
Zhejiang	57.3	9.4	77.2	9.5	88.9	9.3	103.7	8.6	100.7	7.1	99.4	6.2	110.0	6.0	811.8	6.8
Jiangsu	89.5	14.7	131.8	16.3	174.3	18.1	218.9	18.1	251.2	17.7	253.2	15.8	287.0	15.6	1980.4	16.7
Shanghai	63.1	10.4	68.5	8.4	71.1	7.4	79.2	6.5	100.8	7.1	105.4	6.6	111.2	6.0	917.3	7.7
Shandong	86.6	14.2	110.1	13.6	100.0	10.4	110.1	9.1	82.0	5.8	80.1	5.0	91.7	5.0	929.0	7.8
Beijing	25.6	4.2	35.3	4.4	45.5	4.7	50.7	4.2	60.8	4.3	61.2	3.8	63.6	3.4	489.3	4.1
Tianjin	17.2	2.8	22.7	2.8	43.7	4.5	52.8	4.4	74.2	4.3	90.2	5.6	108.5	5.9	558.9	4.7
Hebei	7.0	1.1	19.1	2.4	23.8	2.5	24.2	2.0	34.2	2.4	36.0	2.3	38.3	2.1	257.6	2.2
Liaoning	54.1	8.9	35.9	4.4	59.9	6.2	91.0	7.5	120.2	8.5	154.4	9.7	207.5	11.2	902.8	9.5
Hainan	1.2	0.2	6.8	0.8	7.5	0.8	11.2	0.9	12.8	0.9	9.4	0.6	15.2	0.8	109.4	0.9

(*Continued*)

Table A.1: (Continued)

Regions/Provinces	1996 Value	%	1997 Value	%	1998 Value	%	1999 Value	%	2000 Value	%	2001 Value	%	2002 Value	%	2003 Value	%
All Regions	427.8	100	449.0	100	416.8	100	371.0	100	371.7	100	420.8	100	482.0	100	474.7	100
Central Region	46.5	10.9	56.7	12.6	53.1	12.7	43.8	11.8	42.2	11.4	45.9	10.9	56.0	11.6	63.4	13.4
Shanxi	1.4	0.3	2.7	0.6	2.4	0.6	3.9	1.1	2.2	0.6	2.3	0.6	2.1	0.4	2.1	0.4
Inner Mongolia	0.7	0.2	0.7	0.2	0.9	0.2	0.6	0.2	1.1	0.3	1.1	0.3	1.8	0.4	0.9	0.2
Jilin	4.5	1.1	4.0	0.9	4.1	1.0	3.0	0.8	3.4	0.9	3.4	0.8	2.4	0.5	1.9	0.4
Heilongjiang	5.7	1.3	7.3	1.6	5.3	1.3	3.2	0.9	3.0	0.8	3.4	0.8	3.6	0.7	3.2	0.7
Anhui	5.1	1.2	4.3	1.0	2.8	0.7	2.6	0.7	3.2	0.9	3.4	0.8	3.8	0.8	3.7	0.8
Jiangxi	3.0	0.7	4.8	1.1	4.6	1.1	3.2	0.9	2.3	0.6	4.0	0.9	10.8	2.2	16.1	3.4
Henan	5.2	1.2	6.9	1.5	6.2	1.5	5.2	1.4	5.6	1.5	4.6	1.1	4.0	0.8	5.4	1.1
Hubei	6.8	1.6	7.9	1.8	9.7	2.3	9.1	2.5	9.4	2.5	11.9	2.8	14.3	3.0	15.7	3.3
Hunan	7.5	1.7	9.2	2.0	8.2	2.0	6.5	1.8	6.8	1.8	8.1	1.9	9.0	1.9	10.2	2.1
Guangxi	6.6	1.6	8.8	2.0	8.9	2.1	6.4	1.7	5.2	1.4	3.8	0.9	4.2	0.9	4.2	0.9

(Continued)

Table A.1: (*Continued*)

Regions/Provinces	2004 Value	%	2005 Value	%	2006 Value	%	2007 Value	%	2008 Value	%	2009 Value	%	2010 Value	%	1996–2010 Value	%
All Regions	609.3	100.0	811.0	100.0	960.6	100.0	1210.1	100.0	1419.0	100.0	1597.9	100.0	1845.1	100.0	11866.8	100.0
Central Region	75.0	12.3	125.8	15.5	131.7	13.7	208.0	17.2	265.6	18.7	295.0	18.5	348.5	18.9	1857.3	15.7
Shanxi	2.8	0.5	2.8	0.3	4.7	0.5	13.4	1.1	10.2	0.7	8.3	0.5	7.14	0.4	69.7	0.6
Inner Mongolia	3.4	0.6	11.9	1.5	17.4	1.8	21.5	1.8	26.5	1.9	31.8	2.0	35.59	1.9	155.9	1.3
Jilin	1.9	0.3	6.6	0.8	7.6	0.8	8.8	0.7	9.9	0.7	11.4	0.7	14.06	0.8	87.1	0.7
Heilongjiang	3.4	0.6	14.8	1.8	4.8	0.5	5.3	0.4	25.5	1.8	23.6	1.5	26.62	1.4	138.8	1.2
Anhui	4.3	0.7	6.9	0.9	13.9	1.5	30.0	2.5	34.9	2.5	38.8	2.4	50.14	2.7	207.8	1.8
Jiangxi	20.4	3.4	24.2	3.0	28.1	2.9	31.0	2.6	36.0	2.5	40.2	2.5	51.01	2.8	279.9	2.4
Henan	4.2	0.7	12.3	1.5	12.3	1.3	30.6	2.5	40.3	2.8	48.0	3.0	62.47	3.4	253.4	2.1
Hubei	17.4	2.9	21.8	2.7	12.4	1.3	27.7	2.3	32.4	2.3	36.6	2.3	40.50	2.2	273.7	2.3
Hunan	14.2	2.3	20.7	2.6	25.9	2.7	32.7	2.7	40.1	2.8	46.0	2.9	51.84	2.8	296.8	2.5
Guangxi	3.0	0.5	3.8	0.5	4.5	0.5	6.8	0.6	9.7	0.7	10.4	0.6	9.12	0.5	95.3	0.8

(*Continued*)

Table A.1: (*Continued*)

Regions/Provinces	1996 Value	1996 %	1997 Value	1997 %	1998 Value	1998 %	1999 Value	1999 %	2000 Value	2000 %	2001 Value	2001 %	2002 Value	2002 %	2003 Value	2003 %
All Regions	427.8	100	449.0	100	416.8	100	371.0	100	371.7	100	420.8	100	482.0	100	474.7	100
Western Region	10.2	2.4	15.5	4.1	13.7	3.3	11.4	3.1	12.2	3.3	14.3	3.4	14.1	2.9	12.2	2.6
Shaanxi	3.3	0.8	6.3	1.4	3.0	0.7	2.4	0.7	2.9	0.8	3.5	0.8	3.6	0.7	3.3	0.7
Chongqing			3.9	0.9	4.3	1.0	2.4	0.6	2.4	0.7	2.6	0.6	2.0	0.4	2.6	0.5
Sichuan	4.4	1.0	2.5	0.6	3.7	0.9	3.4	0.9	4.4	1.2	5.8	1.4	5.6	1.2	4.1	0.9
Gansu	0.9	0.2	0.4	0.1	0.4	0.1	0.4	0.1	0.6	0.2	0.7	0.2	0.6	0.1	0.2	0.0
Qinghai	0.0	0.0	0.0	0.0	0.0	0.0	0.0	0.0	0.0	0.0	0.4	0.1	0.5	0.1	0.3	0.1
Xinjiang	0.6	0.1	0.2	0.1	0.2	0.1	0.2	0.1	0.2	0.1	0.2	0.0	0.2	0.0	0.2	0.0
Ningxia	0.1	0.0	0.1	0.0	0.2	0.0	0.5	0.1	0.2	0.0	0.2	0.0	0.2	0.0	0.2	0.0
Guizhou	0.3	0.1	0.5	0.1	0.5	0.1	0.4	0.1	0.3	0.1	0.3	0.1	0.4	0.1	0.5	0.1
Yunan	0.7	0.2	1.7	0.4	1.5	0.3	1.5	0.4	1.3	0.3	0.6	0.2	1.1	0.2	0.8	0.2
Tibet	0.0	0.0	0.0	0.0	0.0	0.0	0.0	0.0	0.0	0.0	0.0	0.0	0.0	0.0	0.0	0.0

(*Continued*)

Table A.1: (*Continued*)

Regions/Provinces	2004		2005		2006		2007		2008		2009		2010		1996–2010	
	Value	%	Value	%	Value	%	Value	%	Value	%	Value	%	Value	%	Value	%
All Regions	609.3	100	811.0	100	960.6	100	1210.1	100	1419.0	100	1597.9	100	1845.1	100	11866.8	100
Central Region	13.3	2.2	27.9	3.4	36.9	3.8	48.7	4.0	84.6	6.0	109.5	6.9	174.4	9.5	598.8	5.0
Shaanxi	1.4	0.2	6.3	0.8	9.2	1.0	12.0	1.0	13.7	1.0	15.1	0.9	18.20	1.0	104.2	0.9
Chongqing	2.5	0.4	5.2	0.6	7.0	0.7	10.3	0.8	24.5	1.7	40.2	2.5	63.70	3.5	173.4	1.5
Sichuan	3.7	0.6	8.9	1.1	12.1	1.3	14.9	1.2	30.9	2.2	35.9	2.2	70.13	3.8	210.3	1.8
Gansu	0.4	0.1	0.2	0.0	0.3	0.0	1.2	0.1	1.3	0.1	1.3	0.1	1.35	0.1	10.3	0.1
Qinghai	2.3	0.4	2.7	0.3	2.8	0.3	3.1	0.3	2.2	0.2	3.1	0.2	3.17	0.2	20.4	0.2
Xinjiang	0.4	0.1	0.5	0.1	1.0	0.1	1.2	0.1	1.9	0.1	2.2	0.1	2.37	0.1	11.7	0.1
Ningxia	0.7	0.1	1.1	0.1	0.4	0.0	0.5	0.0	0.6	0.0	0.7	0.0	0.81	0.0	6.4	0.1
Guizhou	0.6	0.1	1.1	0.1	0.9	0.1	1.3	0.1	1.5	0.1	1.3	0.1	1.35	0.1	11.1	0.1
Yunan	1.4	0.2	1.9	0.2	3.0	0.3	3.9	0.3	7.8	0.5	9.1	0.6	13.29	0.7	49.6	0.4
Tibet	0.0	0.0	0.1	0.0	0.2	0.0	0.2	0.0	0.2	0.0	0.6	0.0	0.00	0.0	1.3	0.0

Source: Statistical Yearbook of China 1997–2011, Ministry of Commerce, and China Economic Information Network 2004–2011.
Note: Before 1997, Chongqing was a part of Sichuan and became a direct-controlled municipality on 14 March 1997.

Appendix B

Table B.1: FDI as a share of total capital formation (%).

	1996	1997	1998	1999	2000	2001	2002	2003	2004	2005	2006	2007	2008	2009	2010
Eastern Region:	19.63	15.96	14.87	12.65	11.77	12.44	12.65	10.15	9.23	9.76	9.84	9.54	8.03	7.42	7.12
Guangdong	41.04	35.47	32.61	29.68	26.78	25.58	22.57	12.18	12.88	12.08	12.02	11.68	10.26	8.93	7.89
Fujian	41.60	25.31	22.10	19.90	15.80	16.72	14.99	8.88	5.58	7.26	7.06	6.56	7.61	6.60	6.66
Jiangsu	17.47	15.40	16.53	14.16	13.84	13.50	17.54	14.00	9.13	11.59	13.02	13.46	11.11	9.84	9.18
Zhejiang	7.08	5.59	4.40	4.05	4.99	6.33	7.34	8.79	8.17	9.81	9.71	9.26	6.89	6.40	5.75
Shanghai	21.12	17.40	15.09	12.17	12.35	15.48	14.68	15.15	14.33	13.40	11.90	10.82	11.48	10.64	10.16
Shandong	9.74	6.45	5.27	5.12	5.86	6.46	7.93	8.51	9.31	9.71	7.36	6.64	3.80	3.02	2.89
Hebei	5.63	4.96	5.74	3.95	2.38	2.21	2.43	2.52	1.43	3.39	3.45	2.72	2.84	2.65	2.35
Beijing	10.28	10.75	12.85	10.72	9.19	8.24	7.10	7.83	7.74	8.08	9.14	8.45	9.82	7.95	7.07
Tianjin	34.11	30.02	23.98	20.21	11.81	18.90	12.41	9.52	8.42	9.45	14.73	13.74	12.42	11.29	10.60
Liaoning	13.81	15.93	14.79	6.84	11.50	12.81	15.38	9.91	13.54	7.35	9.54	10.92	8.01	11.21	12.28

(Continued)

Table B.1: (*Continued*)

	1996	1997	1998	1999	2000	2001	2002	2003	2004	2005	2006	2007	2008	2009	2010
Western Region															
Shaanxi	2.47	2.87	2.21	1.80	1.79	1.76	1.54	1.06	0.95	1.64	1.74	1.84	2.26	2.51	3.13
Chongqing	5.64	9.53	3.87	2.95	2.80	2.99	2.69	1.88	0.63	2.45	2.63	2.73	2.01	1.89	1.80
Sichuan		5.98	5.96	3.34	2.93	2.59	1.64	1.63	1.26	2.18	2.51	2.92	4.28	7.18	9.42
Gansu	2.72	1.64	2.16	1.93	2.44	2.79	2.33	1.47	1.10	2.18	2.35	2.19	3.15	3.19	5.15
Qinghai	3.36	1.06	0.87	0.83	1.18	1.38	0.94	0.31	0.40	0.18	0.22	0.68	0.46	0.48	0.39
Xinjiang	0.11	0.18	0.00	0.27	0.00	1.46	1.59	0.70	5.71	5.90	5.13	4.75	2.38	2.64	1.97
Ningxia	1.12	0.36	0.26	0.34	0.27	0.22	0.18	0.11	0.24	0.24	0.43	0.45	0.59	0.58	0.48
Guizhou	0.56	0.54	1.21	2.99	0.86	0.67	0.74	0.45	1.40	1.96	0.56	0.59	0.47	0.37	0.35
Yunan	1.11	1.31	1.02	0.79	0.42	0.39	0.49	0.49	0.59	0.86	0.64	0.68	0.59	0.44	0.35
Tibet	1.10	1.95	1.57	1.71	1.46	0.57	1.04	0.60	0.80	0.78	1.01	1.13	2.02	1.65	1.61
	0.00	0.00	0.00	0.00	0.00	0.00	0.00	0.00	0.00	0.51	0.50	0.67	0.50	1.04	0.00

Table B.1: (*Continued*)

	1996	1997	1998	1999	2000	2001	2002	2003	2004	2005	2006	2007	2008	2009	2010
Central Region	5.59	5.19	4.33	3.55	3.20	3.22	3.49	3.34	3.01	4.05	3.30	3.89	3.50	3.09	2.94
Shanxi	2.78	3.87	2.63	4.73	2.49	2.42	1.91	1.42	1.41	1.05	1.45	3.19	1.77	1.15	0.76
Inner Mongollia	1.60	1.28	1.43	0.96	1.43	1.44	1.73	0.56	1.46	3.41	4.00	3.64	3.18	2.90	2.67
Jilin	7.92	6.04	5.52	3.79	4.06	3.53	2.25	1.42	1.17	2.99	2.11	1.73	1.27	1.28	1.32
Heilongjiang	6.51	6.63	3.97	2.74	2.51	2.50	2.22	2.02	1.67	6.20	1.65	1.34	4.60	3.21	3.20
Anhui	5.11	3.38	2.05	2.06	2.41	2.35	2.42	2.07	1.77	2.39	3.99	6.67	5.53	5.40	5.50
Jiangxi	5.63	6.15	5.48	3.55	2.62	4.09	8.96	9.75	9.64	10.01	9.50	8.53	7.61	6.60	7.11
Henan	3.50	3.37	2.73	2.20	2.15	1.62	1.32	1.54	0.89	2.01	1.55	2.78	2.57	2.46	2.65
Hubei	5.73	4.37	4.85	4.18	4.00	5.01	5.92	6.00	5.33	6.07	2.76	4.73	3.94	3.66	3.22
Hunan	7.74	7.44	5.98	4.79	4.40	4.70	4.74	4.80	5.15	6.59	6.43	6.17	5.00	4.64	4.00
Guangxi	8.72	12.08	11.28	8.14	6.42	4.13	3.93	3.33	1.80	1.77	1.58	1.71%	1.73	1.22	0.78

Note: FDI was originally in US dollars. The original data on DFI are converted into Chinese Yuan when calculating the share of DFI in total capital formation. The exchange rates used are official rates in each year. Capital formation here refers to total fixed capital investment realized each year. Before 1997, Chongqing was a part of Sichuan and became a direct-controlled municipality on 14 March 1997.

Source: Statistical Yearbook of China 1997–2011, Ministry of Commerce, and China Economic Information Network 2004–2011.

Appendix C

Table C.1: Fixed capital investment and as a share of GDP (100 million yuan, %).

Regions	Indicator	1996	1997	1998	1999	2000	2001	2002	2003	2004	2005	2006	2007	2008	2009	2010
Eastern	Investment	15715	19577	21487	22524	24534	26840	29740	36616	46213	55168	64173	76050	93868	105131	125778
(ER)	% of GDP	0.42	0.46	0.47	0.45	0.44	0.44	0.43	0.46	0.48	0.46	0.47	0.47	0.49	0.50	0.50
Western	Investment	3442	4494	5154	5233	5652	6729	7577	9413	11516	13946	16893	20118	26015	29773	37715
(WR)	% of GDP	0.36	0.42	0.45	0.43	0.43	0.47	0.48	0.52	0.53	0.55	0.56	0.56	0.60	0.60	0.63
Central	Investment	6918	9052	10140	10209	10926	11811	13290	15536	20424	25428	31823	40688	52775	65286	80364
(CR)	% of GDP	0.33	0.38	0.41	0.39	0.39	0.38	0.39	0.41	0.44	0.47	0.50	0.53	0.57	0.63	0.64

Note: Both GDP and fixed capital investment are in current price in each year.
Source: *Statistical Yearbook of China* 1997–2011.

4. Inclusive Growth and SME Finance in China

Wei Li and Hans Hendrischke*

1. Introduction

The concept of inclusive growth has increasingly become accepted by organizations and governments around the world. As China strives to build a 'harmonious society,' while income gaps widen and new social issues emerge, inclusive growth has been promoted by the central government and academics as a way of achieving sustainable growth, in contrast to the traditional model of investment-driven centered growth. China's pivot toward a consumption-driven economy also requires improving income distribution and inclusiveness. Together with general welfare (*minsheng*) and nation building (*kexue fazhan guan*), inclusive growth is one of the three pillars of China's development strategy.

In spite of China's official promotion of inclusive growth, how to achieve it is an under-researched area. Government policies and academic research mainly focus on bringing the state back in, such as through transfer payments to redistribute regional income and reduce individual inequality (Zhou, Zhu and Tai, 2011; Mok, 2012). Mok (2012), for example, argues that marketization and privatization since the late 1990s have led to growing inequality in major fields of social policy, such as health, education and housing. To address the negative consequences, he calls for restoring the role of the state, mainly through central government intervention.

This chapter contributes to the Chinese policy debate on inclusive growth by emphasizing the largely neglected role of local governments and the local private enterprise sector at the county and township level. Local enterprises, specifically small and medium enterprises (SMEs), which constitute the majority of the private sector, and improved public finance

---

*Corresponding author: li.wei@econ.usyd.edu.au.

at the local level play an important role in promoting inclusive growth. We point out that, although central intervention has led to spectacular achievements in poverty reduction over the past two decades, central policies alone are not sufficient to fill the local resource gap to achieve inclusive growth. Instead, collaboration between local governments and a vibrant SME sector with the ability to contribute to local budgets matters for the wider aims of inclusive growth. In illustrating the importance of the local SME sector, we will focus especially on their role in promoting overall economic growth, employment opportunity for a broader population and credit flowing to more productive projects and enterprises. Decentralization in China gives local governments such a degree of autonomy in implementing national policies that the central government faces increasing principal–agent problems with local governments.

The willingness and capacity of local governments to implement reforms facilitating China's inclusive growth agenda are limited, as local governments are traditionally underfunded (Wong, 1992; Shue and Wong, 2007; Wong, 2011) and rely on their self-raised revenue, in particular, extra-budgetary revenue, to fund social policies (Zhao and Zhang, 1999; Zhang *et al.*, 2004; Herrmann-Pillath and Feng, 2004; Ping and Bai, 2006; Foster, 2006). Expanding extra-budgetary revenue relies on local enterprise-related activities, including real estate development and expansion of the local SME sector. Expansion of the private sector, in turn, depends on functioning enterprise finance. Thus, the local SME sector and its revenue contribution are crucial for the delivery of local government measures required to achieve inclusive growth, and local governments are committed to funding and growth of their local SME sector.

This chapter adds a local institutional perspective to the Chinese policy debate on inclusive growth and trajectories of enterprise finance as two interlinked aspects of China's reform agenda. Local and informal institutions are often overlooked in China's official reform policies in favor of central policies and formal institutions imposed by the central government. Institutions are defined here following North's (1990) broad interpretation: human-devised constraints that consist of formal rules, informal constraints and the enforcement characteristics of both. These institutions provide stable designs for chronically repeated activity sequences (Jepperson, 1991) and mitigate uncertainty and opportunistic behavior (North, 1993; Williamson, 1979) over time (Lin, 2011). Evolving institutional arrangements are likely to be path dependent and therefore have a profound impact on the actual trajectories of economic reform.

By taking a local institutional perspective, we explore two reform trajectories relevant for achieving inclusive growth under decentralization: the role of local governments and the importance of private enterprise and enterprise finance. The role of local governments is undervalued in the current top-down policy debate, which focuses on central policy initiatives but overlooks the inability of the central government to fund policy initiatives at the local (county and township) level. Enterprise finance for the local SME sector is a well-known bottleneck for local enterprise development. The top-down perspective envisages a long-term solution in a gradual process of reforming the banking system and stock market. The institutional perspective, in contrast, is able to point to the systemic role of informal finance and to suggest institutional trajectories which suggest alternative reform paths to secure local enterprise finance.

The chapter is organized as followed: Section 2 will introduce Chinese policies aimed at achieving inclusive growth. Section 3 will explore the role of local governments and local enterprises in achieving inclusive growth, followed by Section 4 exploring options for local enterprise funding growing out of the current informal environment. The conclusion will put these points back into the context of current reform debates.

2.   Approaches to Inclusive Growth

Inclusive growth is a relatively new concept in development economics and still lacks theoretical foundation and consensus on what inclusive growth is. The UNDP International Policy Centre for Inclusive Growth (IPC-IG), for example, adopts a general definition of inclusive growth describing it as a growth outcome and process which everyone can participate in and equitably share the benefits (UNDP IPC-IG, 2012). In contrast, the EU interpretation of inclusive growth focuses on improving human capital and specifies that inclusive growth should be achieved through four means: raising employment, helping people of all ages to anticipate change through investment in skills and training, modernizing labor markets and welfare systems and ensuring that the benefits of growth reach all parts of the EU (European Commission, 2010). The UNDP and EU definitions, while appealing to policy makers, fail to provide a clear rationale as to why inclusive growth is needed and what distinguishes inclusive growth from other concepts in development economics such as broad-based economic growth or equal opportunities.

Taking a more specific approach, the World Bank defines inclusive growth with a focus on both the pace and pattern of economic growth by stressing that the poor should benefit from growth in absolute terms as participants of economic growth (Ravallion and Chen, 2003; Kraay, 2003; World Bank, 2009). This inclusive growth definition is in line with World Bank's previous absolute pro-poor growth concept, which requires that the poor benefit in absolute terms. According to this criterion, national policies should be designed to stimulate economic growth, and the extent to which growth is pro-poor depends solely on the rate of change in poverty.

Contrary to the World Bank's absolute pro-poor growth, the Asia Development Bank (ADB) adopts a relative pro-poor approach, which emphasizes growth coupled with shifting distributional patterns. Moving from poverty to inequality reduction, the ADB's perspective of inclusive growth is propelled by the experience of Asian countries where growth was accompanied by falling poverty but rising disparities. The ADB argues that, while growth should benefit all layers of society, it should also disproportionately increase the income of disadvantaged groups (Zhuang and Afzal, 2009; Rauniyar and Ravi, 2010). Inclusive growth is thus defined as a non-discriminatory and disadvantage-reducing growth process which requires meeting three criteria: (1) positive per capita income growth rates; (2) primary income (pre-tax earnings and self-employment income) growth rates for pre-defined, disadvantaged groups that is at least as high as growth rates for per capita income; (3) the expansion of non-income dimensions of well-being that exceed the average rate for pre-defined disadvantaged groups. In this context, inclusive growth not only means poverty reduction for developing countries but also becomes relevant for developed countries as a way to reduce inequality (Klasen, 2010).

China has developed its own definition of inclusive growth (*baorongxing zengzhang*). In 2009, this concept was for the first time officially introduced by President Hu Jintao in a speech he gave at the 17th APEC Economic Leaders' Meeting. The following year, at the 5th APEC Human Resources Development Ministerial Meeting in Beijing, Hu reiterated the concept and further expound its applications in China (Hu, 2010). Hu's speech has been widely quoted in the Chinese press. In academic writing, this definition is used as China's official interpretation of inclusive growth:

> China is actively promoting inclusive growth ... To this end, we must ensure everyone has equal access to development opportunities. We must steadily put in place a system for guaranteeing social equity with a focus on ensuring fairness in rights, opportunities, rules and distribution, and eradicate obstacles that

keep our people from participating in economic development or sharing the fruits of economic development. We should put human capital first, ensure and improve people's livelihood . . . including education, labour and employment, health care, old-age support and housing.

Based on this definition, it is clear that China shares similar views with the ADB by coupling economic growth not just with poverty alleviation but also reduction of inequality. Specifically, equal access to opportunities, improving human capital and promoting full employment are recognized by the Chinese government as major means to promote inclusive growth. Yet, unlike the World Bank and ADB, China's approach also emphasizes reforms to its social safety network to attenuate the negative social impact of economic policies. China's current social security system, which was established during the era of central economic planning, can no longer accommodate the outcomes of societal changes that include state-owned enterprise (SOE) reform, the growth of the private economy and the abolition of state-funded welfare. The Chinese government acknowledges that an effective social security framework that covers retirement, medical insurance, unemployment workers compensation and parental leave insurance is needed to mitigate the risks and vulnerabilities of disadvantaged groups.

It is important to note that, while the above interpretation of China's inclusive growth commits the central government level, the effectiveness of these anti-inequality policies depends largely on the ability of local governments to implement inclusive growth. In the last decades, decentralization in China has heralded a fundamental shift in central-local relations (Baum and Shevchenko, 1999; Saich, 2002; Hillman, 2010). While administrative decentralization has given local governments more decision-making power, fiscal decentralization has meant that local governments rely more on their own resources and less on central government allocations. As each of the measures for inclusive growth requires administrative enforcement and financial commitment at the local government level, the question is whether local governments are willing and capable of delivering needed resources to create economic opportunities, improve human capital, promote employment and build an effective social security framework. The local dimension of is an important feature of implementing inclusive growth in China.

In recent years, income inequality has overtaken poverty reduction as one of the major challenges faced by the Chinese government. In two decades of market-oriented reforms, China has been one of the world's fastest-growing economies with per capita income more than quadrupling and a massive decline in poverty (as shown in Figure 1). The World

Figure 1: China's progressive reduction of poverty.

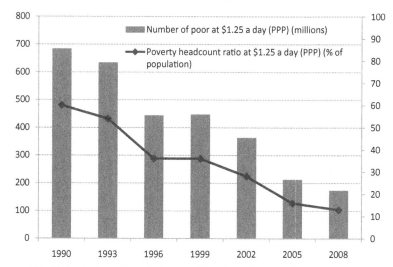

Source: World Bank Data, http://data.worldbank.org/country/china.

Bank estimates that the proportion of people living under the poverty line (US$1.25/day) has been reduced from 60% in 1990 to 13% in 2008, and the absolute number of people living under the poverty line has shrunk to less than 200 million in 2008 (Figure 1). During the same time, however, income inequality in the country has risen rapidly (see for example, Chen and Wang, 2001; Zhang and Kanbur, 2005; World Bank, 1997). The aggregate Gini ratios have increased by one third from 0.32 in 1990 to 0.43 in 2005 (as shown in Table 1). Results from the China Household Finance Survey (CHFS, 2012) also show that household income inequality is vast and serious.[1] CHFS estimates that the top 10% of households

---

[1]The China Household Finance Survey is jointly conducted by Southwestern University of Finance and Economics and the Institute of Finance Research of People's Bank of China. The survey is designed to explore micro areas of household finance in urban and rural China, including housing assets and financial wealth, debts and credit constraints, income, expenditures, social security and insurance and other demographic characteristics and employment. The first survey was carried out in August 2011. In total, 8438 questionnaires were sent to 320 communities (urban and rural) in 80 counties of 25 provinces, autonomous regions and provincial-level municipalities. The total response rate was 88%. The high response rate, according to CHFS, was achieved by having welltrained interviewers and samplers.

Table 1: The growth of China's income inequality, 1990 to 2005.

Indicator name	1990	1993	1996	1999	2002	2005
GINI index	32.4	35.5	35.7	39.2	42.6	42.5

Source: World Bank Data. Available at: http://data.worldbank.org/
indicator/SI.POV.GINI.

took home 57% of the total income in 2010 and control 87% of total
wealth.

Income inequality is generally seen to affect long-term growth. A high
level of inequality changes aggregate consumption and demand structure
through heterogeneous propensities to consume and save (Staehle, 1937,
1938; Zweimüller, 2000), which then lead to inefficient investment allocations, undermining productivity and retarding growth (Campano and
Salvatore, 2006; Baumol, 2007). Using a cross-country growth equation and
controlling a set of explanatory variables, Barro (2008) shows that income
inequality exerts a significant negative effect on economic growth. In the
long term, the effects of excessive inequality will be also transmitted to
greater inequality in schooling attainments and less investment in human
capital (Galor and Zeira, 1993; Benabou, 1996; Galor and Tsiddon, 1997;
Campbell, Hombo and Mazzeo, 2000). Furthermore, as reviewed by Neck-
enman and Torche (2007), a growing body of research shows that inequality
exerts a negative influence in areas such as health, crime, social relations and
politics. Recently, Hacker and Pierson (2011), Noah (2012) and Krugman
(2012) have also affirmed that inequality can interact with a money-driven
political system to grant excessive power to the most affluent, threatening
democratic politics. Stiglitz (2012), for example, in his recent book *The
Price of Inequality* points out the profound consequences of inequality on
values such as fairness, trust and civic responsibility.

For China, similar consequences emerge from increasing inequality.
Several empirical studies produce positive evidence of the growth-inequality
link (i.e., see Qin *et al.*, 2009; Guo, 2013). The findings from these studies show the imperative of pursuing inclusive growth for the Chinese
government. Creating equal access to opportunities, improving human
capital, promoting full employment and building an effective social security framework are tasks that have become more pressing than ever for the
Chinese government in its drive to achieve sustainable economic and social
development.

3.   China's Private SME Sector and Inclusive Growth

China's private SME sector matters for inclusive growth. The contribution of the local SME sector to inclusive growth is visible in a number of areas: broad-based economic growth, equality of opportunities, creation of employment, improvement of human capital and the overall contribution of local enterprises to local public finance. The local dimension in implementing inclusive growth is important because it allows for local differentiation, not only across different economic regions but also between neighboring counties or townships. The actual implementation of economic policies depends on the ability of local governments to fund relevant measures, which in turn depends on non-earmarked local revenue that is generally derived from extra-budgetary sources. Localities therefore vary in their specific policies to achieve inclusive growth, even though all are committed to achieving economic growth, equal opportunities, higher employment, improving human capital and better public finance.

3.1.   *Economic growth*

Chinese SMEs are the main source of the country's overall economic growth. They are estimated to contribute more than 60% of GDP in 2009 (Liang, 2010). In particular, SMEs drive China's economic growth through at least two means: investment and export. To the extent that SMEs perform these functions well, the Chinese economy tends to grow faster. In Table 2, we

Table 2: Investment in urban fixed assets and export, 2004–2010 (percentage by source).

	2004	2006	2008	2010
Total investment (billion yuan)	5902.8	9336.9	14873.8	24141.5
State-owned enterprises	57.8	48.0	43.0	42.3
Foreign-owned enterprises	11.8	10.6	9.5	6.6
Private enterprises (SMEs)	**30.4**	**41.4**	**47.4**	**51.1**
Total export (billion dollars)	762.0[a]	969.1	1428.6	1577.9
State-owned enterprises	22.2[a]	19.7	18.0	14.9
Foreign-owned enterprises	58.3[a]	58.2	55.3	54.6
Private enterprises (SMEs)	**19.6[a]**	**22.1**	**26.6**	**30.5**

[a]2005 figure.
Source: Huang (2012).

show that private enterprises (overwhelmingly SMEs) have overtaken SOEs and become the biggest source of investment in urban fixed assets, accounting for over half of the total investment in 2010. Moreover, SMEs have also surpassed SOEs in generating exports. Their total exports were double the value of exports from SOEs in 2010.

Besides contributing to growth, Chinese SMEs are significant innovators in providing new services and products and facilitating the spread of technology. Innovation is a critical input to deliver long-term growth in modern economies. In particular, SMEs are flexible and able to rapidly adapt new technologies (Chen, 2006; Zhou and Xin, 2003). A case study from Dezhou illustrates that while local large manufacturers such as the local Himin Group have shown leadership in undertaking major R&D projects, small businesses were important in creating industrial agglomeration that catalysed the deployment of innovations in solar technology (Li *et al.*, 2011).

3.2.   *Equal access to opportunities*

One of the ways in which a functioning SME sector promotes inclusive growth is by creating business opportunities in the market. The growth of SMEs means that there are sufficient participants in the market to create competitive market pressure and expanding China's market economy. Together with foreign investment companies (Otani *et al.*, 2011), SMEs make up the bulk of China's privately owned sector. A sufficient number of participants and transactions in the market improves overall efficiencies. Besides, SME development is also essential for simultaneously absorbing resources and re-employing workers laid-off or dispersed from the restructuring of the large enterprise sector, so as to minimize social disruptions. Based on statistics from China's Information Office of the State Council (2004), from 1998 to 2003, nearly 19 million workers laid-off from SOEs were re-employed, and most of them went to SMEs.

3.3.   *Employment*

Employment is a major channel through which SMEs affects inclusive growth. It is generally believed that SMEs are drivers of employment in emerging economies. A World Bank publication (Voices of the Poor, 2000) documented that the most important path out of poverty came in the form of jobs, either through self-employment or through paid employment. Even in developed countries, however, evidence suggests that SMEs contribute more to employment growth. de Kok *et al.* (2011) examine the quantity of jobs created by SMEs in Europe. Given data are corrected for the population effect, de Kok *et al.* find that, between 2002 and 2010, SMEs created more jobs than large enterprises for the 27 EU Member States and the 10 non-European countries participating in the Competitiveness and Innovation Programme (CIP) of DG.

China's SME sector is a large provider of employment, especially of new jobs. Currently, SMEs account for around 80% of China's manufacturing employment and are estimated to have created 80% of new urban employment (Liang, 2010; Chen, 2006). China's Second National Economy Survey shows that from 2005, China's private sector (overwhelmingly SMEs) provided employment for 58 million people, growing to 94 million in 2010 (as shown in Table 3). To put this into context, China's SMEs created nearly 40 million jobs in five years, equivalent to China's total population increase during the same period.

More importantly for inclusive growth, China's SMEs employ more low-income workers and members of socially vulnerable groups and sometimes are the only source of employment in poorer regions. A case study (Yu *et al.*, 2007) in Xiji County, for example, illustrates that, in a less developed region, the development of the SME sector not only reduced poverty by expanding non-agricultural employment but also increased farmers' income through strengthening their connections with external markets and creating new economic opportunities for rural households. In addition, SMEs working in coordination with local governments (Hendrischke, 2011) have been an

Table 3: The rapid development of China's private enterprises (SMEs).

Year	Number (million)	Average register capital (10 thousand yuan)	Number of employees (million)
2002	2.64	94	—
2003	3.29	107.4	—
2004	4.02	119	—
2005	4.72	129.9	58.24
2006	5.44	139.7	65.86
2007	6.03	155.7	72.53
2008	6.57	178.6	79.04
2009	7.4	197.8	86.07
2010	8.45	227.1	94.07

Source: Huang (2012).

Figure 2: Number of employees by education attainment in 2008.

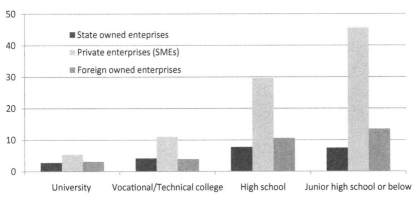

Source: Huang (2012).

increasingly important source of employment for less well-educated people in China. As shown in Figure 2, in 2008, more than 54 million employees with educational attainment of junior high school level and below worked in the SME sector, accounting for half of the SME workforce. This ratio is much lower for other types of enterprises, such as SOEs and foreign-owned enterprises.

3.4. *Improving human capital*

As stated, China's SMEs create employment opportunities, particularly for the disadvantaged. This opportunity to work in SMEs provides disadvantaged groups with the access to knowledge and skills, which comes from formal and informal training by working with other people. Sen (1990) found that being close to educated people generates positive externalities for the less well educated. SMEs offer such a platform for improving human capital through experience, learning-by-doing or vocational education and training. Through continuously drawing in labor to participate in economic development and generating both economic and non-economic benefits, especially for the relatively disadvantaged groups, the sustainable growth of SME sector is important for China's inclusive growth.

3.5. *SME contribution to public finance*

As mentioned earlier, China's SMEs generate a large amount of tax revenue for local governments. Tax revenue collected from SMEs has increased significantly in the last decade (as shown in Figure 3). Average annual growth

Figure 3: Tax contribution from private enterprises (SMEs) in China, from 2005 to 2010.

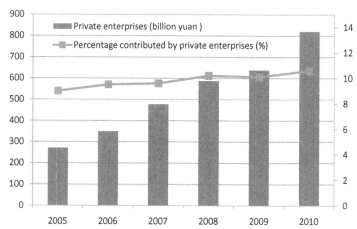

Source: Huang (2012).

rate at around 25% is much faster than the growth rate of GDP. In 2010, tax revenue from private enterprises was over 800 billion yuan, accounting for nearly 14% of total tax revenue (Huang, 2012). Tax revenue from SMEs enabled local governments to roll out fiscal policies to boost growth in consumption and create incentives for investment and export. Moreover, at a time of fiscal consolidation and global financial crisis, the contribution of SME tax revenue to local budgets is important in giving local governments more resources and leverage to implement inclusive growth policies. As discussed in the previous section, the effective implementation of inclusive growth policies is conditional on the willingness and capabilities of local governments to implement them. In particular, China's decentralization since the 1980s meant that local governments are responsible for 80% of government expenditure, but receive reduced funding support from the central government covering around 40–50% of their expenditure (World Bank, 2012, pp. 55–56). They have to raise extra-budgetary revenue to ensure local fiscal stability and growth (Hendrischke, Krug and Zhu, 2011). Since SMEs generate extra-budgetary revenue for local budgets to promote inclusive growth, local governments have a vested interest in SME development.

While administrative decentralization has brought local governments more decision-making authority, fiscal decentralization and fiscal federalism (Qian and Weingast, 1997) have meant that local governments depend less on the central government for funding but have to deploy entrepreneurial strategies to meet local budget need. This significantly alters the incentive structure of local governments and gives them reason to work more closely with local enterprises.

In sum, the above discussion illustrates the contribution of the local SME sector to inclusive growth in a number of areas: broad-based economic growth, equality of opportunities, creation of employment, improvement of human capital and the overall contribution of local private enterprises to local public finance. What is more important, the promotion of inclusive growth through SME sector development depends on expanding local extra-budgetary funds, which in turn creates incentives for local governments to support the local SME sector, which is largely beyond the administrative reach of the central state.

4. Characteristics of SME Finance

Although SMEs are a major source of China's economic growth and con-tribute to inclusive growth, the expanding SME sector faces an increas-ing shortage of finance. Official policies constantly emphasize the need to improve access of SMEs to formal finance in response to on-going com-plaints about underfunding of China's SME sector (e.g., Huang, 2008). There is substantial evidence showing that Chinese SMEs are financially more constrained and are less likely to have access to formal finance than the non-private sector (Lin and Li, 2001; Guo and Liu, 2002; Wang, 2010; Li, 2012). A national survey of 4,283 firms, overwhelmingly SMEs, conducted in 2010 by the China Enterprise Survey System (CESS, 2012) revealed that more than 40% of the surveyed enterprises considered lack of finance to be their biggest constraint. Credit assets of state-owned financial institu-tions are disproportionately composed of loans allocated to SOEs and large enterprises. Consequently, Chinese SMEs rely heavily on sources of finance other than banks and formal financial institutions. The situation worsened after the 2008 global financial crisis, when the monetary tightening policy adopted by the People's Bank of China further marginalized SMEs.

Although there is no empirical study specifically looking at the impact of lack of finance on overall SME growth for China, international research based on firm-level survey data covering 54 countries shows that financ-ing obstacles prevent firms of all types from reaching their optimal size, but are especially growth-constraining for small firms (Beck *et al.*, 2005).

Economic theory suggests that credit market failure, attributed to information asymmetries, is the key cause for lack of SME finance. Lenders are imperfectly informed about borrowers and bank officers do not have 'perfect' information on enterprises and their proposals. This leads to insufficient credit available for sound or 'bankable' propositions (Stiglitz and Weiss, 1981).

Enterprises in their early stages of development such as the SMEs face more acute asymmetric information problems, because information on these enterprises is limited and they sometimes lack transparency (Berger and Udell, 1998). Assets of start-up firms are often knowledge based and exclusively associated with the founding entrepreneurs (Hall *et al.*, 2000; Schmid, 2001; Hsu, 2004). Founders of manufacturing- or technology-based start-up firms will be reluctant to provide full information about their knowledge of opportunities, as disclosure may help competitors (Shane and Cable, 2002). Banking institutions face higher costs in obtaining information and monitoring small enterprises, and thus have less incentive to extend credit to them.

Another issue that hinders Chinese SMEs' access to formal finance is that most of them lack fixed assets for collateral and that their ownership and financial structures tend to be opaque (Jin and Xi, 2006; Chi, 2007). Firms are said to keep two sets of accounting books: one for official declaration, one for internal usage. For example, the co-owner of a small fishing fleet in Zhoushan, Zhejiang Province, explained in 2012 that while the company's registration certificate listed five official shareholders, there were several 'invisible' shareholders behind each of them, who provided start-up and operational funds to the business and received benefits and dividends. This makes it difficult for banks to evaluate operation and assess financial risks (Lin and Sun, 2006). As a result, China's financial institutions lack an adequate credit rating system for SMEs. This lessens the incentives for SMEs to build up a credit reputation.

The policy solution to these problems is seen in extending the reach of the formal banking sector to address SME funding as part of a gradual reform process. Chinese policy makers and international advisers, such as World Bank economists, agree that gradual banking reforms will drive out informal finance and ultimately solve SME credit constraint problems (World Bank, 2012). Assuming that once there are more 'formal' units to provide supporting finance and enhance competition in the enterprises finance market, China's SME finance is expected to converge with Western models.

However, there are institutional obstacles to reforming China's state-owned banking and finance system. China's state-owned financial institutions remain essential tools of China's macroeconomic policies and state intervention. Banks have traditionally been designed to support centrally planned national economic development and fund the SOE sector. Any reform of the financial system in favor of SMEs would have to be aligned with general economic policies and would require a shake-up of existing institutional framework. As a result, while official policies acknowledge that a financial framework that fosters competition and transparency should be the long-term reform direction for China (Hu, 2012), current banking regulations and lending practices continue to disadvantage the SME sector in practical terms.

While formal funding avenues have not improved, SMEs in the meantime have survived and flourished by relying on informal funding channels. There is ample empirical evidence to show that one of the distinct features of China's SME financing structure is the predominance of informal and semi-formal finance (Tsai, 2004; Ayyagari, Demirgüç-Kunt and Maximovic, 2010; Ji, 2009; Yang, 2011) which have evolved endogenously through social and market development and vary from one locality to another. The decentralized and localized nature of informal enterprise finance has led to the complexity of China's informal enterprise finance sector. Enterprise finance in provinces with a large private sector has developed bottom up and without help from the formal sector when local businessmen established mutually reinforcing finance mechanisms embedded in close-knit business communities (Nee and Opper, 2012). As a result, there is much diversification in the informal finance sector, and its institutions vary from region to region across China. Moreover, the boundary between formal and informal finance institutions in China is not always clear. There is a transition from informal to formal finance institutions where finance institutions and practices can be either formal or semi-formal, for example, through small credit associations or firms (China Banking Regulatory Commission and People's Bank of China, 2008). These finance institutions operate under local arrangements, some on a trial basis with local banks without full legal status, under the toleration of local governments. Therefore, policies as well as corporate strategies targeting SME finance need to take into consideration local variations and institutional dynamics.

A closer look into the development and governance mechanisms of these informal and semi-formal financing channels reveals that transforming them by introducing legal rules and regulations is not feasible. For example, equity raised through cross-listed accounts of credits and debits with business partners usually operates without formal contracts or strict enforcement terms, but depends heavily on shared business interests, mutual dependence, reputation and local government backing. These informal governance mechanisms have evolved over time and gained sophistication. Top-down formalization of these financing channels would imply sudden adjustments to the incentive structure of local governments. This complexity of China's informal finance structure makes it unlikely that there will be a smooth gradual transition to a conventional bank and finance system without affecting inclusive growth. Liberalization of financial and capital markets will address the formal financial sector such as banking institutions and stock exchanges, but not the informal and semiformal financing channels, which play an indispensable role for local public finance.

To respond appropriately to SMEs' financing challenges, it is important to consider the path dependency created by China's SME finance structure. Notably, most available studies analyze SME finance patterns through the lens of bank and non-bank financial institutions without taking into account underlying entrepreneurial dynamics. One significant area of research, for example, focuses on disentangling the different roles of finance sources on enterprise growth by using large-scale national survey data (Allen, Qian and Qian, 2005; Lin and Sun, 2006; Maksimovic *et al.*, 2008; Ayyagari, Demirgüç-Kunt and Maksimovic, 2010). Allan, Qian and Qian (2005), for example, use the categorization of bank finance and self-fundraising. Ayyagari, Demirgüç-Kunt and Maksimovic (2010) arrive at six sources of finance by further subdividing self-raised funds into five categories, including informal finance, operations finance, equity finance, investment funds and internal finance (as shown in Table 4).

The problem with this categorization is that different sources of SME finance often overlap with each other. Take informal finance and equity finance as an example. While some informal finance is provided as short-term credit or long-term debt borrowing, there is also a large proportion of informal finance raised through equity channels. Li and Hsu (2009) have shown that, in most provinces in northern China, informal finance involves fundraising societies which provide equity in ways that make it nearly impossible to draw clear borderlines between informal debt finance and equity finance. There is a range of finance institutions operating across the divide between formal and informal finance, such as private equity funding from different sources.

Table 4: Categorization of finance sources used by Ayyagari, Demirgüç-Kunt and Maksimovic (2010).

Finance source	Description
Bank Financing	Local commercial banks, foreign commercial banks
Informal Finance	Financing from informal sources such as a money lender or an informal bank
Operations Finance	Trade credit
Equity Finance	
Investment Funds	Investment funds or special development financing or other state services
Internal Finance	Internal funds or retained earnings, loans from family and friends and the other category.

Official reform trajectories are generally divided into debt financing channels, i.e., the banking sector, and equity finance, i.e., the stock market. This dualistic model fails to take into account the complexity of the informal sector and the resulting path dependency that has been created by entrenched informal finance which its long historic tradition in China (Jiang, 2009). Putting SME finance in a rigid formal framework misses not only the underlying entrepreneurial dynamics and networks but also the interrelationship between local enterprises and local governments. This particular dimension of state–private collusion is missing from official reform scenarios. Its inclusion would produce a set of different reform trajectories.

In response to the issues raised above, we propose an institutional debt-versus-equity finance framework (as shown in Figure 4). The proposed framework can be used to analyze SMEs' finance structure in a more flexible way. Particularly, the institutional approach allows us to take into account two dynamics, which are depicted by the two vertical arrows in Figure 4; one indicating local–national interaction in expanding markets; the other pointing to the complex transition from informal to increasingly formal structures.

Figure 4 questions the received logic of pecking-order theory, which sees financing organized in a hierarchical structure with internal sources first, external debt financing second, with external equity financing a last resort, at least as it applies to SME start-ups (Howorth, 2001; Paul, Whittam and Wyper, 2007; Atherton, 2009). However, SMEs in China face significant distortions in the external credit market where, on one hand, they continue to face significant constraints in accessing debt finance and on the other,

Figure 4: Trajectories of SME finance in China.

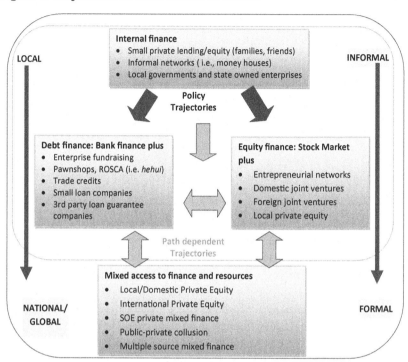

there exists a surplus of private equity capital that is ready to feed through institutionalized mechanisms in search of deployment. These institutionalized mechanisms, similar to private equity and debt market suggested by Berger and Udell (1998), can offer highly structured, complex contracts to SMEs. Thus, with necessary institutional arrangements, SMEs can negate the need for debt finance. Likewise, the variation in local institutions would heavily determine the capacity and incentive of SMEs in moving up the pecking order of financing sources.

The institutional debt-versus-equity finance framework also uncovers the equity and debt sides of SME finance. The framework defines the paths along which SME finance is progressing in China's expanding and deepening markets and how various finance institutions are linked. In general, Chinese SMEs start with internal funding sources, including low-level private equity, informal networks and local governments. When internal funds are insufficient to meet expanding investment needs, SMEs seek funds from external sources with the promise to return the principal, in addition to an agreed-upon level of interest (debt finance). In a conventional financial market, this demand would be covered by bank finance, but for China's SMEs, this gap is filled by various forms of informal finance. Leverage can also be issued by other semi-formal finance institutions which are indirectly linked to banks, such as small loan companies and third-party loan guarantee companies. Alternatively, SMEs obtain funding from investors interested in shares or 'assets' of enterprises in return for their investment (equity finance). Local governments can either be participants in or beneficiaries of such transactions by providing access to resources or simply by non-interference.

In sum, the institutional debt versus equity framework provides an alternative view of the working of SME finance. The framework is based on the idea that SMEs seek finance in an entrepreneurial environment that does not rigidly differentiate debt from equity by giving creditors the option to convert outstanding debt into equity in future business concerns. The finance mechanism is a combination of debt and equity finance with the flexibility to interchange. This creates a rich dynamic in SMEs finance structure.

The contrast between the formal trajectories and actual path dependent trajectories is indicated in Figure 4 by red and green arrows. Red arrows indicate the formal trajectories that envision debt and equity as the two possible avenues for formal funding. The green arrows indicated *de facto* paths of finance which in spite of their informal origin are compatible with formal structures and even international expansion.

This framework is the first step towards a deeper understanding of how SME finance works in China and provides theoretical foundation for further empirical studies.

5. Conclusion

The aim of this chapter is to show the links between inclusive growth as a policy target and China's institutional environment at local level. We demonstrate that China's inclusive growth targets are coupled with not just poverty alleviation but also inequality reduction. Further, we examine why inclusive growth in China is not achievable by central government intervention alone, but depends on local governments and their support for local enterprise development. Finally, we show that this has implications for enterprise finance and requires changes that are not yet part of an official reform agenda.

However, this differentiation between official policies and local enterprise activity and enterprise–government cooperation does in no way indicate that inclusive growth is not achievable in China. Our findings indicate that decentralization, which has been well documented in the literature on fiscal federalism and business studies, is also a feature of implementing inclusive growth in China. Inclusive growth is more likely to be achieved first in better endowed and economically developed regions and later in others.

One line of our enquiry opens the question of China's SME finance. Research in this field is far from conclusive. The formal policy response disregards established informal practices which create their own path dependencies and trajectories. Overcoming the debt versus equity dichotomy provides the first step toward a deeper understanding of entrepreneurial finance in China and its implications for new markets.

In conclusion, a well-functioning finance system for SMEs will allocate resources more efficiently, providing China's SME sector, specifically those better-performing SMEs, with credit and opportunities to grow. In return, SME growth will contribute to achieving inclusive growth by spreading and encouraging entrepreneurial initiatives. Compared with direct central intervention to promote inclusive growth, this bottom-up approach will have more support from local governments in China, as SME development will enhance local revenue, employment and opportunities.

References

Allen, F., J. Qian, and M. Qian (2005). "Law, Finance, and Economic Growth in China," *Journal of Financial Economics*, Vol. 77, pp. 57–116.

Atherton, A. (2009). "Rational Actors, Knowledgeable Agents: Extending Pecking Order Considerations of New Venture Financing to Incorporate Founder Experience, Knowledge and Networks," *International Small Business Journal*, Vol. 27, pp. 470–495.

Ayyagari, M., A. Demirgüç-Kunt, and V. Maksimovic (2010). "Formal Versus Informal Finance: Evidence from China," *Review of Financial Studies*, Vol. 23, No. 8, pp. 3048–3097.

Barro, R. J. (2008). "Inequality and Growth Revisited," Working Papers on Regional Economic Integration.

Baum, R. and A. Shevchenko (1999). "The State of the State," in *The Paradox of China's Post-Mao Reform*, R. Macfarquhar (ed.), Cambridge: Harvard University Press.

Baumol, W. J. (2007). "On Income Distribution and Growth," *Journal of Policy Modeling*, Vol. 29, No. 4, pp. 545–548.

Beck, T., A. Demirgüç-Kunt, and R. Levine (2005). "SMEs, Growth, and Poverty: Cross-Country Evidence," *Journal of Economic Growth*, Vol. 10, No. 3, pp. 197–227.

Benabou, R. (1996). "Inequality and Growth," *NBER Macroeconomics Annual*, Vol. 11, pp. 11–92.

Berger, A. N. and G. F. Udell (1998). "The Economics of Small Business Finance: The Roles of Private Equity and Debt Markets in the Financial Growth Cycle," *Journal of Banking and Finance*, Vol. 22, pp. 613–673.

Campbell, J. R., C. M. Hombo, and J. Mazzeo (2000). "NAEP Trends," *National Center for Education Statistics*, Vol. 2, No. 4, p. 31.

Campano, F. and D. Salvatore (2006). *Income Distribution*, New York: Oxford University Press.

Chen, J. (2006). "Development of Chinese Small and Medium-Sized Enterprises," *Journal of Small Business and Enterprise Development*, Vol. 13, No. 2, pp. 140–147.

Chen, S. and Y. Wang (2001). "China's Growth and Poverty Reduction: Recent Trends Between 1990 and 1999," World Bank Policy Research Working Paper No. 2651, World Bank, Washington DC.

Chi, X. L. (2007). The dilemma and choice of private SME financing, Doctoral dissertation, Jinlin University.

CESS (2012). "2012 Report on the Growth and Development of Chinese Enterprises," China Enterprise Survey System.

China Banking Regulatory Commission and People's Bank of China (2008). "Guiding Opinion on Pilot Operation of Small Loan Companies," No. 23 [2008] of China Banking Regulatory Commission. Available at: http://www. gov.cn/gzdt/2008-05/08/content_965058.htm. Accessed 28 January 2013.

China Household Finance Survey (2011). "China Household Finance Survey," Southwestern University of Finance and Economics and People's Bank of China.

de Kok, J., P. Vroonhof, W. Verhoeven, N. Timmermans, T. Kwaak, J. Snijders, and F. Westhof (2011). "Do SMEs Create More and Better Jobs?" Available at: http://ec.europa.eu/enterprise/policies/sme/factsfigures-analysis/perfor mance-review/pdf/do-smescreate-more-and-better-jobs_en.pdf [accessed on 2 September 2013].

European Commission (2010). *Europe 2020—Europe's Growth Strategy*. Brussels: European Commission.

Foster, K. W. (2006). "Improving Municipal Governance in China Yantai's Path-breaking Experiment in Administrative Reform," *Modern China*, Vol. 32, No. 2, pp. 221–250.

Galor, O. and J. Zeira (1993). "Income Distribution and Macroeconomics," *The Review of Economic Studies*, Vol. 60, No. 1, pp. 35–52.

Galor, O. and D. Tsiddon (1997). "Technological Progress, Mobility, and Economic Growth," *The American Economic Review*, Vol. 87, No. 3, pp. 363–382.

Guo, B. and M. Liu (2002). "Private Finance and Small and Medium-Sized Enterprises Development: Empirical Evidence from Wenzhou Region," *Economic Research Journal*, Vol. 2002, No. 10, pp. 40–46.

Guo, R. (2012). *Understanding the Chinese Economies*, San Diego: Academic Press, pp. 125–143.

Hacker, J. S. and P. Pierson (2011). *Winner-Take-All Politics: How Washington Made the Rich Richer and Turned Its Back on the Middle Class*, New York: Simon & Schuster.

Hall, G., P. Hutchinson, and N. Michaelas (2000). "Industry Effects on the Determinants of Unquoted SMEs' Capital Structure," *International Journal of the Economics of Business*, Vol. 7, No. 3, pp. 297–312.

Hendrischke, H. (2011). "Changing Legislative and Institutional Arrangements Facing China's Workplace," in *China's Changing Workplace: Dynamism, Diversity and Disparity*, P. Sheldon, S. Kim, Y. Li, and M. Warner (eds.), London: Routledge, pp. 51–67.

Hendrischke, H., B. Krug, and Z. Zhu (2012). "China's Local Tax Regimes: Devolution, Tax Farming and Fiscal Federalism," in *Taxation in ASEAN and China: Local Institutions, Regionalism, Global Systems and Economic Development*, N. C. Sharkey (ed.), Milton Park, UK: Routledge, pp. 38–61.

Herrmann-Pillath, C. and X. Feng (2004). "Competitive Governments, Fiscal Arrangements, and the Provision of Local Public Infrastructure in China A Theory-driven Study of Gujiao Municipality," *China Information*, Vol. 18, No. 3, pp. 373–428.

Hillman, B. (2010). "Factions and Spoils: Examining Political Behavior Within the Local State in China," *The China Journal*, Vol. 64, pp. 1–18.

Howorth, C. (2001). "Small Firms' Demand for Finance: A Research Note," *International Small Business Journal*, Vol. 19, No. 4, pp. 78–86.

Hsu, D. H. (2004). "What Do Entrepreneurs Pay for Venture Capital Affiliation?" *The Journal of Finance*, Vol. 59, No. 4, pp. 1805–1844.

Hu, J. (2010). "Deepen Exchanges and Cooperation for Inclusive Growth." The Opening Ceremony of the Fifth APEC Human Resources Development Ministerial Meeting in Beijing, 16 September. Available at: http://english. gov.cn/2010-09/16/content_1704109.htm [accessed on 28 January 2013].

Hu, J. (2012). "Hu Jintao's Report at 18th Party Congress," The Opening Ceremony of the 18th CPC National Congress at the Great Hall of the People in Beijing, 8 November. Available at: http://news.xinhuanet.com/english/ special/18cpcnc/2012-11/17/c_131981259.htm [accessed on 28 January 2013].

Huang, Y. (2008). *Capitalism with Chinese Characteristics*, Cambridge: Cambridge University Press.

Huang, M. (ed.) (2012). *Annual Report of Non-state Owned Economy in China No. 8 (2010–2011)*, Beijing: Social Science Academic Press.

Information Office of the State Council (2004). *China's Social Security and Its Policy*, Beijing: Information Office of the State Council.

Jepperson, R. L. (1991). "Institutions, Institutional Effects, and Institutionalism," in *The New Institutionalism in Organizational Analysis*, W. W. Powell and P. J. DiMaggio (eds.), Chicago: University of Chicago Press.

Ji, C. (2009). "Chinese Informal Financial Systems and Economic Growth — A Case Study of China's Small and Medium Enterprises," *Public Policy Review*, Vol. 5, No. 1, pp. 63–88.

Jiang, S. (2009). "The Evolution of Informal Finance in China, and Its Prospects," in *Informal Finance in China: American and Chinese Perspectives*, J. Li and S. Hsu (eds.), USA: Oxford University Press.

Jin, Y. H. and Y. Q. Xi (2006). "Comparing SME Financing Structure: An International Perspective," *Enterprise Vitality*, 2006(1).

Klasen, S. (2010). "Measuring and Monitoring Inclusive Growth: Multiple Definitions, Open Questions, and Some Constructive Proposals," ADB Sustainable Development Working Paper Series No. WPS102016.

Kraay, A. (2003). "When is Growth Pro-Poor? Evidence from a Panel of Countries," mimeo, Development Research Group, World Bank.

Krugman, P. (2012). *End This Depression Now!* New York: W.W. Norton & Company.

Li, J. and S. Hsu (eds.) (2009). *Informal Finance in China American and Chinese Perspectives*, USA: Oxford University Press.

Li, W., G. Song, M. Beresford, and B. Ma (2011). "China's Transition to Green Energy Systems: The Economics of Home Solar Water Heaters and their Popularization in Dezhou City," *Energy Policy*, Vol. 39, No. 10, pp. 5909–5919.

Li, Y. (2012). "Analysis on Small and Medium Enterprises Finance and Implications," *Co-operative Economy & Science*, Vol. 2012, No. 3, pp. 66–67 (in Chinese).

Liang, J. (2010). "Official: China's SMEs in Best Period," People's Daily Online. Available at: http://english.peopledaily.com.cn/90001/90778/90862/7107295.html [accessed on 2 September 2013].

Lin, J. Y. (2011). *Demystifying the Chinese Economy*, Cambridge: Cambridge University Press.

Lin, J. Y. and Y. J. Li (2001). "Promoting the Growth of Medium and Small-Sized Enterprises through the Development of Medium and Small-Sized Financial Institutions," *Economic Research Journal*, Vol. 2001, No. 1, pp. 10–19 (in Chinese).

Lin, J. Y. and X. Sun (2006). "Information, Informal Finance, and SME Financing," *Frontiers of Economics in China*, Vol. 1, No. 1, pp. 69–82.

Maksimovic, V., A. Demirgüç-Kunt, and M. Ayyagari (2008). "Formal Versus Informal Finance: Evidence from China," World Bank Policy Research Working Paper No. 4465, World Bank, Washington DC.

Mok, K. H. (2012). "Bringing the State Back In: Restoring the Role of the State in Chinese Higher Education," *European Journal of Education*, Vol. 47, No. 2, pp. 228–241.

Nee, V. and S. Opper (2012). *Capitalism from Below: Markets and Institutional Change in China*, Cambridge, MA: Harvard University Press.

Neckerman, K. M. and F. Torche (2007). "Inequality: Causes and Consequences," *Annual Review Sociology*, Vol. 33, pp. 335–357.

Noah, T. (2012). *The Great Divergence: America's Growing Inequality Crisis and What We Can Do about It*, New York: Bloomsbury Press.

North, D. C. (1990). *Institutions, Institutional Change and Economic Performance*, Cambridge; New York and Melbourne: Cambridge University Press.

North, D. C. (1993). *The New Institutional Economics and Development*, Washington University in St. Louis.

Otani, I. (2011). "China's Capital Controls and Interest Rate Parity: Experience during 1999–2010 and Future Agenda for Reforms," Bank of Japan Working Paper Series No. 11-E-8.

Paul, S., G. Whittam, and J. Wyper (2007). "The Pecking Order Hypothesis: Does It Apply To Start-Up Firms?" *Journal of Small Business and Enterprise Development*, Vol. 14, No. 1, pp. 8–21.

Ping, X. Q. and J. Bai (2006). "Fiscal decentralization and local public good provision in China," *Finance & Trade Economics*, Vol. 2, p. 009.

Qian, Y. and B. R. Weingast (1997). "Federalism as a Commitment to Preserving Market Incentives," *Journal of Economic Perspectives*, Vol. 11, No. 4, pp. 83–92.

Qin, D., M. A. Cagas, G. Ducanes, X. He, R. Liu, and S. Liu (2009). "Effects of Income Inequality on China's Economic Growth," *Journal of Policy Modeling*, Vol. 31, No. 1, pp. 69–86.

Rauniyar, G. and K. Ravi (2010). "Inclusive Development: Two Papers on Conceptualization, Application, and the ADB Perspective," January Draft. Independent Evaluation Department, ADB.

Ravallion, M. and S. Chen (2003). "Measuring Pro-poor Growth," *Economics Letters*, Vol. 78, No. 1, pp. 93–99.

Saich, T. (2002). "China's WTO Gamble," *Harvard Asia Pacific Review*, Vol. 4, No. 1, pp. 10–14.

Shane, S. and D. Cable (2002). "Network Ties, Reputation, and the Financing of New Ventures," *Management Science*, Vol. 48, No. 3, pp. 364–381.

Schmid, F. (2001). Equity Financing and the Entrepreneurial Firm," *Federal Reserve Bank of St Louis Review*, Vol. 83, pp. 15–28.

Sen, A. K. (1990). "Development as Capabilities Expansion," in *Human Development and the International Development Strategy for the 1990s*, K. Griffin and J. Knight (eds.), London: MacMillan.

Shue, V. and C. Wong (2007). *Paying for Progress in China*, Oxon: Routledge.

Stiglitz, J. E. (2012). *The Price of Inequality*, New York: W.W. Norton & Company.

Stiglitz, J. E. and A. Weiss (1981). "Credit Rationing in Markets with Imperfect Information," *The American Economic Review*, Vol. 71, No. 3, pp. 393–410.

Staehle, H. (1937). "Short-Period Variations in the Distribution of Incomes," *The Review of Economics and Statistics*, Vol. 19, No. 3, pp. 133–143.

Staehle, H. (1938). "Retail Sales and Labor Income: New Considerations on the Distribution of Incomes and the "Propensity to Consume" (partly in reply to Mr. Dirks)," *The Review of Economics and Statistics*, Vol. 20, No. 3, pp. 134–141.

Tsai, K. S. (2004). *Back-Alley Banking: Private Entrepreneurs in China*, Ithaca, NY: Cornell University Press.

UNDP IPC-IG (2012). "What is Inclusive Growth?" United Nations Development Programme, International Policy Centre for Inclusive Growth (IPC-IG). Available at: http://www.ipc-undp.org/pages/newsite/menu/inclusive/whatisinclusivegrowth.jsp?active=1 [accessed on December 2012].

Wang, R. (2010). "Causes for Financing Difficulties of Chinese Small and Medium Enterprises and the Establishment of an Institutional Environment," *Information of Economics and Law*, Vol. 2010, No. 4, pp. 38–42 (in Chinese).

Williamson, O. E. (1979). "Transaction-Cost Economics: The Governance of Contractual Relations," *Journal of Law and Economics*, Vol. 22, No. 2, pp. 233–261.

Wong, C. (1992). "Fiscal Reform and Local Industrialization: The Problematic Sequencing of Reform in post-Mao China," *Modern China*, Vol. 18, No. 2, pp. 197–227.

Wong, C. (2011). "The Fiscal Stimulus Program and Problems of Macroeconomic Management in China," *OECD Journal of Budgeting*, Vol. 2011, No. 3, pp. 1–21.

World Bank (1997). *Sharing Rising Incomes: Disparities in China*, Washington DC: World Bank.

World Bank (2000). *Voices of the Poor: Volume 1: Can Anyone Hear Us?* Washington DC: World Bank.

World Bank (2009). "What Is Inclusive Growth?" PRMED Knowledge Brief, February 10. Washington, DC: Economic Policy and Debt Department, Washington DC: The World Bank.

World Bank (2012). *China 2030: Building a Modern, Harmonious, and Creative High-Income Society*, Washington DC: The World Bank.

Yang, Y. (2011). "China's Crippled Financial Sector. Project Syndicate." Available at: http://www.project-syndicate.org/commentary/china-s-crippled-financial-sector [accessed on 28 January 2013].

Yu, J., M. Liu, J. Wang, J. Zhu, M. Zhang, H. Li, and E. Cheng (2007). "SME Development and Poverty Reduction: Case Study of Xiji County, China," CFED Project Research Report.

Zhang, X. and R. Kanbur (2005). "Spatial Inequality In Education and Health Care in China," *China Economic Review*, Vol. 16, No. 2, pp. 189–204.

Zhang, X., S. Fan, L. Zhang, and J. Huang (2004). "Local Governance and Public Goods Provision in Rural China," *Journal of Public Economics*, Vol. 88, No. 12, pp. 2857–2871.

Zhao, X. B. and L. Zhang (1999). "Decentralization Reforms and Regionalism in China: A Review," *International Regional Science Review*, Vol. 22, No. 3, pp. 251–281.

Zhou, Y. and T. Xin (2003). "An Innovative Region in China: Interaction Between Multinational Corporations and Local Firms in a High-Tech Cluster in Beijing," *Economic Geography*, Vol. 79, No. 2, pp. 129–152.

Zhou, B., S. Zhu, and J. Tai (2011). Inclusive Growth: The New Paradigm for Social Economic Development," *Contemporary Economic Research*, Vol. 2011, No. 04, pp. 85–88 (in Chinese).

Zhuang, J. and A. Afzal (2009). *Inequality and Inclusive Growth in Developing Asia*, Manila: Asian Development Bank.

Zweimüller, J. (2000). "Inequality, Redistribution, and Economic Growth," *Empirica*, Vol. 27, No. 1, pp. 1–20.

5. Service Sector's Growth in China: The Role of ICT, Non-ICT and Human Capitals

Dilip Dutta* and Guan Long Ren

1. Introduction

It is often claimed that the expansion of an economy's service sector relative to that of its goods-producing sector has a negative effect on the rate of overall economic growth. The argument behind such claims lies in the perishable or non-storable nature of services right after their production, unlike goods that are storable or non-perishable.[1] In a series of pioneering works, William Baumol and his co-authors (Baumol, 1967, 1972; Baumol, Blackman and Wolff, 1985) have hypothesized that the service sector (referred to as 'stagnant'), whose productivity growth rate is below the economy's overall average, would tend to experience above-average cost increases. The resulting 'cost disease' may, therefore, lead the service sector to experience above-average price increases, decline in quality and financial pressure. However, much of the recent research undertaken focusing on the service sector deals with explaining, verifying or falsifying 'cost disease.' Some of these studies suggest that Baumol's 'cost disease' has been cured, primarily due to the application of information and communication technology (ICT) in service sector.[2] ICT has also generated a large number of new services in the forms of e-commerce (in particular, business services), e-finance (financial services), e-government and so forth. The emergence of ICT has thus improved the intrinsic productivity performance of service sector to a large extent.

---

*Corresponding author: dilip.dutta@sydney.edu.au
[1]Dutta (2008, pp. 504–505).
[2]Rowthorn and Wells (1987); Dutta (2008) and Gholami *et al.* (2009).

From another perspective, much of the theoretical literature deals with identifying potential growth engines (such as physical and/or human capital accumulations) and explaining their role in the development process. Recently, with the emergence of producer services,[3] this industry has become a relatively more skill-intensive sector. Therefore, human capital must now act as a powerful engine of labor productivity (LP) growth in the service sector as well. In view of this, we intend to examine the impact of ICT and human capital on the service sector's productivity growth in China. Two central questions are addressed in this chapter: (1) Is there a positive relationship between the intensive use of ICT and service sector's productivity performance? (2) To what extent can this productivity growth be explained by ICT adoption and human capital accumulation, separately and combined? We expect that the answers to these questions could help us in investigating whether Baumol's 'cost disease' prevails in the contemporary Chinese economy.

After presenting a literature review in Section 2, we provide a brief discussion on data, variables and descriptive statistics in Section 3. A methodology of dynamic panel data estimation for the service sector's productivity growth in China is elaborated in Section 4, followed by an analysis of the estimation results in Section 5. Finally, a conclusion is drawn in Section 6.

2. Literature Review

In his seminal paper, Baumol (1967) constructs a model of unbalanced growth in which an oversimplified economy was divided into two differential productivity growth sectors: one 'progressive' and the other 'stagnant.' He assumes that the manufacturing sector is the progressive sector, and that its productivity increases exponentially. The reason for this is that, in the manufacturing industry, labor is instrumental to the product and can be replaced by machinery as technological innovation in capital products. He also assumes that the service sector is a stagnant one, and its productivity remains relatively unchanged over time. The reason for this assumption is that the service industry is predominantly labor intensive and its final services can hardly be provided by machinery itself.

---

[3]Producer services include advertising, computer and data processing services, personnel supply services, management and business consulting services, protective and detective services, accounting and auditing services, and engineering and architectural services (Tschetter, 1987).

There are several conclusions that can be drawn from the unbalanced growth model first set out by Baumol (1967) and further developed in Baumol (1985) and Baumol, Blackman and Wolff (1989). The first and most fundamental proposition was that, with the passage of time, the cost per unit of a consistently stagnant product would rise monotonically and without limit relative to that of a manufacturing product. The rationale behind this stagnationist argument is that, with growing relative productivity, the capital-intensive manufacturing sector would use increasingly less input quantities over time. For example, in circumstances of free movement of the labor force across sectors, rising wages will likely to keep unit costs unchanged in the manufacturing sector due to exponential increase in its productivity, while rising wages will lead to increased costs in the service sector. Since the productivity performance of the service sector is stagnant and the demand for services has relatively small income elasticity and high price elasticity, then such an increased cost is difficult to recover. This is why Baumol has called this phenomenon the 'cost disease' of the stagnant services.

The second stagnationist argument is that, if the output ratio of a stagnant to a progressive product happens to remain constant or does not fall, the share of the combined inputs used by the stagnant sector must rise without limit. As mentioned before, labor in the manufacturing sector can be replaced by machinery as technology advances, while labor in the service sector cannot be replaced and the service products themselves are directly embodied by labor input. Thus, in order to maintain the relative output share of the service sector, more labor is needed in the service industry.

The third stagnationist argument is that, if resources are shifting toward the industry where productivity is growing relatively stagnantly (namely, the technologically stagnant industry), the aggregate productivity growth rate will steadily fall to the rate prevailing in the stagnant industry. Likewise, Nordhaus (2006) argues that a taste for the output of stagnant sectors may lead to secular stagnation and declining real-income growth as consumers increasingly demand labor-intensive services where productivity growth is intrinsically limited.

The primary response to this pessimistic prognostication of Baumol and his co-authors has been an argument that not all service activities have stagnant productivity growth, especially certain emerging industries of producer services do show higher productivity growth (Rowthorn and Ramaswamy, 1997). From this point of view, Baumol (1985) later make a modified hypothesis that service activities are 'asymptotically' stagnant so that he could better explain the coexistence of the emerging service industry and the relatively stagnant growth of the overall economy in the US. Further, Stiroh (1998) argues that the stagnationist argument still implies that the growth of aggregate productivity will slow, unless new technology can be relied on to raise future service sector growth, something it has thus far failed to do so. Additionally, Nordhaus (2006) has verified Baumol's modified hypothesis and LP stagnation in some service industries in the US.

Meanwhile, Oulton (2001) raises a question about the stagnationist argument by pointing out that it is logically correct only if all industries produce final goods. Proceeding from this angle, he assumes exogenously specific sectoral growth rate of productivity in both manufacturing and service sectors, but introduces the hypothesis that a portion of the service sector produces intermediate goods for the manufacturing sector. Then, by testing this hypothesis with data from the UK, he obtains a remarkable result that even if the primary inputs are shifting toward the service industry from the manufacturing sector, the growth rate of aggregate productivity still increases over time. Thus his empirical analysis rules out the negative Baumol effect of the service sector on the UK's overall economic growth. Later on, Wolff suggests that the emergence of the producer service industry causes a divergence in different service industries' labor productivities, and even some of these industries' productivities are relatively higher than that of the manufacturing sector. Furthermore, Markusen and Strand (2007) argue that, when the producer service can be traded as an intermediate input, LP in the service sector will increase, thereby enhancing the aggregate productivity performance. Service industries such as financial and business services that have been expanding rapidly in the recent years are, in fact, the large producers of intermediate inputs.

From the perspective of human capital accumulation, Spithoven (2000) explains the positive effect of the so-called stagnant services on aggregate productivity performance. This appears obvious in the case of educational and health services. Romer (1990) argues that long-term economic growth is driven primarily by the accumulation of knowledge. From this point of view, Pugno (2006) revises and extends Baumol's unbalanced growth framework by combining two hypotheses: (1) consumer preferences shift to services as income increases; and (2) the Lucas-like accumulation function of human capital depends linearly on the employment in service sector. Eventually, he obtains the result that both the productivity and the quality of service production through enhanced human capital accumulation are crucial for long-term economic performance.

There is a large number of recent empirical studies that have investigated the potential relationship between ICT and productivity performance. Oulton (2002) applies a growth-accounting approach to measure the contribution of ICT to the growth of both aggregate output and aggregate input and estimates the contribution of ICT as intermediate input to the UK's aggregate productivity growth. Elasdig (2008) analyzes the role of ICT and human capital intensities on productivity growth in the Malaysian economy over a decade. Seo, Lee and Oh (2009) build a model of cumulative growth to examine the dynamic interdependent relationship between ICT and economic growth for a sample of 29 countries in the 1990s. The findings of the empirical studies on the relationship between ICT and productivity growth carried out appear to be somewhat mixed.

Until now, most studies on the growth of LP in China's service sector have examined whether 'Baumol's cost disease' exists or not. Using provincial data from 1978 to 2000, Cheng (2004) finds that the LP of China's service sector has been relatively stagnant. The income elasticity of demand in most service industries is less than one unit and demand for service is price inelastic, thereby causing 'cost disease'. We intend to examine the earlier stagnationist state of China's service sector at the provincial levels. More specifically, using current data, we will make an effort to evaluate the effects of both ICT and human capital on the service sector's productivity performance in China's provinces.

3. Data, Variables and Descriptive Statistics

Using data in Appendix A, the annual growth rates of LP of the service and manufacturing sectors in China over 34 years (1978–2011) have been computed and then shown in Table 1. As can be seen in this table, the average annual growth rate of LP in the service sector is 6.06%, which is surprisingly higher than that in the manufacturing sector (5.85%), although both sectors had occasionally experienced negative labor productivity growth. However, the 1990s witnessed an increase in worsening of LP growth in service sector compared to that in manufacturing sector. There are three plausible reasons to explain this situation. First, the positive effects of the open-door policy during the early 1980s on service sector seem to have been depleted, leading to worsening of its labor productivity growth. Second, the positive effects from the microeconomic reforms of industrial enterprises, with lay-offs, downsizing and improving efficiency as their core, gradually

Table 1: Aggregate growth rates of employment and labor productivity during 1978–2011.

Year	Ls[a] (%)	LPm[b] (%)	LPs[c] (%)	DiffLPmLPs[d] (%)
1978	—	—	—	—
1979	1.11	3.52	−6.85	10.38
1980	0.01	−0.22	−2.73	2.52
1981	1.98	−3.35	−0.44	−2.91
1982	−1.03	−0.64	3.37	−4.01
1983	2.42	4.57	3.90	0.67
1984	3.28	3.32	10.36	−7.03
1985	−0.14	5.03	20.32	−5.29
1986	−1.36	1.02	3.13	−2.12
1987	1.10	4.11	4.24	−0.14
1988	1.11	1.90	2.27	−0.37
1989	1.86	−5.11	−1.36	−3.75
1990	1.18	−11.77	−12.06	0.29
1991	1.14	12.00	15.36	−3.36
1992	1.72	16.51	12.47	4.04
1993	1.89	16.23	2.64	13.59
1994	3.45	7.14	−0.14	7.28
1995	3.04	6.53	−3.11	9.64
1996	1.23	5.10	1.49	3.62
1997	0.32	5.55	9.05	−3.51
1998	0.93	4.29	11.00	−6.70
1999	1.35	7.58	9.84	−2.26
2000	2.01	11.28	9.77	1.50
2001	0.72	7.55	11.22	−3.67
2002	3.20	12.75	8.71	4.04
2003	0.64	11.96	7.31	4.65
2004	0.11	8.25	5.34	2.91
2005	−1.30	9.08	10.00	−0.92
2006	−1.39	9.24	12.26	−3.02
2007	−2.47	8.02	17.15	−9.12
2008	0.43	9.37	8.02	1.35
2009	0.22	3.81	9.66	−5.84
2010	−0.78	10.49	10.86	−0.37
2011	0.17	7.90	6.98	0.92
Mean	0.85	5.85	6.06	−0.21
Std. Dev.	1.45	5.89	6.91	5.78

[a]Service sector's employment as a proportion of total employment.
[b]Labor productivity in manufacturing sector (LPm).
[c]Labor productivity in service sector (LPs).
[d]Difference between LPm & LPs.
Source: The data source is derived from *Chinese Statistical Yearbooks 1997–2011*.

became apparent in the 1990s. This improved the LP growth rate of the manufacturing sector, thereby increasing its labor productivity relatively more compared to that of the service sector. Third, from the late 1980s, there was a pressure on the service sector to absorb surplus agricultural labor force and laid-off workers from the secondary industries, which greatly hampered the its improvement of LP.

Interestingly, there has been a gradual increase in labor productivity growth in both manufacturing and service sectors since 1996. For the explanation of this sustained growth in labor productivity of the service sector, two main reasons are often noted. First, with the rapid growth of GDP in the past 20 years, peoples' consumption and expenditure levels have begun to rise. This trend (as can be explained by Engle's law) has prompted growth in demand for services. Second, with the wide application of ICT products, the producer services industry has gradually begun to shake off its heavy reliance on labor. Without reducing the aggregate output of services, this might be the main factor that leads to not only the reduction of the labor share of the service industry (see Table 1) but also improvement in labor productivity.

Annual panel data of 31 provinces in China over the period[4] from 2003 to 2010 are used to evaluate the relationship between ICT capital growth, human capital accumulation and economic growth. The data used in this study are all derived from the *China Statistical Yearbooks* (CSYs) from 2004 to 2011. The data on five main specified variables of service sector's gross regional product (Q_S), non-ICT physical capital (K_N), ICT capital (K_C); human capital (H) and total employment (L_S) are tabulated in Appendix B.

3.1. Gross Regional Product (GRP) of service sector (Q_S, measured unit: 100 million yuan)

The data set covers an eight-year period (2003–2010) across 31 provinces in China. Annual GRP data are shown as the value-added at current prices in China Statistical Yearbook (CSY). Using consumer price index (CPI) of

---

[4]The reason for choosing 2003 as the initial year is that, in 2002, the National Bureau of Statistics amended *The National Standards of the National Industry Classification and Codes*, making adjustments and revisions to those original service industry categories and adding six new categories: (i) information transmission, computer services and software industry; (ii) hotels and catering services; (iii) leasing and business services; (iv) management of water conservation, the environment and public facilities; (v) education and (vi) international organizations.

2003 as the base, the GRPs of the subsequent years have been deflated in order to obtain real GRPs.

3.2. Non-ICT Physical Capital of service sector (K_N, measured unit: 100 million yuan)

The standard perpetual inventory approach created by Goldsmith in 1951 is used to estimate the non-ICT capital stock (K_t) for service sector in each year, by applying the basic formula: $K_t = I_t + (1 - \delta) * K_{t-1}$. The first key point is investment of the current year, I_t, which is referred to as gross fixed capital formation at the current price. The calculation of the gross fixed capital formation is based on the total social fixed asset investment (Wang and Yao, 2001). However, in the CSYs, the data regarding the total social fixed asset investment in tertiary industry (i.e., service sector) cannot be found directly. Thus, the data regarding fixed asset investment are obtained by summing the total investment in fixed assets of different subsectors in the tertiary industries, excluding the ICT sector. Next, the price index for investment in fixed assets has been used to compute the real investment. The second key point is choosing the average depreciation rate of non-ICT physical capital, δ, which equals to 6% in this analysis. The third key point is calculating the initial capital stock, K_0. Following the method of Hall and Jones (1999), the initial capital stock equals the fixed capital formation of the basic year (set at 2003 level) divided by the depreciation rate and the average geometric growth rate of fixed capital formation during the subsequent seven years.

3.3. ICT Capital (K_C, measured unit: 100 million yuan)

An approach similar to that mentioned above has been taken for obtaining the real ICT capital, the only difference being that the data of gross fixed capital formation of ICT at current prices are directly obtained by fixed asset investment in the ICT sector. The average depreciation rate for ICT capital is here assumed to be 31.5%, as has been the standard in similar literature (e.g., Gholami *et al.*, 2009).

3.4. Human Capital (H, measured unit: 100 million yuan)

Since the data on schooling information are not comprehensive in the CSYs, neither Gemmell's (1996) adjustment of Barro–Lee's approach, nor

Schultz's (1960) opportunity time cost foregone approach can be used here. Therefore, the data on expenditure in education is used as a proxy for human capital. According to the UNESCO, the years of formal schooling received, on average, by Chinese adults over age 15 is 6.4 years. Following this information, we use labor's educational expenditure with a lag of 6 years for data on human capital.

3.5. Total Employment of Service Sector (L_S, measured unit: 10,000 persons)

The sources of the regional labor statistics in China are reported in the CSYs. Thus, the data regarding total employment in the tertiary industry sector for each region are directly drawn from the CSYs.

In order to illustrate graphically the correlation between the growth of different key variables (mentioned above) and that of service sector's labor productivity (LP), we use scatter diagrams. Figures 1 to 3 show the correlations between LP growth in the service sector with growth in non-ICT capital intensity (measured per capita), ICT capital intensity (measured per capita) and human capital intensity (measured per capita), respectively. Based on Figures 1 to 3, it is easy to find that, as expected, LP growth in the services sector is positively correlated with growth in non-ICT capital

Figure 1: Relationship between growth rates of LP$_s$ and non-ICT capital intensity.

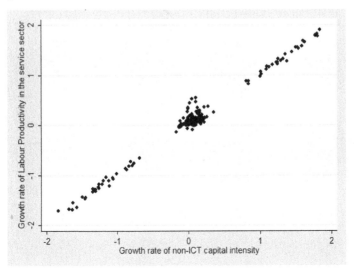

Figure 2: Relationship between growth rates of LP$_s$ and ICT capital intensity.

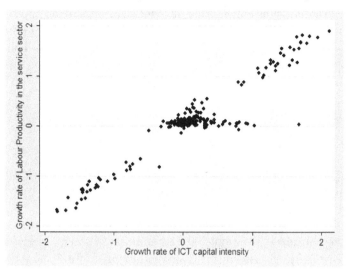

Figure 3: Relationship between growth rates of LP$_s$ and human capital intensity (with a six-year lag in educational expenditure).

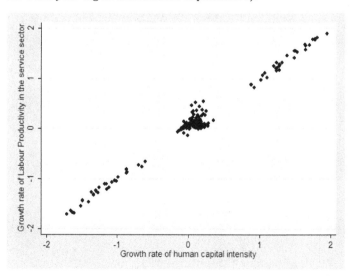

intensity, ICT capital intensity and human capital intensity, respectively. Nevertheless, these results need further verification.

4. Methodology for Empirical Analysis

The new growth theory suggests that the impact of physical investment on productivity growth might be underestimated by traditional growth accounting analysis,[5] due to positive externalities associated with such activities (Romer, 1986; Grossman and Helpman, 1991). Moreover, on an empirical level, Stiroh (1998) argues that there are several reasons why the standard neoclassical growth model fails to capture the contribution of new ICT investment on economy's productivity. As summarized by Wolff (2007), these reasons include the presence of embodied technological change, measurement error in variables and reverse causality, the presence of productivity spillovers from ICT and problems of omitted variables. Keeping the above limitations of the standard neoclassical growth model in mind, we use the following Cobb–Douglas production function of service sector:

$$Q_{Sit} = A_{it} * K_{Nit}^{\alpha} * K_{Cit}^{\beta} * H_{it-6}^{\gamma},$$

where Q_{Sit} = the real output of the services sector, K_{Nit} = the input of non-ICT capital goods, and K_{Cit} = the ICT capital in the ith region at time t; and H_{it-6} = human capital in the ith region at time $(t-6)$. The parameters α, β, γ stand for factor shares (or the output elasticities with respect to non-ICT capital, ICT capital and human capital, respectively). A_{it} is the exogenous technological parameter of the ith region at time t.

Then, taking logs and first differences, the above equation becomes:

$$\Delta \ln Q_{Sit} = \Delta \ln A_{it} + \alpha * \Delta \ln K_{Nit} + \beta * \Delta \ln K_{Cit} + \gamma * \Delta \ln H_{it-6}$$

To capture the LP growth rate in the service sector, we first divide the Cobb–Douglas functional form by total labor force employed in service sector, L_{Sit}:

$$\frac{Q_{Sit}}{L_{Sit}} = \frac{A_{it} * K_{Nit}^{\alpha} * K_{Cit}^{\beta} * H_{it-6}^{\gamma}}{L_{Sit}},$$

---

[5]For a short description of growth accounting, see Appendix A in Chapter 2 by Limin Wang.

and then take logarithm and first differences to obtain the following equation:

$$\Delta \ln \left(\frac{Q_{Sit}}{L_{Sit}} \right) = \Delta \ln \tilde{A}_{it} + \alpha * \Delta \ln \left(\frac{K_{Nit}}{L_{Sit}} \right) + \beta * \Delta \ln \left(\frac{K_{Cit}}{L_{Sit}} \right)$$

$$+ \gamma * \Delta \ln \left(\frac{H_{it-6}}{L_{Sit}} \right)$$

or,

$$\Delta \ln q_{Sit} = \Delta \ln \tilde{A}_{it} + \alpha * \Delta \ln k_{Nit} + \beta * \Delta \ln k_{Cit} + \gamma * \Delta \ln h_{it-6},$$

where the lower cases of Q, K_N, K_C and H all represent intensities in per-capita terms.

Following Griliches and Jorgenson (1962) and Samoilenko and Osei-Bryson (2008), the above equation can be written in a fully fledged translog specification (by including both squared terms and cross-product terms of all the inputs) as:

$$\Delta \ln q_{Sit} = \Delta \ln \tilde{A}_{it} + b_1 * \Delta \ln k_{Nit} + b_2 * \Delta \ln k_{Cit} + b_3 * \Delta \ln h_{it-6}$$

$$+ b_4 * (\Delta \ln k_{Cit} * \Delta \ln h_{it-6}) + b_{11} * (\Delta \ln k_{Nit})^2$$

$$+ b_{21} * (\Delta \ln k_{Cit})^2 + b_{31} * (\Delta \ln h_{it-6})^2.$$

It is to be noted that the coefficients of above equation can no longer be interpreted in terms of elasticity.

The term $\Delta \ln q_{Sit}$ denotes the LP growth of the service sector in China. $b_1 * \Delta \ln k_{Nit} + b_{11} * (\Delta \ln k_{Nit})^2$ is the contribution of non-ICT capital intensity.
$b_2 * \Delta \ln k_{Cit} + b_{21} * (\Delta \ln k_{Cit})^2$ is the contribution of ICT capital intensity.
$b_3 * \Delta \ln h_{it-6} + b_{31} * (\Delta \ln h_{it-6})^2$ is the contribution of human capital intensity.
$b_4 * (\Delta \ln k_{Cit} * \Delta \ln h_{it-6})$ is the contribution of interactive effect between ICT and human capital intensities.

Here, for the dynamic panel data-set, it is difficult to distinguish whether the regressors (explanatory variables) are strictly exogenous or not. If the regressors are strictly exogenous, the error term cannot affect explanatory variables, while if the regressor is predetermined, then the error term may affect explanatory variables. Dynamic panel-data estimators allow for predetermined regressor. In general, dynamic panel-data models have been of interest in a wide range of economic, financial and other applications, including Euler equations for household consumption and empirical models of economic growth (Arellano and Bond, 1991; Ahn and Schmidt, 1995). In order to apply the Arellano–Bond dynamic panel GMM estimation approach,[6] we could include lags of the dependent variable, allowing for error serial correlation of unknown form. This means the basic regression equation of interest now becomes:

$$\Delta \ln q_{Sit} = \psi_1 * \Delta \ln q_{Sit-1} + \psi_2 * \Delta \ln q_{Sit-2} + \Delta \ln \tilde{A}_{it}$$
$$+ b_1 * \Delta \ln k_{Nit} + b_2 * \Delta \ln k_{Cit} + b_3 * \Delta \ln h_{it-6}$$
$$+ b_4 * (\Delta \ln k_{Cit} * \Delta \ln h_{it-6}) + b_{11} * (\Delta \ln k_{Nit})^2$$
$$+ b_{21} * (\Delta \ln k_{Cit})^2 + b_{31} * (\Delta \ln h_{it-6})^2,$$

where the first two terms are lagged dependent variables. The above regression equation captures the essential feature of the model, that is, a dynamic effect of the explanatory variables (i.e., growth rates of K_{Nit}, K_{Cit} and H_{it-6}) on LP growth for which the speed of adjustment is governed by the coefficients of lagged growth in LP.

5. Estimation Results

Table 2 shows the results of dynamic panel GMM estimators using the Arellano–Bond method. Both *Model-1* and *Model-2* estimate effects of the explanatory variables of non-ICT capital intensity, ICT capital intensity and lagged human capital intensity on the explained variable of LP in the service sector. The estimates of all the three explanatory variables are with expected signs and statistically significant. However, *Model-2* adds one interactive term between ICT capital and human capital intensity accumulations. The estimate of the coefficient of this interactive term is positive and statistically significant. This means that the positive coefficient of the

---

[6]Because some input factors in previous period's growth may also affect the growth performance in the following period, economic behavior is inherently dynamic. The generalized method of moments (GMM) approach tackles this kind of problem. Arellano–Bond estimation method is applied specifically in the context of dynamic panel data analysis in order to obtain consistent parameter estimates. Furthermore, Arellano and Bover (1995) and Blundell and Bond (1998) suggest using additional moments condition to obtain an estimator with improved precision and better finite-sample properties.

Table 2: Estimation results of labor productivity growth (as the dependent variable) in China's service sector (2003–2010).

Independent variables:	Model-1	Model-2	Model-3	Model-4
$\Delta \ln q_{St-1}$	0.019**	−0.02*	−0.02	−0.019
	(0.008)	(0.011)	(0.013)	(0.013)
$\Delta \ln q_{St-2}$	0.012	0.005	0.001	0.003
	(0.008)	(0.006)	(0.008)	(0.008)
$\Delta \ln k_{Nt}$	0.679***	0.893***	0.848***	0.866***
	(0.074)	(0.076)	(0.088)	(0.108)
$\Delta \ln k_{Ct}$	0.103***	0.076***	0.122***	0.004
	(0.037)	(0.018)	(0.032)	(0.067)
$\Delta \ln h_{t-6}$	0.315***	0.185**	0.161*	0.125
	(0.090)	(0.081)	(0.088)	(0.088)
$\Delta \ln k_{Ct} * \Delta \ln h_{t-6}$		0.027***	0.409**	
		(0.007)	(0.172)	
$(\Delta \ln k_{Nt})^2$			0.050***	0.050***
			(0.012)	(0.017)
$(\Delta \ln k_{Ct})^2$			−0.210**	−0.008
			(0.084)	(0.011)
$(\Delta \ln h_{t-6})^2$			−0.220**	−0.012
			(0.091)	(0.015)
$\Delta \ln k_{Ct} * \Delta \ln h_{t-6}$ in Eastern				−0.346
				(0.442)
$\Delta \ln k_{Ct} * \Delta \ln h_{t-6}$ in Western				0.18
				(0.592)
$\Delta \ln k_{Ct} * \Delta \ln h_{t-6}$ in Central				−0.177
				(0.585)
constants	−0.006	−0.011	−0.01	−0.012
	(0.008)	(0.008)	(0.007)	(0.011)
Sample number	155	155	155	155
Chi Square	107690.4	194064.6	413883.5	511893.9
Variance of cluster estimators (vce)	robust	robust	robust	robust

Notes: In this table, standard errors are in parentheses. Value marked with (*), (**), (***) are statistically significant at the level of 10%, 5% and 1%, respectively.

interactive term amplifies the total contributions of both ICT and human capital intensity accumulations on labor productivity growth.

In *Model-3*, a fully fledged translog formation is specified. Table 2 shows that non-ICT capital intensity accumulation has a clear positive effect on LP growth in the service sector. Moreover, its quadratic term also enters with the expected positive and significant coefficient. This result reveals that, when the growth in non-ICT capital intensity accumulation reaches a certain degree, its influence on labor productivity growth in the service sector still remains persistent, which leads to further increase in labor productivity growth. In other words, largely, the performance of labor productivity growth in the service sector relies heavily on the growth in non-ICT capital intensity accumulation.

As can be seen from the estimates of *Model-3* in Table 2, ICT capital intensity accumulation has also a significant and positive effect on service sector's LP growth. However, the coefficient of its quadratic term is statistically significant but with negative value. This result reveals that, with the increasing growth rate of ICT capital intensity, LP growth first increases and then decreases when the growth rate of ICT capital intensity reaches a certain level. In other words, this result indicates that when the growth in ICT capital intensity reaches a specific level, its influence on labor productivity growth in the service sector will decline with increasing ICT capital accumulation. One possible reason for this might be the lack of the sustained technical innovation in the service sector in contemporary China.

Likewise, LP growth in the service sector is positively correlated with human capital intensity accumulation but negatively correlated with its quadratic term, although both estimates are statistically significant. This result also indicates that when the growth in human capital intensity reaches a specific level, its influence on LP growth in the service sector will decrease with increasing human capital intensity accumulation. Similar to ICT capital intensity accumulation, this result seems to indicate that the relatively skill-intensive service sector still lacks innovation due to insufficient investment in research and development (R&D) and also competition caused by entry barriers. Lastly, the statistically significant coefficient of the interactive term is positive as expected.

Model-4 includes additional interaction terms between the region-specific dummy variables and both the ICT and human capital intensity accumulations. The interaction terms between both the eastern and central regions and both ICT and human capital intensity are negative, while that between the western region and both ICT and human capital intensity is positive although not statistically significant. The results suggest that in the case of western region, the interactive effect of ICT adoption and human capital actually improves LP growth. As pointed out previously, the ICT- and human-capital-poor regions have a greater potential for enhancing overall performance of LP in service sector due to the catch-up factor. Likewise, the ICT- and human-capital–rich regions need not always be experiencing high growth performance, resulting from either diminishing returns or the catch-up factor.

6. Conclusion

Over the past 20 years, China has experienced a very high GDP growth rate. Since 1996, there has been a gradual increase in labor productivity growth in both manufacturing and service sectors as well. The growth of labor productivity, particularly in the service sector, has been sustained mainly because peoples' consumption and expenditure levels have begun to rise steadily; this trend has prompted growth in demand for consumer services as well. The wide application of ICT products in the producer services industry is also partly responsible for growth in service sector's labor productivity. However, we make an attempt to examine empirically if there is any role of non-ICT capital on labor productivity growth in service sector of China.

Although Baumol's seminal model of unbalanced growth between service and manufacturing sectors does not include any type of physical capital accumulation, our empirical results show that the sustainable growth of LP in China's service sector is predominantly driven by non-ICT capital accumulation. Therefore, it can be concluded that at the present stage of China's service sector, non-ICT capital accumulation is still a powerful engine of labor productivity growth; and the influence of ICT and human capital accumulation on labor productivity growth in this sector has its limit and needs to be further explored.

References

Ahn, S. and P. Schmidt (1995). "Efficient Estimation of Models for Dynamic Panel Data," *Journal of Econometrics*, Vol. 68, pp. 5–27.

Arellano, M. and S. Bond (1991). "Some Tests of Specification for Panel Data: Monte Carlo evidence and an Application to Employment Equations," *Review of Economic Studies*, Vol. 58, pp. 277–297.

Arellano, M. and O. Bover (1995). "Another look at the Instrumental-Variable Estimation of Error-Components Models," *Journal of Econometrics*, Vol. 68, pp. 29–51.

Baumol, W. J. (1967). "Macroeconomics of Unbalanced Growth: The Anatomy of Urban Crisis," *American Economic Review*, Vol. 57, No. 3, pp. 415–426.

Baumol, W. J. (1972). "Macroeconomics of Unbalanced Growth: Reply," *American Economic Review*, Vol. 62, No. 1, pages 150.

Baumol, W. J. (1985). "Productivity Policy and the Service Sector," in *Managing the Service Economy: Prospects and Problems*, P. R. Inman (ed.), Cambridge, MA: Cambridge University Press.

Baumol, W. J. (2001). "Paradox of the Services: Exploding Costs, Persistent Demand," in *The Growth of Service Industries: The Paradox of Exploding Costs and Persistent Demand*, T. Ten-Raa and R. Schettkat (eds.), Cheltenham (UK) and Northampton (MA): Elgar, pp. 3–28.

Baumol, W. J., S. A. B. Blackman, and E. N. Wolff (1985). "Unbalanced Growth Revisited: Asymptotic Stagnancy and New Evidence," *American Economic Review*, Vol. 75, No. 4, pp. 806–817.

Baumol, W. J., S. A. B. Blackman, and E. N. Wolff (1989). *Productivity and American Leadership*, Cambridge, MA: The MIT Press.

Blundell, R. and S. Bond (1998). "Initial Conditions and Moment Restrictions in Dynamic Panel Data Models," *Journal of Econometrics*, Vol. 87, pp. 115–143.

Cheng, D. (2004). "Features, Causes and Effects of Service Industry Growth: Baumol-Fuchs Hypothesis and an Empirical Study," *Social Sciences in China*, Vol. 2, pp. 18–32 (in Chinese).

Dutta, D. (2008). "Services and Development," in *International Handbook of Development Economics*, A. K. Dutt and J. Ros (eds.), United Kingdom: Cheltenham, pp. 497–515.

Elsadig, M. A. (2008). "ICT and Human Capital Intensities Effects on Malaysian Productivity Growth," *International Research Journal of Finance and Economics*, Vol. 13, pp. 152–161.

Gemmell, N. (1996). "Evaluating the impacts of human capital stocks and accumulation on economic growth: some new evidence," *Oxford Bulletin of Economics and Statistics*, Vol. 58, No. 1, pp. 9–28.

Gholami, R., X. Guo, M. A. Higón, and S. Y. T. Lee (2009). "Information and Communications Technology (ICT) International Spillovers," *IEEE Transactions on Engineering Management*, Vol. 56, No. 2, pp. 329–340.

Griliches, Z. and D. W. Jorgenson (1962). "Capital Theory: Technical Progress and Capital Structure, Sources of Measured Productivity Change Capital Input," *American Economic Review*, Vol. 52, No. 1, pp. 50–61.

Grossman, G. M. and E. Helpman (1991). *Innovation and Growth in the Global Economy*, Cambridge, MA: MIT Press.

Hall, R. R. and C. I. Jones (1999). "Why does some countries produce so much more output per worker than others?" *The Quarterly Journal of Economics*, Vol. 114, No. 1, pp. 83–116.

Markusen, J. R. and B. Strand (2007). "Trade in business services in general equilibrium." *National Bureau of Economic Research*, NBER Working Paper No. 12816.

Nordhaus, W. D. (2006). "Baumol's Disease: A Macroeconomic Perspective," National Bureau of Economic Research (NBER) Working Paper No. 12218.

Oulton, N. (2001). "Must the Growth Rate Decline? Baumol's Unbalanced Growth Revisited," *Oxford Economic Papers*, Vol. 53, pp. 605–627.

Oulton, N. (2002). "ICT and Productivity Growth in the United Kingdom," *Oxford Review of Economic Policy*, Vol. 18, No. 3, pp. 363–379.

Pugno, M. (2006). "The Service Paradox and Endogenous Economic Growth," *Structural Change and Economic Dynamics*, Vol. 17, pp. 99–115.

Romer, P. M. (1986). "Increasing Returns and Long-Run Growth," *Journal of Political Economy*, Vol. 94, pp. 1002–1037.

Rowthorn, R. and R. Ramaswamy (1997). "Deindustrialization: Causes and Implications," in *Staff Studies for the World Economic Outlook*, Washington DC: International Monetary Fund.

Rowthorn, R. E. and J. Wells (1987). *De-industrialization and Foreign Trade*, Cambridge, New York and Melbourne: Cambridge University Press.

Samoilenko, S. and K. M. Osei-Bryson (2008). "An Exploration of the Effects of the Interaction between ICT and Labor Force on Economic Growth in Transition Economies," *Inernational Journal of Production Economics*, Vol. 115, pp. 471–481.

Schultz, T. W. (1960). "Capital Formation by Education," *Journal of Political Economy*, Vol. 68, pp. 571–572.

Seo, H. J., Y. S. Lee, and J. H. Oh (2009). "Does ICT Investment Widen the Growth Gap?" *Telecommunications Policy*, Vol. 33, pp. 422–431.

Spithoven, A. H. G. M. (2000). "An Explanation for the Rising Share of Services in Employment," *International Journal of Social Economics*, Vol. 27, pp. 1205–1230.

Stiroh, K. J. (1998). "Computers, Productivity and Input Substitution," *Economic Inquiry*, Vol. 36, pp. 175–191.

Tschetter, J. (1987). "Producer Services Industries: Why Are They Growing So Rapidly?" *Monthly Labor Review*, December, pp. 31–40.

Wang, Y. and Y. Yao (2001). *Sources of China's Economic Growth, 1952–1999: Incorporating Human Capital Accumulation*, The World Bank, pp. 1–24.

Wolff, E. N. (2007). "Measures of Technical Change and Structural Change in Services in the USA: Was There A Resurgence of Productivity Growth in Services?" *Metroeconomica*, Vol. 58, No. 3, pp. 368–395.

Appendix A: Aggregate data on variables for 34 years (1978–2011).

Year	Ls (in 10,000)	Lm (in 10,000)	Qs (Bill. Yuan)	Qm (Bill. Yuan)	CPI	RealQs (Bill. Yuan)	RealQm (Bill. Yuan)	Labor share [Ls/(Ls+Lm)]
1978	4890	6945	872.50	1745.20	100.00	872.50	1745.20	0.41
1979	5177	7214	878.90	1913.50	101.90	862.51	1877.82	0.42
1980	5532	7707	982.00	2192.00	109.50	896.80	2001.83	0.42
1981	5945	8003	1076.60	2255.50	112.20	959.54	2010.25	0.43
1982	6090	8346	1163.00	2383.00	114.40	1016.61	2083.04	0.42 *
1983	6606	8679	1338.10	2646.20	116.70	1146.62	2267.52	0.43
1984	7739	9590	1786.30	3105.70	119.90	1489.82	2590.24	0.45
1985	8359	10384	2585.00	3866.60	131.10	1971.78	2949.35	0.45
1986	8811	11216	2993.80	4492.70	139.60	2144.56	3218.27	0.44
1987	9395	11726	3574.00	5251.60	149.80	2385.85	3505.74	0.44
1988	9933	12152	4590.30	6587.20	177.90	2580.27	3702.75	0.45
1989	10129	11976	5448.40	7278.00	209.90	2595.71	3467.37	0.46
1990	11979	13856	5888.40	7717.40	216.40	2721.07	3566.27	0.46
1991	12378	14015	7337.10	9102.20	223.80	3278.42	4067.11	0.47
1992	13098	14355	9357.40	11699.50	238.10	3930.03	4913.69	0.48
1993	14163	14965	11915.70	16454.40	273.10	4363.13	6025.05	0.49
1994	15515	15312	16179.80	22445.40	339.00	4772.80	6621.06	0.50
1995	16880	15655	19978.50	28679.50	396.90	5033.64	7225.88	0.52
1996	17927	16203	23326.20	33835.00	429.90	5425.96	7870.43	0.53
1997	18432	16547	26988.10	37543.00	441.90	6107.29	8495.81	0.53
1998	18860	16600	30580.50	39004.20	438.40	6975.48	8896.94	0.53
1999	19205	16421	33873.40	41033.60	432.20	7837.44	9494.12	0.54
2000	19823	16219	38714.00	45555.90	434.00	8920.28	10496.75	0.55
2001	20165	16234	44361.60	49512.30	437.00	10151.40	11330.05	0.55
2002	20958	15682	49898.90	53896.80	433.50	11510.70	12432.94	0.57
2003	21605	15927	56004.70	62436.30	438.70	12766.06	14232.10	0.58
2004	22725	16709	64561.30	73904.30	455.80	14164.39	16214.19	0.58
2005	23439	17766	74919.30	87598.10	464.00	16146.40	18878.90	0.57
2006	24143	18894	88554.90	103719.50	471.00	18801.46	22021.13	0.56
2007	24404	20186	111351.90	125831.40	493.60	22559.14	25492.59	0.55
2008	25087	20553	131340.00	149003.40	522.70	25127.22	28506.49	0.55
2009	25857	21080	148038.00	157638.80	519.00	28523.70	30373.56	0.55
2010	26332	21842	173596.00	187383.20	536.10	32381.27	34953.03	0.55
2011	27282	22544	203260.10	220591.60	565.00	35975.24	39042.76	0.55

Sources: Various issues of *China Statistical Yearbook*.

Appendix B: Panel data on 5 variables for 31 provinces over 2003–2010.

Provinces	Year	Region	RealGRPs (Bill. yuan)	Ls (in 10,000)	RealKn (Bill. yuan)	RealKc (Bill. yuan)	RealHC (Bill. yuan)
Beijing	2003	Eastern	2255.60	511.54	7829.13	35.40	116.21
Beijing	2004	Eastern	2473.62	597.05	8963.77	92.47	117.15
Beijing	2005	Eastern	4502.17	631.76	10460.98	137.53	152.98
Beijing	2006	Eastern	5198.09	321.34	12296.57	162.62	195.18
Beijing	2007	Eastern	5992.72	790.50	14048.51	193.79	251.28
Beijing	2008	Eastern	6447.53	851.30	14801.44	205.52	323.05
Beijing	2009	Eastern	7758.98	925.57	17587.26	260.69	353.87
Beijing	2010	Eastern	8674.85	976.82	19725.11	287.39	378.13
Tianjin	2003	Eastern	1112.71	169.35	5593.39	30.11	43.00
Tianjin	2004	Eastern	1221.81	171.10	5651.65	46.28	43.34
Tianjin	2005	Eastern	1450.42	173.06	6013.18	55.93	51.87
Tianjin	2006	Eastern	1632.44	80.69	6475.97	62.72	58.60
Tianjin	2007	Eastern	1819.93	173.60	6965.07	72.95	68.82
Tianjin	2008	Eastern	2023.32	221.16	7464.53	90.87	86.96
Tianjin	2009	Eastern	2878.31	220.16	9233.34	106.46	97.57
Tianjin	2010	Eastern	3468.56	231.41	11023.16	108.71	107.66
Hebei	2003	Eastern	2377.04	782.50	8050.17	37.78	111.98
Hebei	2004	Eastern	2659.50	818.94	8613.02	87.11	112.89
Hebei	2005	Eastern	3177.30	856.58	9719.12	122.62	127.54
Hebei	2006	Eastern	3668.82	283.19	11166.90	158.28	139.76
Hebei	2007	Eastern	4144.35	929.81	12726.71	157.84	156.52
Hebei	2008	Eastern	4512.55	967.78	13945.66	177.17	180.07
Hebei	2009	Eastern	5129.42	1201.41	18277.41	134.63	210.11
Hebei	2010	Eastern	5829.51	1059.51	22884.60	122.12	223.29
Shanxi	2003	Central	852.07	458.68	3553.01	25.61	59.57
Shanxi	2004	Central	942.23	454.46	3652.79	46.68	60.05
Shanxi	2005	Central	1478.66	448.75	3979.81	60.60	62.18
Shanxi	2006	Central	1608.98	184.06	4440.14	78.08	70.22
Shanxi	2007	Central	1799.85	497.07	5009.28	93.72	79.77
Shanxi	2008	Central	1989.53	523.28	5539.61	114.59	99.07
Shanxi	2009	Central	2440.25	544.48	7422.90	153.70	117.69
Shanxi	2010	Central	2792.41	586.66	9232.32	135.11	125.58
Inner Mongolia	2003	Western	756.38	303.92	6883.47	15.93	42.11
Inner Mongolia	2004	Western	840.76	311.73	6841.11	29.44	42.45
Inner Mongolia	2005	Western	1449.20	317.88	7298.02	35.50	47.78
Inner Mongolia	2006	Western	1689.99	127.24	8016.65	42.26	53.88
Inner Mongolia	2007	Western	1932.61	328.59	8923.34	77.79	58.31
Inner Mongolia	2008	Western	2168.56	360.41	9558.53	78.31	72.79
Inner Mongolia	2009	Western	3124.70	391.23	11797.41	94.76	85.50
Inner Mongolia	2010	Western	3444.31	407.47	13920.69	111.00	90.07

(Continued)

Appendix B: (*Continued*)

Provinces	Year	Region	RealGRPs (Bill. yuan)	Ls (in 10,000)	RealKn (Bill. yuan)	RealKc (Bill. yuan)	RealHC (Bill. yuan)
Liaoning	2003	Northeast	2487.85	707.13	6856.44	59.98	97.75
Liaoning	2004	Northeast	2717.93	749.10	7592.13	86.83	98.53
Liaoning	2005	Northeast	3000.29	755.23	8950.00	97.18	114.73
Liaoning	2006	Northeast	3302.15	231.59	10867.24	154.89	126.62
Liaoning	2007	Northeast	3587.98	843.60	13014.85	165.70	146.90
Liaoning	2008	Northeast	3900.59	865.34	15083.95	198.73	172.43
Liaoning	2009	Northeast	4979.75	936.03	19523.46	249.73	194.40
Liaoning	2010	Northeast	5604.96	951.53	24166.15	282.71	217.17
Jilin	2003	Northeast	892.33	338.91	4551.38	31.48	60.40
Jilin	2004	Northeast	979.75	389.64	4574.97	36.82	60.89
Jilin	2005	Northeast	1336.74	373.78	4952.42	47.58	75.11
Jilin	2006	Northeast	1571.37	144.09	5656.57	69.81	84.70
Jilin	2007	Northeast	1800.16	368.77	6539.37	83.34	90.65
Jilin	2008	Northeast	2050.17	404.79	7312.55	89.49	106.44
Jilin	2009	Northeast	2329.81	428.42	9226.21	110.25	122.64
Jilin	2010	Northeast	2545.88	457.50	10798.67	112.71	128.00
Heilongjiang	2003	Northeast	1396.75	477.79	5305.60	64.59	75.84
Heilongjiang	2004	Northeast	1501.39	494.53	5406.70	118.31	76.45
Heilongjiang	2005	Northeast	1754.06	498.41	5747.97	160.38	88.20
Heilongjiang	2006	Northeast	1942.95	198.69	6308.90	204.10	105.62
Heilongjiang	2007	Northeast	2181.09	527.04	6894.04	253.54	117.97
Heilongjiang	2008	Northeast	2396.19	551.55	7309.71	287.63	144.37
Heilongjiang	2009	Northeast	2850.24	562.59	9067.15	323.55	158.78
Heilongjiang	2010	Northeast	3160.01	631.15	10945.62	265.68	181.18
Shanghai	2003	Eastern	3029.45	381.32	7801.67	90.52	120.69
Shanghai	2004	Eastern	3431.58	424.00	8821.49	110.19	121.66
Shanghai	2005	Eastern	4368.96	463.47	10391.92	134.82	152.60
Shanghai	2006	Eastern	4884.57	154.26	11962.81	207.80	176.35
Shanghai	2007	Eastern	5695.72	474.29	13390.72	235.43	201.67
Shanghai	2008	Eastern	6169.19	494.47	14214.08	240.36	234.83
Shanghai	2009	Eastern	7549.06	534.22	16619.84	273.30	273.97
Shanghai	2010	Eastern	8046.93	540.93	17948.11	274.31	295.50
Jiangsu	2003	Eastern	4567.37	1120.79	20634.99	71.56	188.56
Jiangsu	2004	Eastern	5170.15	1218.09	21412.39	108.45	190.08
Jiangsu	2005	Eastern	6135.31	1307.63	23308.61	148.60	233.37
Jiangsu	2006	Eastern	7310.95	289.99	25727.88	178.74	264.57
Jiangsu	2007	Eastern	8548.71	1412.47	28089.89	165.57	291.70
Jiangsu	2008	Eastern	9692.86	1521.62	29747.94	156.80	341.10
Jiangsu	2009	Eastern	11520.37	1608.35	35569.98	232.97	404.43
Jiangsu	2010	Eastern	14018.96	1706.51	40561.44	290.31	447.92

(*Continued*)

Appendix B: (*Continued*)

Provinces	Year	Region	RealGRPs (Bill. yuan)	Ls (in 10,000)	RealKn (Bill. yuan)	RealKc (Bill. yuan)	RealHC (Bill. yuan)
Zhejiang	2003	Eastern	3726.00	991.89	19022.19	59.58	126.27
Zhejiang	2004	Eastern	4217.60	1031.60	19904.39	139.04	127.28
Zhejiang	2005	Eastern	5085.58	1071.84	21653.69	183.62	155.08
Zhejiang	2006	Eastern	5875.27	234.40	23648.72	218.67	184.82
Zhejiang	2007	Eastern	6795.55	1268.59	25169.59	255.37	220.90
Zhejiang	2008	Eastern	7395.18	1304.78	25657.56	270.45	286.35
Zhejiang	2009	Eastern	8384.14	1370.39	29586.14	323.00	339.61
Zhejiang	2010	Eastern	9872.03	1441.29	32543.89	340.92	396.13
Anhui	2003	Central	1458.97	893.33	6264.53	13.62	80.03
Anhui	2004	Central	1646.27	948.48	6646.49	35.74	80.68
Anhui	2005	Central	2068.19	943.75	7512.98	55.71	93.12
Anhui	2006	Central	2302.42	179.67	8728.66	74.33	104.55
Anhui	2007	Central	2555.13	1020.63	10251.40	89.93	113.44
Anhui	2008	Central	2785.41	1017.53	11725.80	104.08	135.82
Anhui	2009	Central	3095.54	1068.39	15248.95	149.14	164.05
Anhui	2010	Central	3431.76	1175.82	18551.92	167.14	176.61
Fujian	2003	Eastern	2046.50	522.62	5674.43	14.65	84.03
Fujian	2004	Eastern	2237.72	551.55	6047.51	82.09	84.71
Fujian	2005	Eastern	2389.66	583.69	6770.66	118.87	91.91
Fujian	2006	Eastern	2770.67	146.23	7892.62	146.73	105.36
Fujian	2007	Eastern	3286.34	644.72	9421.11	162.44	123.05
Fujian	2008	Eastern	3566.66	692.24	10518.31	206.98	146.85
Fujian	2009	Eastern	4267.38	754.55	13115.99	268.87	177.93
Fujian	2010	Eastern	4787.66	728.90	15868.15	291.29	189.20
Jiangxi	2003	Central	1043.08	632.39	7124.29	64.63	47.11
Jiangxi	2004	Central	1143.91	647.86	7308.50	103.38	47.49
Jiangxi	2005	Central	1334.93	675.84	7910.70	131.70	57.21
Jiangxi	2006	Central	1456.42	152.51	8700.54	139.11	66.58
Jiangxi	2007	Central	1558.52	702.95	9337.58	148.00	75.57
Jiangxi	2008	Central	1682.85	709.80	9679.87	119.50	99.92
Jiangxi	2009	Central	2229.06	726.36	11575.03	125.91	116.98
Jiangxi	2010	Central	2554.30	754.79	13237.17	136.55	129.92
Shandong	2003	Eastern	4298.41	1301.29	14592.53	86.05	162.18
Shandong	2004	Eastern	4800.78	1384.80	15742.10	110.15	163.49
Shandong	2005	Eastern	5601.69	1495.65	17879.14	102.21	185.85
Shandong	2006	Eastern	6694.38	380.13	20392.90	107.71	211.02
Shandong	2007	Eastern	7714.79	1580.27	22839.04	106.26	247.24
Shandong	2008	Eastern	8701.17	1659.79	25410.54	111.00	291.53
Shandong	2009	Eastern	9947.40	1714.14	32083.35	137.07	333.88
Shandong	2010	Eastern	11737.24	1810.37	38426.65	137.47	360.04

(*Continued*)

Appendix B: (*Continued*)

Provinces	Year	Region	RealGRPs (Bill. yuan)	Ls (in 10,000)	RealKn (Bill. yuan)	RealKc (Bill. yuan)	RealHC (Bill. yuan)
Henan	2003	Central	2256.95	1120.25	9765.77	97.28	131.91
Henan	2004	Central	2552.76	1199.67	10217.47	120.94	132.97
Henan	2005	Central	3007.81	1271.88	11420.37	144.47	146.11
Henan	2006	Central	3466.23	391.15	13175.11	213.84	154.85
Henan	2007	Central	4010.13	1365.45	15058.82	193.55	171.59
Henan	2008	Central	4423.98	1424.21	16629.35	166.85	198.27
Henan	2009	Central	4818.86	1509.21	20911.45	180.37	228.84
Henan	2010	Central	5407.35	1576.47	24959.59	166.55	244.94
Hubei	2003	Central	2022.78	919.25	8034.41	48.46	110.68
Hubei	2004	Central	2209.05	960.31	8284.90	99.64	111.57
Hubei	2005	Central	2484.71	1020.55	8965.25	113.47	144.67
Hubei	2006	Central	2864.90	249.33	10020.19	147.32	155.52
Hubei	2007	Central	3453.78	1072.27	11233.35	145.91	171.31
Hubei	2008	Central	3849.66	1152.15	12150.76	142.90	201.46
Hubei	2009	Central	4333.85	1219.70	15371.83	158.97	230.20
Hubei	2010	Central	4953.58	1288.04	18541.40	165.79	243.28
Hunan	2003	Central	1958.05	952.23	7358.16	17.60	109.41
Hunan	2004	Central	2157.89	1037.51	7717.68	53.64	110.29
Hunan	2005	Central	2496.51	1056.86	8571.64	85.69	124.09
Hunan	2006	Central	2873.40	233.49	9629.41	112.55	141.26
Hunan	2007	Central	3250.29	1114.63	10782.52	131.61	152.90
Hunan	2008	Central	3538.61	1158.80	11761.96	153.43	179.29
Hunan	2009	Central	4566.88	1216.32	14856.88	194.91	210.49
Hunan	2010	Central	5212.08	1274.97	17555.54	218.33	226.62
Guangdong	2003	Eastern	5225.27	1410.09	16823.58	229.62	246.63
Guangdong	2004	Eastern	5682.26	1519.56	18078.65	411.62	248.62
Guangdong	2005	Eastern	9074.98	1710.35	20085.48	490.09	299.46
Guangdong	2006	Eastern	10427.77	455.91	22653.57	530.56	317.89
Guangdong	2007	Eastern	11953.80	1969.46	25369.23	537.70	362.38
Guangdong	2008	Eastern	12861.03	2093.99	27247.11	533.68	426.40
Guangdong	2009	Eastern	15259.48	2183.94	32921.47	608.78	520.34
Guangdong	2010	Eastern	16948.62	2275.63	37810.30	606.88	598.92
Guangxi	2003	Western	1074.89	765.49	4604.74	89.32	68.11
Guangxi	2004	Western	1174.67	830.21	4807.34	103.54	68.66
Guangxi	2005	Western	1562.46	882.22	5358.42	103.01	77.37
Guangxi	2006	Western	1785.97	169.53	6047.93	101.88	84.93
Guangxi	2007	Western	2034.41	681.09	6877.26	95.71	93.84
Guangxi	2008	Western	2249.26	695.84	7568.94	91.68	113.70
Guangxi	2009	Western	2467.48	719.26	9742.26	142.85	134.60
Guangxi	2010	Western	2768.46	754.66	12184.20	161.83	138.38

(*Continued*)

Appendix B: (*Continued*)

Provinces	Year	Region	RealGRPs (Bill. yuan)	Ls (in 10,000)	RealKn (Bill. yuan)	RealKc (Bill. yuan)	RealHC (Bill. yuan)
Hainan	2003	Eastern	271.44	108.47	1690.02	6.97	16.27
Hainan	2004	Eastern	293.66	116.96	1672.99	16.11	16.40
Hainan	2005	Eastern	353.37	122.47	1734.46	23.96	18.86
Hainan	2006	Eastern	391.67	40.78	1857.82	30.19	21.46
Hainan	2007	Eastern	442.57	148.56	2012.92	31.64	22.40
Hainan	2008	Eastern	492.85	143.96	2182.24	32.99	25.97
Hainan	2009	Eastern	632.77	156.08	2761.84	39.48	29.72
Hainan	2010	Eastern	780.40	170.08	3377.70	40.22	31.68
Chongqing	2003	Western	936.90	532.93	6267.72	23.84	43.73
Chongqing	2004	Western	1013.33	546.18	6586.34	62.07	44.08
Chongqing	2005	Western	1274.47	570.65	7287.28	79.57	54.10
Chongqing	2006	Western	1457.48	108.62	8179.96	94.08	60.79
Chongqing	2007	Western	1553.60	624.42	9136.41	99.53	70.14
Chongqing	2008	Western	1752.44	667.26	9848.19	109.32	87.82
Chongqing	2009	Western	2091.59	703.23	12053.95	121.08	106.65
Chongqing	2010	Western	2357.64	723.73	14123.54	141.59	116.25
Sichuan	2003	Western	2061.65	1273.39	10998.75	127.27	104.21
Sichuan	2004	Western	2379.03	1334.59	11285.44	155.03	105.05
Sichuan	2005	Western	2682.06	1427.79	12268.51	172.60	123.49
Sichuan	2006	Western	3043.09	263.57	13680.21	177.81	139.01
Sichuan	2007	Western	3405.79	1570.17	15149.42	171.28	162.63
Sichuan	2008	Western	3650.94	1613.47	16228.48	184.86	205.30
Sichuan	2009	Western	4394.44	1676.87	21082.57	248.97	243.74
Sichuan	2010	Western	4934.79	1701.92	25216.57	254.33	256.26
Guizhou	2003	Western	478.43	587.00	3618.25	26.70	29.50
Guizhou	2004	Western	522.75	663.66	3664.36	41.10	29.74
Guizhou	2005	Western	740.77	715.32	3883.02	55.48	36.67
Guizhou	2006	Western	845.78	121.75	4156.39	78.02	43.83
Guizhou	2007	Western	1019.65	812.84	4445.23	85.39	53.05
Guizhou	2008	Western	1155.58	834.38	4625.11	92.07	68.08
Guizhou	2009	Western	1594.02	862.35	5587.07	115.05	86.76
Guizhou	2010	Western	1781.53	925.06	6554.66	113.55	91.82
Yunnan	2003	Western	893.16	430.68	5592.48	49.58	74.83
Yunnan	2004	Western	1001.91	471.11	5696.40	76.22	75.43
Yunnan	2005	Western	1295.60	507.03	6215.89	96.22	83.02
Yunnan	2006	Western	1438.41	155.92	6941.58	108.73	91.07
Yunnan	2007	Western	1646.80	614.64	7708.69	120.81	98.00
Yunnan	2008	Western	1870.01	672.69	8196.75	125.83	117.14
Yunnan	2009	Western	2129.78	704.09	10127.21	141.02	129.50
Yunnan	2010	Western	2366.83	759.95	11979.40	134.85	139.41

(*Continued*)

Appendix B: (*Continued*)

Provinces	Year	Region	RealGRPs (Bill. yuan)	Ls (in 10,000)	RealKn (Bill. yuan)	RealKc (Bill. yuan)	RealHC (Bill. yuan)
Tibet	2003	Western	95.89	33.69	1467.77	9.93	4.45
Tibet	2004	Western	106.45	36.24	1423.92	13.05	4.48
Tibet	2005	Western	132.04	41.20	1441.33	20.43	6.23
Tibet	2006	Western	149.04	14.39	1500.83	23.67	7.78
Tibet	2007	Western	167.82	48.95	1536.86	27.07	8.19
Tibet	2008	Western	184.34	54.38	1504.05	25.10	10.43
Tibet	2009	Western	203.59	58.73	1659.31	25.61	14.12
Tibet	2010	Western	224.89	62.66	1741.17	25.87	18.04
Shaanxi	2003	Western	944.99	598.92	6829.58	51.41	60.12
Shaanxi	2004	Western	1031.50	594.32	6959.25	76.00	60.61
Shaanxi	2005	Western	1314.79	578.16	7533.14	95.76	74.32
Shaanxi	2006	Western	1485.40	187.39	8345.86	109.25	86.18
Shaanxi	2007	Western	1696.32	608.27	9340.56	133.21	101.85
Shaanxi	2008	Western	1893.05	632.63	10301.43	119.34	137.04
Shaanxi	2009	Western	2657.34	609.34	13002.78	132.69	159.77
Shaanxi	2010	Western	3018.72	608.19	15631.79	151.47	178.96
Gansu	2003	Western	460.37	356.69	3130.30	13.71	34.71
Gansu	2004	Western	499.87	366.20	3147.10	30.39	34.99
Gansu	2005	Western	744.43	392.30	3343.24	35.69	39.68
Gansu	2006	Western	838.43	107.84	3540.39	42.10	48.20
Gansu	2007	Western	921.76	427.94	3733.22	43.78	53.74
Gansu	2008	Western	1042.14	455.72	3877.31	39.69	69.50
Gansu	2009	Western	1152.34	462.51	4615.90	44.11	83.64
Gansu	2010	Western	1257.34	484.11	5358.26	47.74	88.00
Qinghai	2003	Western	159.80	76.41	1367.06	14.73	7.98
Qinghai	2004	Western	174.07	85.00	1332.93	13.43	8.04
Qinghai	2005	Western	201.74	89.57	1368.34	10.66	9.72
Qinghai	2006	Western	224.27	26.63	1425.05	11.14	10.78
Qinghai	2007	Western	251.01	96.92	1468.69	10.26	12.87
Qinghai	2008	Western	274.07	94.53	1471.70	8.90	16.65
Qinghai	2009	Western	336.88	100.11	1717.18	8.76	19.04
Qinghai	2010	Western	385.33	104.31	1937.33	7.78	19.21
Ningxia	2003	Western	137.84	76.87	1752.84	9.24	9.14
Ningxia	2004	Western	149.95	85.51	1745.22	14.23	9.21
Ningxia	2005	Western	239.01	87.79	1811.14	16.71	11.03
Ningxia	2006	Western	262.09	30.11	1906.30	16.86	12.96
Ningxia	2007	Western	301.73	97.84	1951.07	16.23	14.92
Ningxia	2008	Western	333.43	91.36	1957.96	16.56	19.74
Ningxia	2009	Western	476.52	112.98	2250.05	22.51	22.96
Ningxia	2010	Western	574.83	111.47	2573.72	27.34	23.56

(*Continued*)

Appendix B: (*Continued*)

Provinces	Year	Region	RealGRPs (Bill. yuan)	Ls (in 10,000)	RealKn (Bill. yuan)	RealKc (Bill. yuan)	RealHC (Bill. yuan)
Xinjiang	2003	Western	667.87	228.39	5077.91	92.16	45.99
Xinjiang	2004	Western	717.42	242.69	5030.28	94.18	46.36
Xinjiang	2005	Western	878.73	255.42	5242.52	101.22	54.86
Xinjiang	2006	Western	985.59	119.26	5493.19	104.66	61.30
Xinjiang	2007	Western	1108.21	275.05	5597.87	105.79	70.50
Xinjiang	2008	Western	1196.48	282.32	5572.98	109.51	94.92
Xinjiang	2009	Western	1342.07	287.18	6375.28	115.13	108.24
Xinjiang	2010	Western	1445.71	296.64	6995.26	109.85	113.52

Source: Various issues of *China Statistical Yearbook*.

Part III

Structural and Institutional Analysis of Contemporary India's Growth and Development

6. Compressed Capitalism and the Challenges for Inclusive Development in India

*Anthony P. D'Costa**

1. Introduction

Since the European enlightenment era, the notion of egalitarianism in the West and beyond has become entrenched. Beginning with the nobility and proprietary classes and upcoming bourgeoisie, the notion has gradually encompassed middle classes and dominant social groups before spreading out selectively to other ethnic minorities as part of a wider political democratic process. In tandem, capitalism as an expanding economic system, which rested on the freedom of capital in organizing production and consumption, contributed to the upward mobility of selective social groups. However, the underpinning liberal political philosophy was a major leveler of social differences, even if status as an intrinsic social marker and the power that flowed from it did not completely disappear even in the West. In the post-colonial (non-Western) world, egalitarianism has been far more difficult to achieve politically, socially and economically, although the vocabulary of equality has been politically internalized in many former colonies. Some East Asian countries (and China, until recently) had attained a fair degree of income and social equality, but politically, most of them remained illiberal or outright authoritarian.

In India, the weight of history, cultural legacies, ethnic diversity and regional differences have stubbornly worked against both the aspirations of Indians to be treated equally and state efforts to create a more inclusive society. The Indian political leadership has always been acutely aware of

*adcosta@unimelb.edu.au

the deeply ingrained hierarchical caste system in India.[1] Granted, the task of creating a just, egalitarian society remains elusive in most places, just as sustaining those that were has become difficult today under globalization even in liberal, economically advanced capitalist countries. Worsening income distribution in the US since the end of the golden age in the 1970s is one such example. However, the notion of "inclusive" development is widely accepted by development scholars and, if more rhetorically and less instrumentally, by both multilateral and Indian development establishments and politicians. The issue has become all the more important as India experiences unprecedented high economic growth rates with favorable predictions. The question is whether such high growth is leading to broader socio-economic transformation. To put it differently, is such growth equitable? If not, what are some of the political-economic underpinnings for the inability to translate growth into meaningful development?

There is, of course, a fundamental difference between equality and inclusive development.[2] The former is more of an outcome, while the latter is more of a process which presumably leads to the former. Compounding the matter, there are multiple meanings associated with inclusive development such as "national integration," "social security provisioning" and tackling "poverty, inequality, and growth" (Subramanian, 2011, p. 69). There are other forms of exclusive development (the negation of inclusiveness) or social exclusion (Chronic Poverty Research Centre, 2008, p. 39) such as slum clearance to beautify cities (Kundu and Samanta, 2011).

The dominant discourse is that growth is necessary and that such growth will ultimately lift all boats as long as the fetters to the smooth operation of market forces are removed. There is no doubt that growth under certain conditions is necessary for an impoverished country such as India. In practical terms, deregulation creates more space for capital accumulation and higher growth. But there is no guarantee that this growth will be shared since the reward system under capitalist markets tends to favor winners and not losers. Worse, there is an unstated false assumption that

---

[1] K. N. Raj, one of India's finest intellectuals, had already mainstreamed 'inclusive' development soon after India's independence (see Kannan, 2011).
[2] There is also a difference between hierarchy (stratification) and inequality (Gupta, 1993, p. 9). Theoretically, social differentiation need not mean inequality. However, in India, differences are celebrated and tolerated in some spheres. But in the domains of economics, politics and society, difference is largely about status and power. Hence, hierarchy or stratification is about inequality.

economic freedom equates social leveling and thus by extension denies the existence of the structures of social, political, and economic domination. A stronger version of the argument would be that growth rates are likely to sweep away even long-standing structures since economic freedom would also be integral to a liberal socio-political system.

I would argue that we cannot make such assumptions about the relationship between economic growth and social leveling. There are strong social structures of domination even in advanced capitalist countries, let alone in late industrializing peripheral economies. Even if we accept longer-term outcomes of structures gradually dissolving due to enlightened government policy and genuine democratic upsurges, I would argue that there are forces of global capitalism, which I label 'compressed capitalism,' that generate new mechanisms of unshared growth, which make even relentless and systematic countervailing interventions ineffective.[3]

The purpose of this chapter is to relate contemporary capitalism unfolding in India to the various forms of exclusionary social and economic differentiation underway due to the specific nature of contemporary capitalism. The latter is captured from observable data on the economic, social, and political standing of various minority groups (see Mohanty, 2011, pp. 5–18), particularly in the areas of employment and well-being (Balakrishnan, 2011, p. 236).[4] Contemporary capitalism in India is theorized to take a compressed form, in which the conventional dual economic structure is accentuated to create a three-legged structure of capitalism comprising primitive accumulation, state-led capitalist maturity and petty commodity production. These have been discussed more fully elsewhere (D'Costa, 2013) and are briefly presented in Section 2. The argument is not that compressed capitalism *per se* is responsible for exclusion but rather it reinforces pre-existing structures of inequality through differential rewards to factors of production and social groups associated with those factors. As shown by Saith (2011), inequality is a contextual feature of global capitalism, exacerbated by the untrammeled expansion of finance capital. Discussing inclusive development compels the investigation into who are the poor and what are some of the social mechanisms by which they remain poor and marginalized

---

[3]This concept has been developed in D'Costa (2013).
[4]The word 'inclusive' is politically laden and has been interpreted as depoliticizing the demands for social justice and equity. However, human dignity and some semblance of social equality as part of such development are likely to enhance politicization rather than diminish it.

relative to dominant groups even with macroeconomic growth and development (see Chronic Poverty Research Centre, 2008, pp. 73–74). Two obvious questions that come up for discussion: If inclusive development is politically and socially internalized by the state and put into practice in India, what has been the result thus far? And, if the record illustrates the failure of inclusive development, what might be some of the key proximate causes?

I begin with the second question first to briefly underscore the built-in structural processes under compressed capitalism operating at the local/national and global levels that render the notion of "inclusive" development elusive. This chapter presents some of the empirical dimensions of and proximate causes of the employment and education status of underprivileged groups and advances some of the reasons why exclusivity remains a persistent feature of contemporary India's high-growth process even as the government attempts to alter the economic and social imbalances. For some of the empirical details, I rely on two important Government of India reports: "The Challenge of Employment in India: An Informal Economy Perspective" (2009) produced by the National Commission for Enterprises in the Unorganized Sector (NCEUS), and "Social, Economic and Educational Status of the Muslim Community in India" (2006) by a Prime Minister's High Level Committee (PMHLC).[5] These two reports admit the failure of the Indian state to foster inclusive development and illustrate its willingness to seek solutions for an intractably difficult problem: employment generation to promote the economic and social mobility of marginalized social groups.

In Section 2, I develop a framework to show why inclusive development in India is difficult, bringing in not only the economic but also social and political dimensions of exclusion. Inclusive development is contextualized by examining briefly how global capitalism operates in developing India. I call it compressed capitalism (defined below), which structurally offers differential opportunities for the highly skilled and educated higher castes and classes compared to less-skilled and educated lower-caste and other minorities and imposes varied constraints on advanced skill-using and labor-intensive sectors when it comes to employment and social mobility. One result of these dynamics is the reinforcement of pre-existing forms of social, economic, and political inequality, albeit unevenly. In Section 3, I present some empirical details of exclusionary tendencies in two parts. The first

---

[5]I thank Sushil Khanna for directing me to the NCEUS report on the unorganized sector and Amiya Bagchi for other pertinent literature on inclusive development.

examines the IT industry and the second the informal sector to illustrate how contemporary capitalism pulls in relatively more high-skilled workers and thereby excludes the vast majority of unskilled and low-skilled workers who are absorbed by the *expanding* unorganized sector with small units.[6] Both discussions bring out the economic and social profile of marginalized populations known as scheduled castes (SC), scheduled tribes (ST), and OBCs, as well as Muslims in India.[7] Both the development of the IT industry and the concomitant expanding unorganized sector are integral to the dynamics of compressed capitalism in India and they both reflect and reinforce the exclusionary tendencies by creating a vast pool of unskilled, unorganized workers while absorbing a small share of the workforce in high-skill activities commensurate with global demand.

2. Compressed Capitalism and Inclusive Development

India has been undergoing rapid economic and social change for several decades. From an economic point of view, there have been two major turning points: 1947, the year of Indian independence, and 1991, the year of a major policy overhaul in favor of market forces. Both turning points mark the beginning of comparatively limited yet historically impressive social development due to formal planning for development and to trickledown effects via new market opportunities. Both phases, after the turning points, have had their class biases and thus, as discussed below, have not contributed substantially to inclusive development, although initially India did experience some degree of equality. From a political and social standpoint, 1947 is also an important marker. Indian independence guaranteed every citizen's right to vote, and thus created the political conditions for economic and social uplift of the poor and the downtrodden. However, it is difficult to identify any specific turning point thereafter, if we consider social change more broadly.

Social change has been an ongoing process of modernization, sometimes marked by particular social policy decisions and at other times by political

---

[6]See Bagchi (2007a) on the process of exclusion due to financial development.

[7]There are of course other minorities such as Sikhs and Christians, depending on what kind of categories are used. However, these minorities are not necessarily marginalized in the same way as the four aforesaid groups.

turns aimed favorably at the poor. For example, the *garibi hatao* (eradicate poverty) program by Indira Gandhi in 1971 was one such instance. However, it accomplished little for the poor other than to embolden them politically and ensure Mrs. Gandhi's election victory.[8] The political mobilization of the rural and urban poor, however, did create some political space, pushing some forms of inclusive development and social justice. One area of inclusive development has been the implementation of the Mandal Commission's report in 1990, a decade after its completion, which extended reservations of government jobs and placement in state colleges and universities to OBCs, a right already given to SCs and STs. The fact that it took a decade before the recommendations of the report were implemented, and they were met with violent responses by the middle and upper classes in the country, reflect the often politically explosive nature of inclusive development in the Indian context. Coincidentally, the comprehensive economic reforms of 1991 creating new economic spaces unwittingly coincided with the unrelated selective social reforms of 1990.

It is clear that class difference is not the only reason for social conflicts: caste still remains a uniquely Indian institution around which many of the social battles are fought. It is also a category fraught with difficulties since castes in India have been fluid, influenced by self-claimed identities, often shifting ones, government decrees and social recognition by peer and dominant groups. Nevertheless, at some broad level, caste identities have become hardened by official policy and the benefits extended; as a result, in some perverse way, both caste and class seem to have reinforced social and economic stratification simultaneously, with lower income and caste groups jostling with the upper income and caste groups for access to income, employment, education and security. Admittedly, such strict correspondence between class and caste might seem simplistic. But there is evidence to suggest that higher castes have generally done better economically than lower castes, suggesting mechanisms for translating social and political position into economic power. Furthermore, gender and ethnicity are two other dimensions that add to the complexity of social and economic stratification and thus inclusiveness.[9] In India, the place of Muslims, a large

---

[8]Prime Minister Indira Gandhi's 1969 bank nationalization also created some space for rural residents by ensuring the establishment of rural bank branches of public sector banks.

[9]I leave gender and child labor issues out of my discussion in this chapter.

but geographically scattered minority with a few identifiable urban pockets, is also problematic for historical, social and regional-political reasons. But any discussion of inclusive development in India, must include Muslims as well as SC, ST and OBCs, since how well these subordinate and dominated groups fare today will be an indication of how inclusive the process of development has been thus far in India.

In this chapter, I will discuss four points that are germane to the discussion of inclusive development under compressed capitalism. First, the lack of inclusive development is due to endogenous processes such as the relative positioning of each class and caste group *vis-à-vis* others in the wider society. Second, inclusiveness is a contentious process since it tends to upset the status quo by redistributing resources and power. Third, there are severe pre-existing social and economic differences that make the task of achieving inclusive development difficult, if not impossible, as it requires intergenerational transfer of financial, educational, and other endowments. Fourth, in combination, the first and third points suggest that inclusive development is also structurally determined by contemporary capitalist dynamics in which India is positioned. Since capitalism is a worldwide system, it suggests contrary to the first point, that internal forces are to blame, exogenous processes interact with endogenous pre-existing inequalities to reinforce exclusive development.

Inclusive development is a challenge under economic reforms — not because it does not create new opportunities but rather because it does. By ushering in capitalist market forces in a big way, barriers to accumulation at home are cleared and doors to and for the world economy are opened. Indian businesses are now subject to the competitive pressures of the global economy. This means, among other things, that costs must be controlled, new technologies adopted to be internationally competitive, rate of investments raised for increased productivity and access to raw materials and the supply of skilled labor ensured through the expansion of higher education to meet growing demand. All these activities in a global context tend to promote capital-intensive industrialization and generate demand for high-skilled workers. When viewed in the context of compressed capitalism, which is the coexistence of a select few advanced sectors and an expansive low-technology, low-wage informal sector (a form of exacerbated dualism), the chances of being included for the poor and marginalized can be low.

I have argued elsewhere (D'Costa, 2013) that late industrialization is a process where capitalism is 'compressed.' By this, I mean that the various phases of historical capitalism are experienced simultaneously in countries such as India. There are three integrated parts to this compression: first, primitive accumulation (the recent rapidity of the alienation of land from the peasantry); second, capitalist maturity (a process by which local/national capitalists, with the help of the state and foreign capital, have matured technologically and commercially) and third, petty commodity production (the informal, unorganized sectors with low wages) remains a persistent feature in spite of high growth due to capital intensive production, limiting formal employment and primitive accumulation forcing workers off the land. These three legs of accumulation provide the dynamism of growth in India in an interdependent, reinforcing way. The state socializes costs for private accumulation, contributing to capitalist maturity and competitiveness, while primitive accumulation, which is really a pre-historic stage of capitalism completed more than a century ago in the now advanced capitalist economies (Bose, 1988) continues sustaining petty commodity production.

High growth is consistent with such an economic structure as the labor-intensive sector supports the capital-intensive sector in the overall capital accumulation process, without itself being formalized. However, the displacement by dispossession (loss of land) under primitive accumulation and the permanency of petty commodity producers also pull back the development potential of these countries because of low income and extensive forms of precarious employment in the informal sector. In the social context of class, caste, and cadre exploitation (as in China), the effects of compressed capitalism on minorities can at best be neutral and at worst highly polarizing for large numbers of rural residents and migrants. Given the pre-existing inequality among classes, castes and regions, economic reforms such as deregulation and liberalization are likely to not only create new accumulation opportunities but also exacerbate inequality. This is because of the two interrelated developments: increasing demand for too few high-skilled workers linked to the formal global capitalist sector, while labor displacement and dispossession in the countryside expands the number of low-skilled workers for the informal sector. Figure 1 presents the key processes underlying compressed capitalism.

There are multiple implications for inclusive development under compressed capitalism, as outlined below.

First, cost reductions suggest the systematic pressure to keep wages down. Even if high economic growth is likely to pull wages in the opposite direction, labor abundance and the persistence of petty commodity production (PCP), for reasons discussed below, keep wages low.

Figure 1: Compressed capitalism in action.

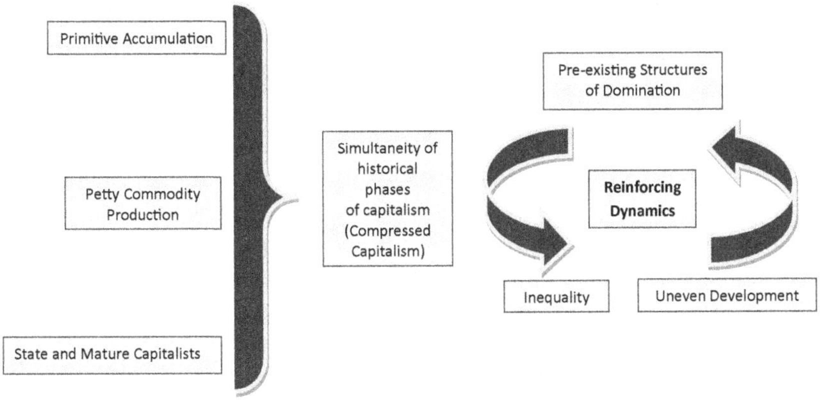

Second, to be internationally competitive, firms must continue to invest in new technologies, thus contributing to the capital intensity and automation of production. Also, international outsourcing contributes to the demand for higher skilled workers, even though the demand for higher skilled professionals is not large enough to be significant in the generation of decent jobs (Mazumdar and Sarkar, 2008, p. 9). Inequality under compressed capitalism is also inevitable, as illustrated by Apple's sophisticated production system using subcontracting arrangements with Taiwanese firms in China. On the one hand, Chinese labor is exploited through low wages and harsh working conditions, and on the other, Apple charges high prices to affluent consumers worldwide (Barrientos, 2008, p. 981; Wingfield, 2012, Duhigg and Barboza, 2012). Globalization also means skill-intensive goods are imported, which reduces the demand for low-skill services thus the demand for low-skill labor. Capitalists also hedge against production disruption by maintaining a small elite workforce at high wages, who are also productive (Mazumdar and Sarkar, 2008, p. 14). The net impact is relative reduction in the demand for low-skill wage workers, even as the demand for high-skill jobs remains small as a whole.

Third, compressed capitalism, when juxtaposed with pre-existing inequality in income, education and social position, marginalizes those who are already on the margins of society. Middle class bias inherent in tertiary education restricts access of lower castes and classes to tertiary education, especially technical education and thus limits their entry into high-wage labor markets (see Bhushan, 2008, p. 299). Hence, groups with better education, skills, income and social position are better able to capture economic growth.

As argued by Bardhan (2010, pp. 95–103), the source of inequality is generally not globalization: rather, it is lack of investments in infrastructure, restricted access to education and poor distribution of land.[10] However, as the discussion above indicates, contemporary global capitalism cannot be altogether a disconnected process that generates exclusive development. After all, some of the most egalitarian societies such as Japan, South Korea and China are experiencing worsening inequality (see D'Costa, 2012), partly because of their increasing integration with the world economy and consequent disruptive effects on labor markets. Similarly, rising agricultural prices, partly due to subsidies in the advanced capitalist countries, and increasing luxury food production illustrate new sources of global inequality (Rao, 2009, pp. 1279, 1281). In India, the lack of inclusive development is a result of endogenous structures of pre-existing inequality, which is reinforced by the structural imperatives of global capitalism today, mainly by the increased power of capital (Banerjee, 2005).

3.   India's Record of Inclusive Development

In this section, I present the structure and pattern of, for lack of a better term, exclusive development. The discussion is divided into three parts. First, I present briefly the Indian information technology (IT) sector, India's glamorous high-growth sector, to illustrate the mechanisms behind its exclusivity. This discussion largely relies on D'Costa (2011a), which brings out the significance of pre-existing inequality as a factor for entry into the IT workforce, demonstrating that there are many social groups that cannot access the necessary education to join the industry. The premise is that the IT sector is a high-wage, white-collar professional domain to which many Indians aspire to join but few are actually able to. Second, I present empirical materials on the scale and scope of the informal sector, highlighting the fact that the bulk of India's recent employment has been in this precarious low-wage sector. Here I also indicate some of the reasons for the persistence of this petty commodity production sector as an integral

---

[10]Elsewhere, Bardhan, Bowles and Wallerstein (2006) go further, optimistically arguing that freer mobility of resources (globalization) would bring about greater equality.

part of contemporary (compressed) capitalism in India.[11] Theoretically, it is
linked to the urban informal sector through rural–urban migration. Third,
I present additional evidence on the workings of exclusive development in
India by focusing on the social and economic plight of Muslims, SC and
ST and OBC in India. The empirical analysis underscores not only the
magnitude of the problem but also highlights the difficulties of inclusive
development in a global setting.

3.1. High-growth IT and middle class inclusion

India's recent high rate of economic growth has gone hand in hand with
heightened social differentiation especially in class terms. A household survey by the National Council of Applied Economic Research (NCAER) shows
that high-income households grew much faster than low-income households. In fact, the higher the household income, the faster their numbers
expanded compared to lower-income households (see D'Costa and Bagchi,
2012). Households earning more than Rs. 5 million annual income increased
by almost 25% a year between 1995–1996 and 2001–2002 compared to all
other household groups earning less than Rs. 5 million. The same survey,
when extrapolated, indicated even faster growth of the high-income groups
in recent years. This development is consistent with the view, as posited
earlier, that most growth has benefited the better-off economic classes.
While a number of sectors expanded after the economic reforms of 1991
had settled in, the most spectacular growth has been in the IT industry
(Figure 2). The IT sector has grown from 1.2% of GDP in 1998 to 6.4% in
fiscal year 2011.[12] The share of IT exports to total exports increased from
4% to 26% during the same period. India exported over 67% of IT sector
output in the last few years and a third of India's total exports comprised IT
services.

Structurally India's high-growth IT sector is consistent with compressed capitalism due to the role of the state in promoting skill-driven
technologically advanced sectors, including IT. However, the sector's inability to absorb large numbers of people is also compatible with compressed
capitalism since the sector relies on the supply of technical graduates, which

---

[11]Based on D'Costa (2013), primitive accumulation in the countryside and in mining
areas is assumed and not discussed here.

[12]Nasscom Indian IT-BPO Industry. See http://www.nasscom.in/indian-itbpo-industry
[accessed on 10 October 2011].

Figure 2: India IT growth in recent years.

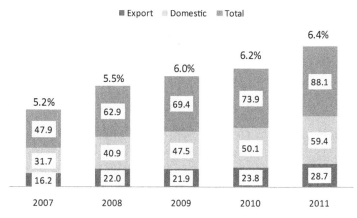

Source: NASSCOM.

at the minimum means a college degree beyond high school. The middle class bias is evident since access to tertiary technical education depends on socio-economic status determined by schooling, family status and income. The relative scarcity of college and university seats makes them all the more coveted and contentious. This middle class bias, while lifting the upwardly mobile classes, tends to leave behind large numbers of uneducated and unskilled people.

According to the National Association of Software and Services Companies (NASSCOM), the industry lobby, about 2.5 million jobs have been created by the IT sector and indirectly another 8 million have been created to support the sector.[13] While these numbers are respectable, their share of total employment is only 2.4% (based on 2004–2005 total employment of 455.7 million) (see Table 1). Direct employment is barely 0.5% of total employment. A simple calculation shows that revenue per employee in the IT industry is US$35,240 (US$88.1 billion generated by 2.5 million employees). This is comparable to OECD per capita income, a level only a handful of Indian households earn.

Direct employment in the IT industry demands college graduates. However, pre-existing inequality imposes entry barriers, especially because IT is education and skill driven (Basu, 2006, p. 1364). The interlocking nature of poverty linking low-caste standing and illiteracy (Reed, 2008; Thorat and Newman, 2010; UNDP, 2006) structurally disadvantages the

---

[13] *Ibid.*

Table 1: Employment and workforce by sectors, 2009–2010.

	Numbers in millions	in %
Total population	1093.0	
Total workers	457.9	100
Agriculture and allied activities	258.7	56.5
Manufacturing	**55.9**	**12.2**
Construction	26.0	5.7
Services	105.8	23.1
Workers in organized sector, 2007	27.2	5.9
Workers in factory sector, 2007–2008	**10.4**	**2.3**
Total jobs in the IT sector, 2008–2009	2.2	0.5

Source: Key Indicators of Employment and Unemployment in India 2009–2010, National Sample Survey Organization. Annual Survey of Industries for Workers in factory sector, from Thomas (2011 conference presentation). Sundaram (2007) based on NSS 61st round; See Table 1 for estimate of population and Table 10 for estimates of workers by sector.

poor (D'Costa, 2003) in seeking higher education. As can be seen from Table 2, literacy rates as well as college graduates vary by socio-religious groups and caste standing. While at lower age groups, literacy rates do not vary much by social groups, they diverge substantially at higher age groups. For example, for age group 23 years and above, OBCs, SCs and STs and Muslims have literacy rates of 50.6%, 36.5% and 46.1% respectively, compared to 74% for the general category of Hindus (generally middle and upper castes). For graduates, the main minority groups have even smaller shares than the general Hindu category, ranging from roughly one-third for OBCs to nearly one sixth for the SC/ST category of the general Hindu category.[14] Disaggregating further, the share of SC/ST students combined in technical education did not vary much and reached 10% of total between 1986–1987 and 2002–2003 (D'Costa, 2011a, p. 246). In recent years, with the expansion of the elite state-owned technical institutes, known as IITs, the share of SC and ST students together was almost 16%.[15]

---

[14]The place of women from underprivileged groups, given both the overt as well as structural discrimination by various classes and socio-religious communities, is also likely to be worse.

[15]Indiastat.com 2011 [accessed on 15 October 2011]. There is no disaggregated data for Muslim enrolment in technical education. This is perhaps due to the absence of state-mandated reservations for the community.

Table 2: Literates and graduates as proportion of population by age groups, 2004–2005.

Age groups	Literates				
	Hindus			Muslims	Other minorities
	General	OBC	SCs/STs		
6–13 years	90.2	80.8	74.7	74.6	88.5
14–15 years	95.7	87.5	80.0	79.5	91.9
16–17 years	95.0	85.2	78.6	75.5	91.3
18–22 years	91.4	76.9	65.0	70.5	85.8
23 years and above	74.0	50.6	36.5	46.1	67.0
Total	80.5	63.4	52.7	59.9	75.2
	Graduates				
20–30 years	18.6	6.5	3.3	4.5	11.6
30–40 years	16.8	4.6	2.3	3.3	9.2
40–50 years	14.6	3.2	1.5	2.8	8.1
51 years and above	9.8	1.9	0.9	2.1	5.7
Total	15.3	4.4	2.2	3.4	8.9

Source: Prime Minister's High Level Committee (PMHLC, 2006, pp. 54, 67).

India's high growth is partly due to the IT industry. However, when it comes to employment, the sector demands a very specific type of workforce that only a small segment of the population can fulfill. This is a classic form of exclusive development since the benefits of growth accrue to a small minority even as the volume of business continues to expand. The inability to include minorities in this sector is mainly due to social-structural reasons of caste standing, poverty, lack of access to education, and the limited number of seats available in elite government educational institutions. However, even if wider access to technical education were possible in the near future, the demand for such education might not materialize if India continues to rely so heavily on the US for nearly 65% of its software service output.[16]

3.2. Low employment growth and the persistence of the informal sector

One of the troubling aspects of compressed capitalism is the co-existence of small advanced industries along with a vast informal sector. Informal enterprises in the Indian case are defined as: lacking regularity of employment,

---

[16]The shortcomings of relying excessively on exports in a single market can be found in D'Costa (2004, 2009, 2011a).

income security, social security, decent conditions of work and legally unprotected enterprises and which have less than 10 workers (see National Commission for Enterprises in the Unorganised Sector (NCEUS), 2009, pp. 7, iv). The expectation is that, with sustained economic growth, the demand for labor would push wages up and structurally alter the economy toward increasing capital-intensive formal sectors with increasing diversity. Such a transition in India has been limited and truncated in that, as we shall see below, India is experiencing rising capital intensity in the formal sector, even as the informal sector expands. The capital output ratio far outstrips labor productivity since the 1990s (Das, 2008, p. 123). Inclusive development is thus structurally constrained due to limited employment growth. Between 1987–1988 and 2001–2002, the census data show that the average number of employees in micro, small, and medium enterprises fell from 6.3 to 4.6, while the number of small units increased substantially (Das, 2008, p. 120).

The paradox of high rates of economic growth and limited expansion of 'decent' jobs is therefore not a surprise (Table 3). First, employment growth was 2.03% over the 1983/84–1993/94 period compared to 1.85% between 1993/94–2004/05 (NCEUS, 2009, p. 9). Second, the informal or unorganized sector absorbed most workers (86% in 2004–2005) with only 6% and 7% by the formal sector in 1999–2000 and 2004–2005, respectively (NCEUS, 2009, p. 13, also Table 3). If unorganized workers in the formal sector are not included in the formal sector figures, the share of employment in the informal sector increases to 93%. Agriculture accounted for 64% of the unorganized workers, implying a long uphill task of formalizing economic activities in India.

There are several reasons for the persistence of the informal sector. One is labor abundance, fuelled by high rural fertility rates, and ongoing rural to urban migration due to primitive accumulation, supplying workers to the informal sector. In the absence of dramatic productivity increases, labor abundance remains a structural feature of the countryside. However, as noted, primitive accumulation combined with an agrarian crisis in India also contribute to the urban informal sector.[17] The other reason for the growth

---

[17] There are multiple causes of the agrarian crisis in India, and it is not easy to separate out the different factors. However, one of the contributing factors, which may leave a deep impact, is the large-scale transformation of tribal and agricultural lands for mining and industrial purposes. The setting up of factories and special economic zones, as in China, is a form of contemporary primitive accumulation, which is an integral part of what I call compressed capitalism (see D'Costa, 2013; also Mohanty, 2011, pp. 7–8, 14–15; Ramakumar, 2010).

Table 3: Relationship between sector and type of employment (UPSS) [all workers 1999–2000 and 2004–2005].

Formal/informal sector	Total employment (millions) and employment share by Category (%)		
	Informal/ unorganized worker	Formal/ unorganized worker	Total
	1999–2000		
Informal/unorganized sector	339.7 [93.6%]	1.8 (5.4%)	341.5 (100.0%) [86.2%]
Formal/organized sector	23.1 [6.4%]	31.8 (94.6%)	54.9 (100.0%) [13.8%]
Total	362.8 (100.0%)	33.6 (100.0%)	396.4 (100.0%)
	2004–2005		
Informal/unorganized sector	391.8 [93.1%]	1.4 (4.0%)	393.2 (100.0) [86.3%]
Formal/organized sector	28.9 [6.9%]	33.7 (96.0%)	62.6 (100.0) [13.7%]
Total	420.7 (100.0%)	35.0 (100.0%)	455.7 (100.0)

Note: NSSO 55th and 61st Round Survey on Employment-Unemployment, computed. UPSS = Usual Principal and Subsidiary Status.
Source: National Commission for Enterprises in the Unorganised Sector (NCEUS, 2009, p. 13).

in the urban informal sector is the inability of the Indian corporations to create labor-absorbing industries on a large scale as China has done on the export front. India's agriculture continues to employ over 50% of India's total workforce, which structurally keeps wages low, contains cost of production, and contributes additional workers to the urban informal sector.

As discussed earlier, high-growth sectors such as IT have not been adequate drivers of job growth. Other formal economic enterprises in the private and public sectors also have been unable to generate jobs in recent years (Table 4). This is counterintuitive, since high growth rates would suggest otherwise. Not only have formal sector jobs declined in absolute terms, from 27.4 million in 1993–1994 to 26.5 million in 2004–2005, but both the private and public sectors have fewer employees on their rolls today (Table 4). Schedule castes tend to suffer more as they depend on the state sector for the better jobs (Jodhka, 2011, p. 57). While one can

Table 4: Comparative statistics of formal sector workers and formal workers in the non-agricultural sector.[a]

Source	Number of workers (millions) and percentage share in total workforce		
	1993–1994	1999–2000	2004–2005
Private sector	7.93 (2.13)	8.65 (2.18)	8.45 (1.85)
Government/public sector	19.45 (5.22)	19.31 (4.87)	18.01 (3.95)
Public and private sector	27.38 (7.35)	27.96 (7.05)	26.46 (5.81)
Total workforce (UPSS)	372.42 (100.0)	396.39 (100.0)	455.70 (100.0)

[a]Based on Directorate General of Employment & Training (DGET) Ministry of Labour & Employment, Government of India and NCEUS estimates.
Note: Total workforce estimates are based on NSS Employment-Unemployment Surveys in the respective years and include informal sector workers.
Source: National Commission for Enterprises in the Unorganised Sector (NCEUS, 2009, p. 15).

hypothesize that neoliberal reforms impose job cuts on the public sector, it is unusual that the private sector would be shedding jobs despite high economic growth. Moreover, the number of formal sector jobs remains a small fraction of the workforce — 8.5 million for the private sector and 18 million for the public sector. The private sector employs more than twice the number of people as the public sector. This reflects the importance of the state in continuing to maintain high-value formal sector jobs in the country. However, from an employment point of view, the process of inclusive development by the organized sector — both private and public — is seriously wanting, contributing less than 6% of total employment. With weak employment growth, a good part of new employment involves contract and casual employment and self-employment or precarious employment (see Roy, 2008, pp. 212–214).[18] Consequently, the average daily earning of workers in the non-agricultural sector grew slowly relative to economic growth. For example, while GDP grew by 7.5% during 1993–1994/2004–2005, urban wages for both male and female and both regular and casual workers grew by less than 2% (NCEUS, 2009, p. 10).

---

[18]According to one estimate for 2004–2005, self-employment was 56% and casual employment 33%, which together represent 89% of all workers (Ghose, 2011, p. 117).

These broad patterns of economic growth and employment suggest lack of inclusive development, but they do not reveal how different socio-economic groups are doing. It has been argued that the better-off classes (upper and middle-income groups) have captured most of India's high growth, evident by the faster growth of high-income households compared to lower income ones. As shown in the case of the IT industry, the middle class bias is intrinsic in the workings of the narrow high-wage employment market. The task is to disaggregate the other classes and minorities such as SCs, STs, OBCs and Muslims to see how they are doing when it comes to upward mobility through education. Any discussion of inclusive development in India must account for their well-being in the wider employment and education sphere.

3.3. *Growth and inclusive development of minorities*

Officially, three social groups in India receive state protection through a variety of transfer programs and reservations policies — SCs, STs, and OBCs. Muslims are a religious minority and hence are not subject to special programs, unless identified under official categories such as OBC. Targeting particular socio-religious communities (SRCs) for state benefits has been motivated both by severe pre-existing inequality and blatant discrimination and by a liberal disposition of the political leadership and the constitution, resulting in ·political appeasement for electoral gains, given the numerical strength of minorities. Despite such social intervention, the impact of economic growth has been highly uneven across SRCs and socio-religious regions. While the data on minorities at the national level generally illustrate their exclusion from the wider process of growth and development, regionally there are a few states where they have made some gains. For example, Muslims in Kerala have an urban poverty rate of 24%, compared to Chattisgarh's 61%, a state carved out of Madhya Pradesh in 2000 with a very high share of SC and ST populations and a small share of Muslims, and the national Muslim urban poverty average of 38.4% (PMHLC, 2006, p. 159).

Worker participation data, disaggregated by industry and social group, shows that Muslims work predominantly in agriculture (38.6%), manufacturing (21.5%) and trade (17.2%) (NCEUS, 2009, p. 63). Scheduled tribes are found in agriculture (78.6%), construction (5.8%) and manufacturing (4.7%); corresponding figures for SCs are 59.6% (agriculture), 8.9% (construction) and 10.7% (manufacturing). Without additional information, not much more can be said about this pattern other than to assert that Muslims are employed less in agriculture and more in manufacturing and trade relative to STs and SCs. The absence of the Hindu concept of ritual purity and thus greater acceptance of some businesses that Hindus find "polluting" (such as working with leather), allows for greater participation in manufacturing and trade. OBCs are employed more in agriculture and less in the other two industries when compared to Muslims. By some measures, Muslims appear to be more mobile than STs, SCs and OBCs. However, landlessness afflicts both Muslims and the SCs (NCEUS, 2009, p. 140), hence they are compelled to pursue non-agricultural employment, most likely in the informal sector if their educational level is low. Drop-out rates for Muslims are higher than for other socio-religious groups at all educational levels (Jodhka, 2011, p. 54; Ahmad, 2011, p. 123). Consequently, the impact of economic growth has been marginal on poverty reduction in part due to pre-existing structural inequality and hence limited intergenerational mobility (see Bardhan, 2010, pp. 96, 103).

The extent to which Muslims have entered the civil service, a public sector that ought to reflect inclusiveness given the Indian state's social commitments, is presented in Table 5. Muslims make up 3.2% of the workers in the three major civil services; only 1.8% of the Indian Foreign Service workers are Muslim.[19] Similarly, Muslims represent only 3.3% of all workers in central public sector units, compared to 10.8% for state government units. In universities, upper-caste Hindus dominate, while Muslims and SC/ST are under-represented. In the four different categories of government jobs, SC candidates have made improvements, with 12% share in the highest category of jobs and 18% in the lowest category (which does not include

Table 5: Share of Muslims in all India civil services, 2006.

Service	All officers	No. of Muslim officers	Share of Muslims to all (%)
Civil service officers	8827	285	3.2
Indian administrative service	4790	142	3.0
Indian foreign service	828	15	1.8
Indian police service	3209	128	4.0

Source: Prime Minister's High Level Committee (PMHLC, 2006, p. 166).

---

[19]Complications arising from being a Muslim in India's regional geopolitical relations might have a bearing on this.

sweepers, a principal occupation for many scheduled castes) (Jodhka, 2010, p. 54). These shares, however, are much lower for Muslims (see PMHLC, 2006, Table 9.4, p. 168).

It should be noted that, within the Muslim community, there is a similar social hierarchy based on self-claimed social descent and by conversions from specific caste groupings associated with particular occupations, although this hierarchy is not as elaborate as the Hindu caste system. This is due to the difficulty in erasing one's lowly social status by changing one's religion. Thus, caste fluidity can be found across religious groups but just as Dalits (SC), who are the worst off within the Hindu hierarchy, the *arzals* are former Dalits who converted to Islam but continue to experience similar hardships because of their low status. Unfortunately, they cannot access some of the state benefits given to SCs because there are no official benefits given under religion in a 'secular' India, even though there is public recognition of their economic and social plight. When Muslims are divided into general and OBC categories, the latter group does worse than the Hindu OBC group in terms of education at almost every level (Table 6). The proportion of persons aged 20 years and above with higher education also reveals that Muslims in general do worse than Hindu OBCs and Muslim OBCs do worse than the general Muslim population (PMHLC, 2006, p. 206). While there are multiple reasons for Muslim exclusion, including overt and tacit discrimination and their own preference to maintain certain autonomy from India's (Hindu) social fabric, such initial conditions reproduce and exacerbate compositely poverty, unemployment and illiteracy among Muslims today. Such state of affairs indicates the future social composition of the

Table 6: Education levels of Muslims and other backward castes.

Education level	Hindu-OBCs	Muslim-general	Muslim-OBCs	Total
Illiterate	33.4	33.3	37.4	31.6
Just literate	1.2	2.2	2.9	1.4
Below primary	0.8	1.7	1.5	1.0
Primary	15.9	18.0	17.5	15.4
Middle	16.0	18.6	16.0	15.7
Secondary	15.0	12.6	13.1	14.2
Higher secondary	7.4	5.9	5.1	7.8
Diploma/certificate	3.9	2.8	2.5	4.4
Graduate and above	3.2	2.4	1.9	4.3

Source: Prime Minister's High Level Committee (PMHLC, 2006, p. 206).

workforce, especially in the professional services, which continue to favor the better-off social groups. All three groups — Hindu OBCs, Muslims in general, and Muslim OBCs — individually and collectively, have extremely low shares of 'technical graduates,' with 0.3% or less (PMHLC, 2006, Table 10.6, p. 206). This once again confirms the middle class bias of India's tertiary education system and the exclusionary tendencies of high-growth IT and other sectors that require high skills (see D'Costa, 2011a).

4. Looking Ahead at Compressed Capitalism and Inclusive Development

This chapter has examined India's record in inclusive development, a state of affairs that has resulted from multiple processes of economic development, social change and political participation in a global setting. It introduced briefly the nature of compressed capitalism in which export-oriented advanced economic sectors coexist with a persistent low-wage unorganized sector. By examining the IT industry, it showed the mechanisms by which exclusion occurs. Pre-existing inequality makes technical tertiary education for most Indians and certainly minorities daunting, despite reservations for some. To further demonstrate these exclusionary processes, the details of informal employment were presented to underscore that India's high growth is not producing formal sector jobs. Although compressed capitalism cannot be solely responsible for exclusion, when growth in the unorganized sector and high growth in high-value formal sectors are juxtaposed, the result is increasing inequality and exclusion. Furthermore, both the private and state sectors employed a small share of the total workforce, which is a structural imperative of compressed capitalism where states must reduce their deficits and the private sector must adopt technology and capital-intensive methods for competitiveness. The third step in illustrating the challenges of inclusive development in India was to assess how well India's minorities were doing. While the pre-existing structures of inequality are squarely responsible, the process of marginalization of minorities and the impoverished is exacerbated by compressed capitalism. The search for raw materials, commercial farming, encroachment of agricultural land for large-scale special economic zones and the inability of India's formal sector to generate adequate employment all contribute to the exclusionary forces. Without altering the socio-economic conditions of India's minorities and reconfiguring India's participation in global capitalism, inclusive development will remain mere rhetoric.

India's record on social development was abysmal at the time of independence, but has substantially improved in certain areas in the last six decades. However, there is also a massive deficit in employment and education opportunities for India's minority communities. Inclusive development falls considerably short of targets and expectations despite the many state programs to help these groups. The presumption that states are capable of inducing inclusive development appears to be overly optimistic since the wider political economy forces often trump more narrow policy goals. In this sense, we are compelled to moderate our expectations. As I have shown with the IT sector, there are structural determinants of contemporary exclusion, endogenous and exogenous; however, this cannot be an excuse for failing to achieve inclusive development, an expectation that has been internalized by the impoverished and exploited masses.

Compressed capitalism is a systemic process that works to generate particular forms of exclusion even as it pulls educated, high-skilled workers into the global economy. By playing the global market game, Indian firms in the formal sector are becoming more capital-intensive and relying on contract workers. These are business strategies to lower costs and enhance profits, a feature that is integral to contemporary capitalism. There are various reasons for rising capital intensity and declining employment (NCEUS, 2009, p. 16). The formal sector is increasing productivity with rising capital intensity, while government policy, under capitalist imperatives, favors technological upgrading and efficiency. The shedding of redundant workers in the organized sector also raises capital intensity. Rising capital intensity is also due to changing composition of exports that are skill and capital intensive. This is because consumers are located in rich countries and thus products must meet certain international quality standards, which entails automation and other capital-intensive methods and demands skilled labor (Mazumdar and Sarkar, 2008, p. 8). The increase in the production of white goods for the growing Indian middle class also induces capital deepening of production. It is evident that such an industrial trajectory is unlikely to be reversed in the near future, making employment prospects in the formal sector elusive.

The unskilled, uneducated and poor, who comprise the vast majority of Indian workers, are absorbed by the large and expanding unorganized sector. They are casual workers, contract workers and the self-employed, categories that by definition are vulnerable, impoverished and close to destitution. India's official minorities and Muslims fall largely in this unorganized sector. Furthermore, liberalization is hurting the minorities more, partly because of cutbacks in social spending. Consequently, as advanced sectors coexist with traditional ones, with the latter not absorbed by high-growth formal sectors, the wealth and income gaps in India continue to widen.

The mechanisms for such polarization are complex and the reasons many, but pre-existing inequality, poverty, low social status and outright discrimination work against minorities in obtaining adequate education and employment. Government programs aimed at minorities such as the SCs, STs and OBCs have somewhat improved their social and economic standing in certain spheres but remain woefully inadequate. Muslims, on the other hand, have fared worse than other government-targeted minorities due to divisive regional and national politics and the constitutional imperative of not recognizing religion as a criterion for state-mandated reservations. Some have argued to dispense with static constitutional design and instead favor change to match today's societal expectations (Ahmad, 2011, p. 128) since Muslims, despite their abject economic conditions, are unable to access state programs aimed at castes and tribes. Consequently, there are demands for reservations for Muslims with the implication that positive discrimination by the state can work.[20]

The argument against reservation for Muslims is that discrimination occurs mainly because of social attitudes and poverty, and positive discrimination in an economy of scarcity benefits the better off among the discriminated groups while the majority resists minority empowerment (Chronic Poverty Research Centre, 2008, p. 77). However, this is politics at its core and the state, if it is to play its developmental role, must rise above it and put into place new social policies with legal teeth behind them with the knowledge that the current exclusive form of growth cannot be morally, economically, and politically sustained.

Being low caste and Muslim is the 'other' in India, which works against ushering in genuine inclusive development. On the one hand, we know that the poor, the vulnerable and the minorities within this group need direct support so that they can exercise their capabilities and freedom: on the other hand, the state must tread carefully in balancing the different needs of India's multinational society in economic, political, and financial terms. Further, India's insertion in the world economy means that the state has reduced space for social policy. The good news is that the Indian state

---

[20]There are also talks about reservations in the private sector for SCs but businesses see this as state interference. Instead businesses want the state to provide equal access to education.

has made efforts to address some of these issues and if India is to be the juggernaut of the world economy it is clear that the state must do much more. India's rural sector and the urban informal sector are necessary starting points in this quest to meet societal needs. One recent initiative, the National Rural Employment Guarantee Act, is a step in the right direction, though its impact has been uneven across states and it has often excluded women since the head of the household (typically a male) is offered the first option of working for 100 days in the year (Ghosh *et al.*, 2008). It is also too early to tell what the overall transformative impact will be, whether 100 days of guaranteed employment will lift people well above the poverty line, and if the rural infrastructure that results from such employment will create the basis for agrarian prosperity.

The government's 11th Five-Year Plan, 'Towards a Faster and Inclusive Growth' is also on the mark. Among other things, scholarships for SCs and big spending on higher and technical education are envisaged. The presumption is that this will create greater access for marginalized communities. This plan meets the need for increasing the number of seats in quality higher education but whether minorities will be able to access them is an open question. Availability of seats at the college level addresses neither the issue of availability of good education at the primary and secondary levels nor the high dropout rates of school-going children among the poor and minorities. Assisting with credit and technology upgrading for small enterprises and minority-owned business in the informal sector will be another important measure to strengthen the sector (Das, 2008, pp. 130–132; Bagchi, 2007b, p. 328).

It is counterintuitive that a labor-abundant economy such as India would follow a capital-intensive trajectory. There is an oft-repeated argument that labor rigidities (such as trade unions and job security) are one reason why India's informal sector remains vast and the formal sector is unable to increase employment. Allegedly, India's labor regulations, which make the firing of workers (in enterprises with 100 or more workers) or hiring of contract workers difficult, discourage hiring and encourage capital-intensive production processes. However, studies show that most firms seeking retrenchment of workers obtained permission to do so (Nagaraj, 2007). Also, contrary to bad industrial relations, an excuse for hiring contract workers, firms have hired contract workers under conducive production environment overall (NCEUS, 2009, p. 15). The crux of the matter is that, under compressed capitalism, the power of capital is strong even in statist economies such as India, due to the maturity of capitalists and their increasing partnership with international capital. Consequently, the process of capital accumulation might be intensified. For example, in particular sectors such as the high-growth auto industry, labor–management relations have been conflict prone (D'Costa, 2011b). Witness the recent unrest at Maruti-Suzuki's Manesar plant due to management's refusal to recognize an alternative trade union even though the company has been in existence since 1982 with the partnership of the Indian government. What this suggests is that the lack of inclusive development is partly a result of corporate profit strategies and partly an exercise of power in keeping labor at bay. Such a structural condition is evident from the share of wages to net value added, which fell between 1981–1982 and 2003–2004, while that of profits in the same period initially fell in the first half of the 1980s but rose continuously and steeply since 2000–2001 (Roy, 2008, p. 219).

Looking ahead, there is no ready-made solution in sight since inclusive development is a tapestry of social, economic and political processes influenced by policy interventions or lack thereof and the structural conditions impinging on the very process of late capitalist development (see Balakrishnan, 2011, pp. 235–249; Dev, 2012, pp. 285–290). But if historical enlightenment against all odds fundamentally altered the status quo by unshackling the grip of slavery and feudal oppression, there is no reason, why, when the collective consciousness is so much richer in its aspirations about enhancing the quality of life of the diverse world we want to inhabit, we cannot change the way most Indians live. It is an arduous process, with deeply embedded structures, but a committed state and a strong civic society can ensure the basic fundamental right for all to live in human dignity.

Acknowledgments

I thank Dilip Dutta for inviting me to participate at the workshop on 'Inclusive Growth in China & India: Role of Institution Building and Governance' in Sydney in 2011 and Janette Rawlings for meticulously editing the manuscript. The usual caveats apply.

References

Ahmad, R. (2011). "Of Minorities and Social Development: The Case of India's 'Missing' Muslims," in *India, Social Development Report 2010: The Land Question and the Marginalized*, M. Mohanty (ed.), New Delhi: Oxford University Press for Council for Social Development, Delhi, pp. 121–143.

Bagchi, A. K. (2007a). "Global Financial Integration — I: The Overlooked Historical Context of the Current Period," in *Capture and Exclude: Developing Economies and the Poor in Global Finance*, A. K. Bagchi and G. A. Dymski (eds.), New Delhi: Tulika Books, pp. 3–20.

Bagchi, A. K. (2007b). "Finance: Lessons for India," in *Capture and Exclude: Developing Economics and the Poor in Global Finance*, A. K. Bagchi and G. A. Dymski (eds.), New Delhi: Tulika Books, pp. 317–336.

Balakrishnan, P. (2011). *Economic Growth in India: History and Prospect*, New Delhi: Oxford University Press.

Banerjee, D. (2005). *Globalisation, Industrial Restructuring and Labour Standards: Where India Meets the Global*, New Delhi: Sage Publications.

Bardhan, P. (2010). *Awakening Giants, Feet of Clay: Assessing the Economic Rise of China and India*, Princeton: Princeton University Press.

Bardhan, P., S. Bowles, and M. Wallerstein (eds.) (2006). *Globalisation and Egalitarian Redistribution*, Princeton: Princeton University Press.

Barrientos, S. (2008). "Contract Labour: The 'Achilles Heel' of Corporate Codes in Commercial Value Chains," *Development and Change*, Vol. 39, No. 6, pp. 977–990.

Basu, K. (2006). "Globalization, Poverty, and Inequality: What is the Relationship? What Can Be Done?" *World Development*, Vol. 34, No. 8, pp. 1361–1373.

Bhushan, S. (2008). "Proposing Reforms in Higher Education," in *Alternative Economic Survey, India, 2007–2008: Decline of the Developmental State*, Alternative Survey Group (ed.), Delhi: Daanish Books, pp. 297–309.

Bose, S. (1988). "The Problem of Primitive Accumulation," *Economic and Political Weekly*, Vol. 23, No. 23, pp. 1169–1174.

Chronic Poverty Research Centre (2008). *The Chronic Poverty Report 2008–09: Escaping Poverty Traps*, Manchester: Chronic Poverty Research Centre.

Das, K. (2008). "Micro, Small and Medium Enterprises: Unfair Fare," in *Alternative Economic Survey, India, 2007–2008: Decline of the Developmental State*, Alternative Survey Group (ed.), Delhi: Daanish Books, pp. 119–135.

D'Costa, A. P. (2003). "Uneven and Combined Development: Understanding India's Software Exports," *World Development*, Vol. 13, No. 1, pp. 211–226.

D'Costa, A. P. (2004). "Export Growth and Path-Dependence: The Locking-in of Innovations in the Software Industry," in *India in the Global Software Industry: Innovation, Firm Strategies and Development*, A. P. D'Costa and E. Sridharan (eds.), Basingstoke: Palgrave Macmillan, pp. 51–82.

D'Costa, A. P. (2009). "Extensive Growth and Innovation Challenges in Bangalore, India," in *The New Asian Innovation Dynamics: China and India in Perspective*, G. Parayil and A. P. D'Costa (eds.), Basingstoke: Palgrave Macmillan, pp. 79–109.

D'Costa, A. P. (2011a). "Geography, Uneven Development and Distributive Justice: The Political Economy of IT Growth in India," *Cambridge Journal of Regions, Economy and Society*, Vol. 4, No. 2, pp. 237–251.

D'Costa, A. P. (2011b). "Globalization, Crisis and Industrial Relations in the Indian Auto Industry," *International Journal of Automotive Technology and Policy*, Vol. 11, No. 2, pp. 114–136.

D'Costa, A. P. (ed.) (2012). *Globalization and Economic Nationalism in Asia*, Oxford: Oxford University Press.

D'Costa, A. P. (2013). "Compressed Capitalism and Development: Primitive Accumulation, Petty Commodity Production, and Capitalist Maturity in India and China," *Critical Asian Studies* (forthcoming).

D'Costa, A. P. and A. K. Bagchi (2012). "Transformation and Development: A Critical Introduction to India and China," in *Transformation and Development: The Political Economy of Transition in India and China*, A. K. Bagchi, and A. P. D'Costa (eds.), New Delhi: Oxford University Press, pp. 1–38.

Dev, S. M. (2012). *Inclusive Growth in India: Agriculture, Poverty, and Human Development*, New Delhi: Oxford University Press.

Duhigg, C. and D. Barboza (2012). "In China, Human Costs Are Built Into an iPad," *New York Times*, 25 January. Available at: http://www.nytimes.com/2012/01/26/business/ieconomy-apples-ipad-and-the-human-costs-for-workers-in-china.html?ref=technology&nl=technology&emc=techupdate-emal [accessed on 12 April 2012].

Ghose, A. K. (2011). "Informal Employment in India," in *India, Social Development Report 2010: The Land Question and the Marginalized*, M. Mohanty (ed.), New Delhi: Oxford University Press for Council for Social Development, Delhi, pp. 116–120.

Ghosh, S., T. Satpathy, and A. K. Mehta (2008). "National Rural Employment Guarantee Scheme," in *Alternative Economic Survey, India, 2007–2008: Decline of the Developmental State*, Alternative Survey Group (ed.), Delhi: Daanish Books, pp. 245–262.

Gupta, D. (1993). "Hierarchy and Difference: An Introduction," in *Social Stratification*, D. Gupta (ed.), Delhi: Oxford University Press, pp. 1–21.

Jodhka, S. S. (2011). "Dalits and Development," in *India, Social Development Report 2010: The Land Question and the Marginalized*, M. Mohanty (ed.), New Delhi: Oxford University Press for Council for Social Development, Delhi, pp. 51–61.

Kannan, K. P. (2011). "K. N. Raj: Development with Equity and Democracy," *Development and Change*, Vol. 42, No. 1, pp. 366–386.

Kundu, D. and D. Samanta (2011). "Redefining the Inclusive Urban Agenda in India," *Economic and Political Weekly*, Vol. XLVI, No. 5, pp. 55–63.

Mazumdar, D. and S. Sarkar (2008). "Introduction: An Overview of Globaliza-
tion, Reforms and Macro-economic Developments in India," pp. 1–18, in
Globalization, Labour Markets and Inequality in India, D. Mazumdar and
S. Sarkar (eds.), Oxon: Routledge for International Development Research
Centre.

Mohanty, M. (2011). "Social Development and the Story of the Marginalized:
An Introduction," pp. 3–18, in *India, Social Development Report 2010: The
Land Question and the Marginalized*, M. Mohanty (ed.), New Delhi: Oxford
University Press for Council for Social Development, Delhi.

Nagaraj, R. (2007). "Are Labour Regulations Holding up India's Growth and
Exports? A Review of Analysis and Evidence," Paper Prepared for National
Commission for Enterprises in the Unorganised Sector (NCEUS), New Delhi.

National Commission for Enterprises in the Unorganised Sector (NCEUS) (2009).
*The Challenge of Employment in India: An Informal Economy Perspective,
Volume I Main Report*, New Delhi: National Commission for Enterprises in
the Unorganised Sector, Government of India.

Prime Minister's High Level Committee (PMHLC) (2006). "Social, Economic and
Educational Status of the Muslim Community in India," New Delhi: Cabinet
Secretariat, Government of India.

Ramakumar, R. (2010). "Continuity and Change: Notes on Agriculture in 'New
India'," in *A New India? Critical Reflections in the Long Twentieth Century*,
A. P. D'Costa (ed.), London: Anthem Press, pp. 43–70.

Rao, J. M. (2009). "Challenges Facing World Agriculture: A Political Economy
Perspective," *Development and Change*, Vol. 40, No. 6, pp. 1279–1292.

Reed, A. M. (2008). *Human Development and Social Power: Perspectives from
South Asia*, New York: Routledge.

Roy, S. (2008). "Employment and Labour Market: The Myth of 'Rigidity',"
Alternative Survey Group, *Alternative Economic Survey, India, 2007–2008:
Decline of the Developmental State*, Delhi: Daanish Books, pp. 209–222.

Saith, A. (2011). "Inequality, Imbalance, Instability: Reflections on a Structural
Crisis," *Development and Change*, Vol. 42, No. 1, pp. 70–86.

Subramanian, S. (2011). "Inclusive Development and the Quintile Income Statis-
tic," *Economic and Political Weekly*, Vol. XLVI, No. 4, pp. 69–72.

Sundaram, K. (2007). "Employment and Poverty In India: 2000–2005," Centre
for Development Economics, Department of Economics, Delhi School of Economics, University of Delhi Working Paper No. 155.

Thomas, J. J. (2011). "Public Sector Units in India and China: Inefficient Producers or Creators of Crucial Knowledge Assets?" Paper Presented at Globalization and Public Sector Reforms in India and China, Copenhagen: Asia
Research Centre, Copenhagen Business School, 23–24 September.

Thorat, S. and K. S. Newman (eds.) (2010). *Blocked by Caste: Economic Discrimination and Social Exclusion in Modern India*, New Delhi: Oxford University
Press.

UNDP (2006). *Human Development Report 2006 Beyond Scarcity: Power, Poverty and the Global Water Crisis*, New York: UNDP.

Wingfield, N. (2012). "Apple's Chief Puts Stamp on Labor Issues," *New York Times*, 1 April. Available at: http://www.nytimes.com/2012/04/02/technology/apple-presses-its-suppliers-to-improve-conditions.html?_r=1& nl=todaysheadlines&emc=tha26_20120402 [accessed on 12 April 2012].

7. Socio-Economic Dynamics of the ICT Industry's Regional Growth in India

Dilip Dutta* and Supriyo De

1. Introduction

The information technology (IT) industry in India has grown rapidly and has increased its economic impact in recent years. Its contribution to national income (measured in terms of GDP) has increased from 3.41% in the financial year 2000–2001 to 5.86% in the financial year 2007–2008 (Chandrasekhar, 2010). More interestingly, a recent news in 2012 made a headline: *Indian IT industry revenues set to cross US$100 billion.*[1] This sizable economic phenomenon has naturally left its mark on the socio-economic fabric of India.[2] During the last decade of the 20th century, the software sector of India's information technology services (ITS) industry had developed as one of the fastest growing sectors in the economy. Since the beginning of 2001, the traditional ITS companies have been focusing more on the IT-enabled services (ITeS) sector in general and business process outsourcing (BPO) sector in particular. In fact, the ITeS-BPO segment has quickly emerged as a key driver of growth for India's ITS industry.[3] This chapter describes the overall socio-economic effects of the

---

*Corresponding author: dilip.dutta@sydney.edu.au.
[1]Karnik (2012).
[2]As Karnik (*op. cit.*) notes, the achievement of India's IT industry, set to cross a milestone of its revenue exceeding US$100 billion, is better appreciated when one recalls that just 20 years ago, its size was only about half-a-billion dollars. Not only that, this sector is providing livelihood to about 10 million people (including 2.8 million directly employed), it is also the largest recruiter in India's organized private sector, as well as one of India's major foreign exchange earners.
[3]Dutta (2008, pp. 315–316).

information and communication technology (ICT) industry[4] in India, with particular reference to the complementary relationship between human resource development and economic well-being highlighted by the advent of high-technology industries.[5]

It is evident from the Indian growth experience that ICT-services-driven growth shows certain patterns (Arora and Athreye, 2002; D'Costa, 2003, 2011; Arora and Gambardella, 2004; World Bank, 2004; Basant and Chandra, 2007). The growth of high-technology services, like ICT, has been accompanied by increased employment, urban consumption growth and demand for technical education, at the national and the regional levels. Regions endowed with better educational facilities have generally grown faster. Research on the US economy also shows a correlation between higher education and productivity growth in IT-producing industries (Jorgenson, Ho and Stiroh, 2005).

In India, growth in urban consumption at the regional level shows a correlation with the growth of the ICT industry. The growth of business services and physical capital investment also shows correlation with the rise of the ICT industry. While exports were the initial impetus for the ICT industry in India, domestic demand is now growing steadily. The high-technology-services-driven growth witnessed in India, spearheaded by the vibrant ICT sector, appears to be less intensive in physical capital than the manufacturing-industry-oriented growth efforts of China and other East Asian economies. This allows for relatively lower physical investment and therefore higher current consumption (McKinsey and Company, 2007). It appears that this is due to the higher human and organizational capital intensity of ICT-driven growth in India (De and Dutta, 2007).

Several authors have explored the link between the institutional environment, policy initiatives and human resource development in India, and its effect on the growth of the Indian IT industry. Lal (2001) studies the institutional environment and its effect on the growth of the Indian IT

---

[4]ICT industry is a combination of information technology (IT) and communication (C) technology network. While the former is an interconnected intelligent network of various components such as sensors and detectors, computers and knowledge-based systems and control and display systems, the latter includes telephone, wireless transmission and reception (as in television), satellite and mobile telecommunications, fibre optic communication system, computer-modem, Internet, World Wide Web, etc.

[5]Contemporary high-technology industries usually include industries like information and communication technology, biotechnology and nanotechnology.

industry. His paper discusses various policy initiatives to promote exports, technology policies to encourage IT, human resource development, industry structure and performance. Arora *et al.* (2001) provide a detailed analysis of the nature of the Indian software industry, including the importance of human capital, the nature of services exported, structure of the industry and customer experience with the Indian IT industry. Arora and Athreye (2002) assess the contribution of software to India's economic development, paying particular attention to human capital formation. Patibandla and Petersen (2002) also take a human-capital-oriented view but see investment by transnational corporations (TNCs) as a major driving force.

D'Costa (2003) highlights the remarkable disparities generated by the development of the Indian software industry in terms of the urban–rural divide and unequal geographical distribution of software firms. He lays emphasis on the role of technical skills and human capital in increasing regional disparities. In his recent paper, D'Costa (2011) applies a political economy framework both to explain the rise of the Indian IT industry and to analyze the spatial and developmental consequences of this growth. Caniëls and Romijn (2003) study the prominent IT cluster in the southern Indian city of Bangalore. They examine the beneficial effects of regional industrial clusters from the viewpoint of passive and active collective efficiencies. Van Dijk (2003) also analyzes the Bangalore IT cluster from the viewpoint of the role of national, state and local government policies. He finds that policy incentives, such as targeted training, marketing support, subsidies, industrial promotion and infrastructure support, may have contributed to the growth of the IT industry. Parthasarathy (2004) also examines the development of the IT cluster in Bangalore from the viewpoint of the social embeddedness of economic activity. The broad hypothesis relates to the evolving endogeneity of policy making. His paper envisages state policy as slowly losing autonomy and embedding itself in private capital in order to encourage economic growth.

Basant and Chandra (2007) explore the role of educational and research institutions in high-technology city clusters in India. Their research develops a framework for analyzing the role of academic institutions in city clusters. This framework describes various linkages between the institutions, the clusters and the national and global economies. They use survey data of electronics and IT firms in three city clusters. They provide a description of the major research and educational institutions in the clusters. Their findings show that the globalization of IT markets has resulted in the corresponding deepening of labor markets, resulting in increased requirements for specialized skills. In this regard, academic institutions have provided a crucial role in addressing the need for rapid enhancement of skills.

Most of the existing literature analyzes specific aspects of the ICT industry in India. In contrast, our chapter places the Indian ICT industry within a broader socio-economic perspective. In our study, we examine a wider socio-economic dynamics that propels the policy environment and at the same time benefits from it. A composite actor-network theory (ANT) cum national innovation systems (NIS) framework is used to analyze this dynamics. This composite framework helps capture the dynamic cross-flow of influences that determine socio-economic outcomes of technological advancement. Our analysis reveals that the Indian policy environment, shaped by national and regional imperatives, contributed significantly to the development trajectory of the Indian ICT industry. ICT industry development has a dynamic, interdependent relationship with region-specific human resource potential and regional economic development. States endowed with strong human resource potential attract ICT investment. This, in turn, results in higher income and further human capital accumulation. However, this process creates disparities between the regional states: some are the sites of ICT industry activity, while some other states are with relatively little ICT investment. Policy initiatives are suggested to address these imbalances and helps societies cope with the skewed development impact of ICT industry growth.

Of the following four sections, Section 2 describes the analytical framework. Section 3 gives details of the policy environment, human resource development and the growth of the ICT industry in India. Section 4 analyzes the impact of the IT industry on socio-economic development and regional growth. Section 5 distils the policy implication of the research and concludes with new vistas for enhancing India's overall economic growth and improving social welfare.

2.   Analytical Framework

The emergence and development of new technologies is a complex and dynamic socio-economic process. It is imperative that the development of high-technology industries, like ICT, especially in developing countries, be studied in a holistic manner. Any methodological approach for studying the social shaping of technology needs to take into account the social forces that influence economic and policy matters, while simultaneously acknowledging the impact of economic factors and policy initiatives on the evolution of society.

The analytical framework adopted in this study, uses a combination of ANT and NIS approach to capture the essence of the socio-economic dynamics of the evolution of the ICT industry in India. This composite framework is well suited to the analysis of the ICT sector in India (Dutta, 2009). The basis of ANT is the idea that society and technology are composed of networks linking various actors and actants (Ryder, 2003). The actors and actants can be human beings as well as non-human entities. According to ANT, human beings are not the only elements that act. Non-human physical elements of the network also influence the social possibilities. In fact, ANT does not posit a stable social structure; rather a constant interaction between different elements is posited. This interaction is the channel through which technological innovation translates into social transformation. For instance, the advent of the Internet, an inanimate technological system, has spawned changes in social networking possibilities and opened new vistas for personal communications.

The policy-oriented approach of NIS focuses on national level analysis for examining the impact of technology on society. NIS is defined by Metcalfe (1995) as a set of institutions, which jointly and individually, contribute to the development of new technologies and provides the framework within which governments form and influence the innovation process. He states that the division of labor and peculiarities of information, which result in a predominance of coordination by non-market means, shape the nature of each country's NIS. The institutions like private firms, universities, public research centers, etc., which constitute the NIS make complementary contributions, but may differ in terms of their motivation for and commitment to the dissemination of knowledge (Cimoli, 1998).

In adopting a composite ANT–NIS framework for this study, the dynamic cross-flow of influences that shape social, economic and policy outcomes is captured (Figure 1). The framework adopted conceives of certain local characteristics attributable to the actors and actants belonging to both private and public sectors[6] as ultimately influencing NIS through the socio-political process. The NIS matrix, in turn, influences the public sector and private sector outcomes in terms of investment location, technology choice, human capital intensity, etc. The public and private sectors also impinge

---

[6]The public sector is widely defined to include the administrative machinery of the government as well as public enterprises.

Figure 1: Analytical framework.

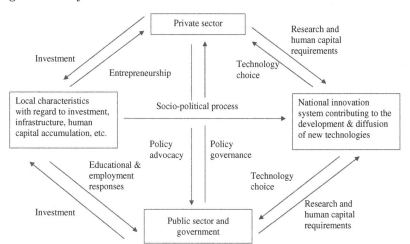

upon the local characteristics with regard to investment, availability of educational and research infrastructure, incentives for human capital accumulation, rewards for entrepreneurship, governance structures, etc. The local characteristics also shape private sector development via, for instance, entrepreneurial activity. They also influence the success of public sector endeavors by responding appropriately to the available educational and employment opportunities. The private sector plays a role in public sector activities through the formal and informal policy advocacy process. The public sector, on its part, influences the private sector through procurement decisions, policy directions and provision of governance and public services. Thus, in this framework each element in the network influences the other. The socio-economic outcome, in terms of technology choice, innovation activity, entrepreneurial initiatives, human capital investment, policy-making, economic growth and income distribution, is the result of a complex interactive process.

This framework provides a broad matrix that can be used to analyze the socio-economic aspects of the ICT industry's growth in India. The Indian social, political and economic system as it emerged following the end of colonial domination was somewhat diverse. The broad national endeavor was to create a unified socio-political entity without sacrificing the underlying diversity of the nation. It resulted, among other things, in the persistence of diversities and the adoption of a federal political system. In this regard, it is notable that certain southern Indian states had a lead in terms of technological capabilities and institutions.[7] A strong desire for rapid technological progress also formed the basis of the Indian NIS. The public sector, which dominated the economy, made major investments in the southern states in terms of research centers and production facilities. Subsequently, private sector investments in the ICT sector also showed a distinct preference for the southern region. This, in turn, encouraged the growth of the private engineering colleges and resulted in further human capital accumulation. This appears to have had a huge spillover effect and a major impact on economic growth. These aspects are analyzed in detail in Sections 3 and 4 of this chapter.

3. Policy Environment, Human Resource Development and the ICT Industry

The overall policy environment contributed significantly in shaping various trends of ICT industry growth in India. The policy matrix resulted in specific choices of production sites, markets, technologies, delivery models, human capital availability and financing patterns in the ICT industry. This policy environment needs to be viewed from the perspective of the socio-economic and political foundations of the Indian state as conceived in the 1950s, as well as the more pragmatic market-oriented structure that evolved following the liberalization process initiated in the 1980s and then adopted more comprehensively in 1991.

India, as conceived by its founding statesmen, including the first Prime Minister Pandit Jawaharlal Nehru, was a developmental state that was geared to place the country on a path of less dependency on the industrialized nations. This almost grandiose vision imbued the policy-making process of independent India. While this vision may appear quixotic in retrospect, the resultant policy environment laid the foundations for the contemporary human capital attainments along with ICT service development. The cornerstones of this policy environment were public sector dominance in major industries, a stress on higher education, import substitution industrialization, and scientific research and development. These initial

---

[7]For instance, the states of Karnataka and Andhra Pradesh, which were largely composed of the erstwhile princely states of Mysore and Hyderabad, respectively, had a strong public works infrastructure, complementary engineering talent and educational institutions.

policies facilitated the development of a fairly sophisticated network of public universities, research institutions, management institutes, research staff, technical personnel and information technology professionals.

The initial development of India's technical education apparatus occurred under the auspices of the colonial state. The All India Council for Technical Education (AICTE), which is the apex statutory body for coordinating and planning the development of technical education, was established in 1945. After India's independence from British colonial rule in 1947, several premier institutions of national importance were established to spearhead the technical education system. These include the Indian Institutes of Technology (IITs) and Indian Institutes of Management (IIMs). The former specialize in providing high-quality training in engineering and technology. They also serve as centers for research and knowledge dissemination. The IIMs provide management education, executive training and consultancy services. The Indian education system thus achieved a head start by establishing IITs since 1951 and IIMs since 1961 (Department of Education, 2005).

Technology strategy in India was focused on providing technological development and research support to the domestic industrial and agricultural sectors. As with other policy initiatives, self-reliance and import substitution were major goals. Broad policy directions were provided by a specific ministry and implemented through activities of the Council for Scientific and Industrial Research (CSIR). Research activities were spearheaded by a set of specialized institutions like the Indian Institute of Science (IISc) and the National Chemical Laboratory (NCL). Following the technological advances and global changes in the 1990s, newer institutions have been created to carry out research in emerging areas of technology. These include, the National Centre for Biological Science, created in 1991 to carry out research in biochemistry, bio-informatics and genetics and Centre for Liquid Crystal Research, set up in 1991 to do basic research on the physical properties of liquid crystal. The International Advanced Research Centre for Powder Metallurgy and New Materials had been operational since 1995 for research and development in advanced materials and associated processing technologies.[8]

The most widespread effect of these technological institutions is probably the development of crucial human capital including software experts,

---

[8]Department of Science and Technology website. See http://dst.gov.in.

data analysts, programmers and data entry operators. Furthermore, it encouraged a culture of scientific research and offered employment opportunities for qualified individuals. This in turn gave households an incentive to engage in human capital creation activities. Recent research indicates that several public and private education and research institutions are now turning to industry-related research especially in the ICT sector (Basant and Chandra, 2007). The technological infrastructure created due to state policies therefore provide the IT industry with human resources as well as research inputs.

There seems to have a widespread agreement in academic discussions, general media, government reports and corporate appraisals that a strong human resource base is probably the greatest strength of the Indian ICT industry. Paradoxically, while 52% of India's working population is illiterate, it has a vast pool of engineers and technical personnel. The education system graduates over 160,000 engineers per year. Most of these graduates are well versed with the English language. These engineers, together with an even larger pool of non-technical graduates, initially provided the ICT industry with high-quality, low-cost human capital (Arora and Athreye, 2002). There are indications that, given the rapid demand for human capital in the IT industry, even this huge output of qualified personnel may not be enough. The rapid growth of ICT and other high-technology industries in India has resulted in a situation whereby state sponsored institutions have been unable to meet the massive demand for qualified technical personnel. Private institutions accredited by government agencies have stepped in to meet this demand. Therefore, accredited engineering seats increased from about 60,000 in 1987–1988 to approximately 340,000 in 2003 (Arora and Gambardella, 2004).

Being aware of the critical need for high-quality human resources for the ICT industry, the government has recently responded by setting up a task force to suggest improvements in the quality and quantity of technical manpower. In its interim report, the committee has suggested that a synergy be developed between the strengths of the government and private institutes. It has also recommended development of faculty to meet shortages in teaching staff (Ministry of Human Resource Development, 2007).

Several state and local governments also provided incentives to the ICT industry like, subsidized land, focused infrastructure, assured electricity supply and exemption from local taxes. In addition, some states have provided 'soft' facilities, like innovation promotion and incubation centers, information technology policy guidelines, marketing support and inter-firm

Figure 2: Location-wise share of revenue and employment generated by major centers of software development in India in 2001.

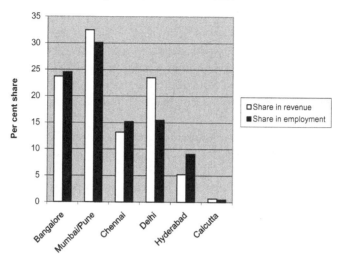

Note: Data from Athreye (2005).

cooperation facilities. States that render significant support measures have become major centers for IT industry activities. These include Andhra Pradesh, Gujarat, Karnataka, Maharashtra and New Delhi. In fact, the capital of Karnataka state, Bangalore, has become almost synonymous with the Indian software success story (Van Dijk, 2003).

Indian software firms show distinct preferences for certain locations. The industry is concentrated around the cities of Bangalore, Mumbai, Pune, Chennai, Delhi, Hyderabad and Kolkata (erstwhile Calcutta) (Figure 2). These areas appear to have been chosen for advantages of human resource availability, commercial importance, proximity to academic institutions, availability of infrastructure and support from local governments (Athreye, 2005). While the city of Bangalore has captured worldwide media attention as a software development and outsourcing destination, the largest share in terms of revenue and employment comes from the city of Mumbai and its nearby town Pune. In terms of revenue the national capital, New Delhi and satellite towns of Noida and Gurgaon have as much importance as Bangalore.

Generally speaking, the early stress on technological research and advanced educational institutions provided by the government, laid the foundation for knowledge-intensive, human resource driven industries like the information technology software sector (Arora *et al.*, 2001; Lal, 2001; Arora and Athreye, 2002; Heeks and Nicholson, 2004). State and local governments buttressed the national level efforts through favorable policies like provision of land, infrastructure support and establishment of avenues for inter-firm cooperation.[9] Certain areas, which were well endowed in terms of educational institutions, research establishments and human resource potential, provided ideal spots for development of high-technology industries like ICT (Van Dijk, 2003; Parthasarathy, 2004). These strengths were further leveraged by the private sector to enhance productivity, create an international reputation and exploit the tremendous opportunities provided by the globalization of the software production process.

The role of high-quality technical personnel in contributing to the success of the Indian software industry has been stressed by several studies. This, in turn, shows the importance of entrepreneurship, organizational skills and management education in the ICT industry. The policy makers responsible for India's initial human resource development strategy were extremely prescient in anticipating that besides technical education, development of managerial skills was a precondition for sustained economic growth. The early lead in both technical and management education by establishing first the IITs and then the IIMs gives Indian high-technology industries a strategic advantage over other competitors in the developing world. This matrix of human resource development where technical skill enhancement and managerial education go hand-in-hand has been replicated by subsequent private sector initiatives following the liberalization and increasing globalization of the Indian economy. This is seen in the advent of several high-quality private management institutes and private technical institutes.

The demand-side influence of this phenomenon is also significant. Probably driven by the need for middle- and upper-level managers with competence in both technical and managerial skills, most firms pay them a significant premium in terms of high salaries and perquisites for recruiting such personnel. It has resulted in a situation where typically most technical personnel aspiring for better career prospects strive to acquire a Master in Business Administration (MBA) degree or an equivalent. This combination of supply and demand for personnel skilled in technical as well as

---

[9]The Indian federal system has a three-tier structure, with the national level referred to as the Central government, various federal constituents referred to as State governments and local levels variously called municipalities, district administrations, etc.

managerial attributes probably endows the Indian human resource base with great flexibility and productivity potential. In a nutshell, this unique human resource base has been harnessed by the Indian ICT industry to improve its production capabilities.

The influence of the IT industry is also reflected in the productivity and living standards of regions that are associated with the production of IT-related goods and services. The ICT industry in India demonstrates significant regional concentration and clustering tendencies. Therefore, the ICT industry is likely to have a major impact on regional economic growth and development. At the same time, regional endowments in terms of educational institutions, technological infrastructure and organizational support are likely to influence the development of high-technology industries like ICT.

4. Regional Development and Socio-Economic Effects

The dramatic but uneven development consequences of the growth of the ICT industry in India has been noted by several studies (Arora and Athreye, 2002; D'Costa, 2003, 2011; Arora and Gambardella, 2004). It is apparent that the rise of the ICT industry provides unique opportunities and challenges to the Indian socio-economic fabric. On one hand, the rise of ICT firms and related high-technology services has resulted in huge opportunities for employment, economic growth and human capital development. On the other hand, certain regions and sections of society have been unable to reap the economic benefits of the ICT sector boom. This has resulted in large disparities in incomes and living standards.

The advent of high-technology services like software and business process outsourcing has been accompanied by increased employment and urban consumption growth. It has also resulted in corresponding increases in the demand for technical education resulting in significant human capital accumulation in certain areas. It is apparent that this has contributed to a virtuous cycle of high human capital investment and corresponding high-technology investment in certain regions. States endowed with better educational facilities have attracted greater ICT investment, resulting in human capital growth. As a consequence, urban consumption has increased dramatically in ICT-industry-intensive regions. The impact of this phenomenon has been so significant that it has also attracted the attention of the popular media, besides academic and policy circles.

In a report on the social and economic performance of Indian states (Debroy, Bhandari and Saran, 2006), certain prominent Indian economists have identified the remarkable growth of the southern Indian states, particularly Karnataka and Andhra Pradesh, with the rise of the ICT industry. While the former has been singled out for the positive impact of state policy initiatives for encouraging IT industries, the latter has shown a significant growth in human capital investment at the household level. Overall, the performance of the southern states in terms of investment, income growth and human capital formation has been remarkable. The development of the ICT industry has probably contributed immensely to this phenomenon. An analysis of the mechanics of ICT-driven economic growth is carried out below using available data and statistics.

The growth of ICT services has been accompanied by increased per capita incomes, manufacturing output growth and demand for technical education. Table 1 depicts the correlation between the aforementioned variables. Per capita income growth has a stronger correlation with ICT services growth (0.510) than manufacturing sector growth (0.071). This indicates that ICT services have a greater impact on per capita income growth and living standards than manufacturing industries. The relationship between ICT services and human capital accumulation is also significant. The number of engineering colleges per million population and the number of engineering students per million population can be considered as proxies for the human capital production apparatus and human capital output, respectively. ICT services growth is positively correlated with engineering colleges (0.326) and engineering students (0.281). Both these variables have a strong positive correlation with per capita income growth (0.523 and 0.591). A clear pattern appears to emerge. States endowed with good educational facilities, and thereby a significant human resource potential attract ICT investments. This in turn, contributes to higher incomes and further accumulation of human capital.

There is also a distinct correlation between manufacturing output growth and ICT services growth (0.449).[10] There are several forces contributing to this effect. First, states with high investment in technological

---

[10]The weak negative correlation between engineering colleges and the manufacturing sector has a simple explanation. Manufacturing output growth does not require a large pool of engineers but is intensive in raw labor. Furthermore, state-sponsored policies of encouraging public sector investment in low-growth states may have contributed to substantial manufacturing sector growth in these states, despite the comparative paucity of engineering talent.

Table 1: Correlation matrix of state per capita income growth, manufacturing output growth, ICT growth, number of engineering colleges and number of engineering students.

	Per capita income growth	Manufacturing growth	ICT growth	No. of engineering colleges per million population	No. of engineering students per million population
Per capita income growth	1.000				
Manufacturing growth	0.071	1.000			
ICT	0.510	0.449	1.000		
No. of engineering colleges per million population	0.523	−0.111	0.326	1.000	
No. of engineering students per million population	0.591	−0.021	0.281	0.866	1.000

Note: This table is based on information given in Appendix A.

fields may be attracting more manufacturing investment from domestic and foreign investors. The attractiveness of these states as sites for manufacturing activity can be due to better reputation and a larger consumer base as a result of higher incomes. At the same time, the development of a corresponding technologically advanced manufacturing base can be due to externalities associated with ICT services, in terms of institutions and human resources. The southern Indian states, which have recently attracted some technologically, advanced manufacturing investment in areas like automobiles, aerospace, etc., may be benefiting from spill-overs of this nature. Furthermore, these industries in turn create more demand for technologically advanced services. It appears that ICT services, like IT software, the advanced manufacturing sector and the technical education sector are propelling each other in a virtuous growth cycle.

This process can also be analyzed by examining the nature of IT output growth at the regional level. The southern region, which is abundant in human capital, initially attracted software sector investment and subsequently displayed rapid growth. The northern region, where the process of ICT sector growth started later has recently shown rapid growth in the demand and supply of private technical education (Arora and Gambardella, 2004). These regional aspects are reflected in Figure 3. The figure shows that for the period 1995–1996, the South and the West had a large proportion of private technical education institutes, and this was correlated with the high growth of IT sector output.[11] In contrast, the North and the East lagged behind in both private technical education and IT output growth. For the period 2002–2003, the South and the West maintained their lead while the North and the East were beginning to catch up in terms of private technical education. The North also showed some growth in IT output but the East was yet to come on par. This probably indicates that human capital creation precedes increases in ICT sector output.

The most apparent socio-economic effect of the ICT boom in India has been the increased salary and thereby improved spending power of ICT professionals. It is estimated that the average monthly spending potential

---

[11]The North comprises Jammu and Kashmir, Himachal Pradesh, Punjab, Haryana, Uttar Pradesh, Uttaranchal, Rajasthan, Bihar, Delhi and Chandigarh. East comprises West Bengal, Odisha, Chattisgarh, Assam, Sikkim, Arunachal Pradesh, Tripura, Manipur, Meghalaya, Mizoram and Nagaland. West is composed of Gujarat, Maharashtra, Madhya Pradesh, Dadra and Nagar Haveli, Daman and Diu. South is composed of Karnataka, Kerala, Tamil Nadu, Andhra Pradesh, Goa and Puducherry.

Figure 3: Relation between regional IT sector growth and technical education.

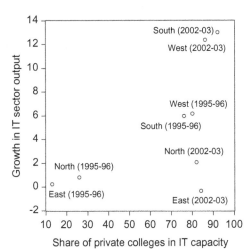

Share of private colleges in IT capacity

Note: Growth in IT sector output: Sales growth of major IT companies (authors' calculation based on Centre for Monitoring Indian Economy, 2005). Number of engineering colleges: Share of privately financed colleges in Indian IT capacity, by region and year from Arora and Gambardella (2004). See Appendix B for data.

of ICT sector employees in the city of Bangalore is Rs. 23,000 per person (or per household if the person is the sole earner). This is computed after setting aside 30% as estimated savings. In contrast, the average affluent category household in Bangalore spends only Rs. 19,500 per month. Therefore, the consumption potential of ICT employees is around 18% higher than that of other urban professionals (Choudhary and Premsingh, 2004). Furthermore, this increased spending power is now available to younger people, which was unthinkable in the past. Due to the availability of jobs for young graduates in the business process outsourcing and call center industry, persons in their early twenties can receive monthly salaries of Rs. 7000–10,000. The newfound spending power has led to a consumption boom characterized by designer wear, branded goods, parties, discos and multiplex cinema theaters. At the same time, the availability of finances has given the youth economic independence from their parents, which in turn is also reflected in greater social and cultural freedom (Ghatak, 2004a). The new high-profile, high-pressure job environment has also increased the ambitions and career goals of the new breed of IT professionals. Frequent changes of jobs are the norm and the more adventurous are looking for extra money and satisfaction as freelancers (Aneja, 2004b; Ghatak, 2004b). At the same time, a new work ethos that values talent, innovation and continuous upgrading of skills has emerged. This has led to a transition in the workforce mindset from one that valued consistency to a less risk-averse attitude as found in conventional models of labor economics. Corporate employers have tried to respond by offering better compensation, training opportunities and also adjusting to the fact that no employee is likely to remain forever (Aneja, 2004a; Ghatak, 2004b).

5. Policy Implications and Conclusion

The preceding analysis has significant policy implications. With particular regard to the Indian economy, it shows that high-technology services like ICT and quality technical education have a large impact on state-level economic prosperity. It explains the disparities in income and growth among Indian states to a large extent. This substantial growth effect has created certain imbalances between states where ICT industries are prevalent and those that have not benefited from such industries due to lack of investment. The process of ICT-driven economic growth in India is clearly leading to significant disparities. Policy makers need to heed these warning signs. In a society that is already segregated along lines of class and caste, this may create a further sub-division between the upwardly mobile haves and the stagnant have-nots of the Indian society.

Our study provides a basic solution to the problem. It is apparent that development of high-technology industries, like information technology, requires a strong human resource base, good educational and research institutions and proactive support from state governments in terms of infrastructure, administrative environment and legal framework. It is apparent that ICT services have contributed significantly in improving incomes and living standards. Therefore, it is imperative that Indian states that hitherto had low investments in this area need to focus on policies to attract ICT industries like software and business process outsourcing. Policy initiatives likely to benefit these states are as follows:

(i) Greater stress on improvement of educational standards at basic as well as advanced levels.
(ii) Encouragement of ICT investment through incentives like provision of software technology parks (STPs), better Internet connectivity and assured power supply.

(iii) Administrative and legal norms with regard to Internet security, enforcement of intellectual property rights and appropriate legislation for workplace relations can provide a strong enabling environment for growth of the information technology industry.

The link between human capital accumulation, ICT investment and economic well-being described above can also serve as a paradigm for the increasing disparities in incomes, access to ICT and human capital investments seen at a global level. At one level, this is seen in disparities between countries that have taken a lead in ICT industries and those that have failed to benefit from the technological revolution. At another level, even in developed countries, there appears to be increasing disparities in living standards between households that have gained from technological advancement and those that have not (Pohjola, 2002; Wolff, 2002).

These disparities may be due to skill-biased technical change (SBTC) that accompanies adoption of information technology (Bresnahan, Brynjolfsson and Hitt, 2002). This may be contributing to higher wages for employees with ICT skills, higher returns to households holding technology related assets and corresponding redundancy of low skilled workers. The analysis of Indian regions described in this chapter shows that the digital divide and the educational divide are interlinked. Improving access to both quality education and better information technology assets is a viable formula for addressing the issue of disparities in income brought about by the ICT revolution.

Policy makers in developed as well as developing countries need to focus on means to counter this imbalance between households that possess material and human assets that are valuable in the ICT-driven economy, and those that are unable to keep up with these changes. Useful policy interventions in this regard are as follows:

(i) Public initiatives for re-training and skill enhancement of redundant workers.

(ii) Greater stress on technology-oriented education for socio-economically backward sections of society.

(iii) Encouraging firms to provide skill-enhancement for existing workers and new employees through provision of educational content and subsidies for workplace training expenses.

It is also apparent that even in Indian states that are well endowed in terms of educational institutions and ICT industry activities, human resource shortages are reaching critical levels. The educational institutions for technical and management education established with government support are unable to keep up with the growing demand for human resources. Private training institutions fill in some of the shortfall, but their contribution continues to be inadequate. In particular, given the rapid technological development in the ICT industry, educational content, academic staff expertise and infrastructure need to be updated on a continuous basis.

Faced with this critical constraint, the larger companies are trying to coordinate with educational institutions to provide up-to-date industry relevant curricula (Basant and Chandra, 2007). However, these instances appear to be sporadic and ad hoc in nature. Furthermore, it is unlikely that smaller companies would benefit from such arrangements. A long-term strategy to combat this problem requires coordinated action between public and private institutions to jointly develop educational content, train academic staff, optimally use available infrastructure and keep abreast with technological advancements in the field.

Following the ANT–NIS framework's dynamic cross-flow of influences that mould socio-economic outcomes, policy makers need to ensure that the valuable combination of high technical and managerial skills in the human resource base is sustained. Several measures can be initiated to encourage firms to undertake a combination organizational and human resource adjustment necessary for ICT adoption. It is apparent that ICT-driven productivity growth is based on a dynamic process combining ICT investments, complementary human capital accumulation and relevant organizational innovations (Bresnahan, Brynjolfsson and Hitt, 2002; De and Dutta, 2007; Dutta, 2009). These aspects are mutually dependent. Therefore, policy initiatives focusing on means to improve productivity through the usage of information technology need to lay stress on all these interlinked approaches. The following relevant policy measures are likely to yield significant dividends in the field of human resource development for high-technology industries like the information technology industry:

(i) Since, the Indian government already has in place ministries for information technology and human resource development, joint action by the two can address the issue of human resource development for ICT industries.

(ii) Advice and consultation can also be elicited from industry bodies like the National Association of Software and Service Companies (NASS-COM), academic institutions and software companies.

(iii) The development and continuous review of nationwide standards of educational content, academic standards and staff requirements would provide the industry with a valuable benchmark for setting the human resource requirement parameters. At the same time, it would provide quality human capital that is required to maintain and enhance the reputation of the Indian software industry in the international market.

(iv) The public and private institutions can develop programs to cross-train academic staff, organize seminars, workshops and conferences for knowledge dissemination, and share infrastructure like libraries, computing facilities and communication networks.

(v) Given the importance of both technical education and management related knowledge, it is necessary to develop educational content that focuses on both aspects with regard to the needs of the software industry. Such programs can be used for management trainees and skill enhancement of existing staff.

Our analysis also calls into question current incentive policies like tax holidays, which only help firms that are already making profits. Rather, revenues gained from taxing ICT companies should be deployed to fund public efforts for human resource enhancement as described above.

It is also evident that, in the ICT industry, higher productivity has been achieved through a combination of superior human resource quality and investments in intangible assets like organizational capabilities (De and Dutta, 2007). First, improvements in ICT sector productivity obviously increases aggregate productivity after the performance of all economic sectors is combined. Furthermore, the organizational attributes and human resource practices of the ICT industry, which contribute to higher productivity, can be emulated by other industries in the services and manufacturing sectors. Certain organizational capabilities like supply chain management (SCM) systems, quality assurance methods and customer relationship management (CRM) techniques have economy-wide applications. Adoption of these methods by other industries can lead to significant productivity gains in those industries.

Arora and Athreye (2002, p. 266) indicate that the organizational practices of software firms have had a "demonstration effect" on other industrial sectors in India. They indicate that certain segments of India's older manufacturing sector are adopting business practices and management styles of the newer ICT companies. It is likely then, that this diffusion of management practices from the ICT sector to other sectors of the economy can have significant productivity effects at the regional and the national level. Policy makers can hasten the diffusion of good organizational practices and better human resource management systems through specific initiatives and improved administrative structures. In particular, while larger companies with their vast resources find it easier to access and implement these practices, smaller firms suffer from lack of information and implementation capabilities. Policy initiatives likely to help in this regard are as follows:

(i) Setting up a system to collate and disseminate organizational best practices. Relevant measures include organization of workshops, seminars and online discussion sites.

(ii) Providing benchmarks for appraisal of organizational and management systems. This can be supplemented by a system for certification that can be used to signal quality. It would also provide customers, potential shareholders and other stakeholders with a transparent system for judging the organizational capabilities of a company.

(iii) Firms should be encouraged to provide in-service training. Generally, certain firms are hesitant to spend on in-service training since employees may quit at a later stage. To address this issue, norms for a certain period of mandatory service following the training period needs to be established.

(iv) To encourage in-service employees to improve their skills and managerial abilities more part-time and executive management programs need to be formulated.

(v) A system of loans should be instituted so that employees can finance their own human capital accumulation.

The development of the ICT industry poses significant challenges to the economy and the society in terms of heightening income disparities and undermining social cohesiveness. At the same time, it opens new vistas for enhancing economic growth and improving social welfare. The socio-economic outcomes that are achieved through the diffusion of ICT depend critically on crucial coordinated action in the public and private spheres. The state, on its part, can help by providing a conducive and enabling environment for private initiatives for development of high-technology industries like ICT. Private firms, on their part, need to acknowledge their social responsibilities in ensuring that purely profit-driven business strategies do not skew the socio-economic substratum on which their investments are based. Ultimately though, the final socio-economic outcomes depend on the way households and individuals respond to the new opportunities, particularly with regard to their choices of human capital investment and labor market participation.

References

Aneja, M. (2004a). "Young IT Pros Reinventing the Workplace," *The Economic Times*, 1 June.

Aneja, M. (2004b). "Why Techies are Quitting Jobs to Freelance," *The Economic Times*, 8 June.

Arora, A., V. S. Arunachalam, J. Asundi, and R. Fernandes (2001). "The Indian Software Services Industry," *Research Policy*, Vol. 30, pp. 1267–1287.

Arora, A. and S. Athreye (2002). "The Software Industry and India's Economic Development," *Information Economics and Policy*, Vol. 14, pp. 253–273.

Arora, A. and A. Gambardella (2004). "The Globalization of the Software Industry: Perspectives and Opportunities for Developed and Developing Countries," NBER Working Paper Series, Working Paper No. 10538.

Athreye, S. (2005). "The Indian Software Industry," in *From Underdogs to Tigers: The Rise and Growth of the Software Industry in Brazil, China, India, Ireland, and Israel*, A. Arora and A. Gambardella (eds.), Oxford: Oxford University Press, pp. 7–39.

Basant, R. and P. Chandra (2007). "Role of Educational and R&D Institutions in City Clusters: An Exploratory Study of Bangalore and Pune Regions in India," *World Development*, Vol. 35, No. 6, pp. 1037–1055.

Bresnahan, T., E. Brynjolfsson, and L. Hitt (2002). "Information Technology, Workplace Organization and the Demand for Skilled Labor: Firm-Level Evidence," *Quarterly Journal of Economics*, Vol. 117, No. 2, pp. 339–376.

Caniëls, M. and H. Romijn (2003). "Dynamic Clusters in Developing Countries: Collective Efficiency and Beyond," *Oxford Development Studies*, Vol. 31, No. 3, pp. 275–292.

Central Statistical Organisation (2004). "Statistical Abstract India 2004," New Delhi (www.mospi.nic.in).

Central Statistical Organisation (2007a). "State Domestic Product (State series)," New Delhi. Available at: http://www.mospi.nic.in/cso_rept_pubn.htm.

Central Statistical Organisation (2007b). "Annual Survey of Industries," New Delhi. Available at: http://mospi.gov.in/asi_index.htm.

Centre for Monitoring Indian Economy (2005). "Prowess (Release 2.4)," Mumbai, India.

Chandrasekhar, C. P. (2010). "How Significant is IT in India," *The Hindu*, 31 May.

Choudhary, R. and M. Premsingh (2004). "B'lore Geeks Richest Among Techies," *The Economic Times*, 23 June.

Cimoli, M. (1998). "National System of Innovation: A Note on Technological Asymmetries and Catching-Up Perspectives," *Interim Report, IT-98-030/June*, Laxenburg, Austria: International Institute for Applied Systems Analysis.

D'Costa, A. P. (2003). "Uneven and Combined Development: Understanding India's Software Exports," *World Development*, Vol. 31, No. 1, pp. 211–226.

D'Costa, A. P. (2011). "Geography, Uneven Development and Distributive Justice: The Political Economy of IT Growth in India," *Cambridge Journal of Regions, Economy and Society*, Vol. 4, No. 2, pp. 237–251.

De, S. and D. Dutta (2007). "Impact of Intangible Capital on Productivity and Growth: Lessons from the Indian Information Technology Software Industry," *Economic Record*, Vol. 83, September, Special Issue, pp. S73–S86.

Debroy, B., L. Bhandari, and R. Saran (2006). "Of Performance, Potential & Policies: The State of the States," *India Today*, 11 September.

Department of Education (2005). "Department of Education: Annual Report 2004–05," Department of Education, Government of India: New Delhi.

Dutta, D. (2007). "Role of ICT in Development Process: A Review of Issues and Prospects in South Asia," in *Information and Communication Technologies for Economic and Regional Developments*, H. Rahman (ed.), Hershey, Pennsylvania: Idea Group Publishing.

Dutta, D. (2008). "Business Process Outsourcing Under Globalization: Is the Conflict between India and the USA Receding?" in *Conflict and Peace in South Asia*, Bingley, Manas Chatterji and B. M. Jain (eds.), UK: Emerald Group Publishing Limited.

Dutta, D. (2009). "Social Shaping of India's Computer Software Technology Sector: A Methodological Analysis in terms of Actors and Networks," in *Post-Reform Development in Asia — Essays for Amiya Kumar Bagchi*, Hyderabad, India: Orient Longman.

Heeks, R. and B. Nicholson (2004). "Software Export Success Factors and Strategies in 'Follower' Nations," *Competition & Change*, Vol. 8, No. 3, pp. 267–303.

Jorgenson, D., M. Ho, and K. Stiroh (2005). "Growth of U.S. Industries and Investments in Information Technology and Higher Education," in *Measuring Capital in the New Economy*, C. Corrado, J. Haltiwanger and D. Sichel (eds.), Chicago: University of Chicago Press, pp. 403–472.

Karnik, K. (2012). "Indian IT Industry Revenues Set to Cross $100 billion," *The Economic Times*, 7 March.

Lal, K. (2001). "Institutional Environment and the Development of Information and Communication Technology in India," *The Information Society*, Vol. 17, pp. 105–117.

Lopamudra, G. (2004a). "IT lets 21-Year Olds Spend Like 35-Year Olds," *The Economic Times*, 22 June.

Lopamudra, G. (2004b). "IT Pros Learn Job Hopping From BPO Bros," *The Economic Times*, 29 June.

McKinsey & Company (2007). "The 'Bird of Gold': The Rise of India's Consumer Market." Available at: www.mckinsey.com/mgi/publications.

Metcalfe, S. (1995). "The Economic Foundations of Technology Policy: Equilibrium and Evolutionary Perspectives," in *Handbook of the Economics of Innovation and Technical Change*, P. Stoneman (ed.), Oxford, UK: Blackwell, pp. 410–512.

Ministry of Human Resource Development (2007). "IT Manpower, Challenge and Response: Interim Report of the Task Force on HRD in IT," Ministry of Human Resource Development, Government of India: New Delhi.

Parthasarathy, B. (2004). "India's Silicon Valley or Silicon Valley's India? Socially Embedding the Computer Software Industry in Bangalore," *International Journal of Urban and Regional Research*, Vol. 28, No. 3, pp. 664–685.

Patibandla, M. and B. Petersen (2002). "Role of Transnational Corporations in the Evolution of a High-Tech Industry: The Case of India's Software Industry," *World Development*, Vol. 30, No. 9, pp. 1561–1577.

Pohjola, M. (2002). "The New Economy: Facts, Impacts and Policies," *Information Economics and Policy*, Vol. 14, pp. 133–144.

Reserve Bank of India (2007). *Handbook of Statistics on Indian Economy*. Available at: http://www.rbi.org.in/scripts/publications.aspx.

Ryder, M. (2003). "What is Actor-Network Theory?" Available at: http://carbon.cudenver.edu/~mryder/itc_data/ant_dff.html1.

Van Dijk, M. P. (2003). "Government Policies With Respect to An Information Technology Cluster in Bangalore, India," *European Journal of Development Research*, Vol. 15, No. 2, pp. 93–108.

Wolff, E. (2002). "The Impact of IT Investment On Income and Wealth Inequality in the Postwar US Economy," *Information Economics and Policy*, Vol. 14, pp. 233–251.

World Bank (2004). "Sustaining India's Services Revolution: Access to Foreign Markets, Domestic Reform and International Negotiations," The World Bank.

Appendix A: Diversity in India's states & union territories.

States	Per capita income growth	Manufacturing growth	ICT growth	No. of engineering colleges per million population	No. of engineering students per million population
Andhra Pradesh	0.058522	0.679734	2.0552	3.201631	930.7845
Arunachal Pradesh	0.010821	0	4.562586	1.075269	0
Assam	0.013141	1.018472	3.590241	0.127224	134.0939
Bihar	0.017122	1.118698	2.188594	0.058451	26.96068
Jharkhand	0.031118	0.206086	0.053721	0.087993	232.2144
Goa	0.084237	1.267669	3.609894	2.48139	1415.219
Gujarat	0.071294	0.831724	1.570071	0.598422	676.5621
Haryana	0.042179	0.82964	1.314883	1.597262	1126.64
Himachal Pradesh	0.062198	1.019385	0.76334	0.37037	376.4815
Jammu & Kashmir	0.020403	0.408399	0	0.594813	199.2624
Karnataka	0.067658	0.750192	1.401684	1.780302	1740.055
Kerala	0.054428	0.523722	3.056492	1.472606	703.3703
Madhya Pradesh	0.02582	0.495311	1.746158	0.950589	363.7069
Chhattisgarh	0.0282	0.684411	0.964832	0.645161	357.5806
Maharashtra	0.035262	0.478616	1.916861	2.035173	1506.016
Manipur	0.04982	0.290805	1.392635	1.53657	553.1653
Meghalaya	0.056608	7.334143	5.564004	0.526593	639.8104
Nagaland	0.038498	0.585638	0	0	0

(Continued)

Appendix A: (*Continued*)

States	Per capita income growth	Manufacturing growth	ICT growth	No. of engineering colleges per million population	No. of engineering students per million population
Orissa	0.032496	0.707913	2.763734	0.5748	400.0605
Punjab	0.026821	0.432345	0	1.126926	769.4084
Rajasthan	0.056665	0.57997	1.186025	0.384008	309.5533
Sikkim	0.043133	0	0	2.309469	1972.286
Tamil Nadu	0.044902	0.694442	1.660045	2.601006	2515.519
Tripura	0.089045	1.580696	5.460213	0.341764	160.9706
Uttar Pradesh	0.017943	0.607034	3.565547	1.071199	166.9214
Uttaranchal	0.041256	1.278662	3.845096	0.674855	836.5501
West Bengal	0.071877	0.539424	1.172983	0.404819	242.277
Andaman & Nicobar Islands	0.005032	−0.07713	0	0	0
Chandigarh	0.067233	0.052797	0.603208	4.322767	1717.579
Delhi	0.184399	0.087037	3.568547	1.149315	1279.284
Pondicherry	0.187363	1.040828	8.260035	5.897617	3433.593

Note: Per capita income growth is annual rate from 1993–1994 to 2003–2004. Authors' calculations are based on data from Reserve Bank of India (2007). Both manufacturing and ICT growths are for the period from 1998–1999 to 2003–2004. Authors' calculations are based on data from Central Statistical Organisation (2007a, 2007b). Details of communication services in Central Statistical Organisation (2007a) are used to represent ICT growth. Details for engineering colleges, students and population are for 2000–2001 from Central Statistical Organisation (2004). Zero represents unavailable data.

Appendix B: India's regional diversity.

Year & regions	Share of private engineering colleges (%)	IT sector output growth
1995–1996:		
North	26 ·	0.8178
South	76	5.9729
West	80	6.1704
East	13	0.2559
2002–2003:		
North	82	2.082
South	92	13.0155
West	86	12.3766
East	84	−0.3205

Note: Growth in IT sector output: Sales growth of major IT companies (authors' calculation is based on data from Centre for Monitoring Indian Economy, 2005).

Source: Private engineering colleges: Share of privately financed colleges in Indian IT capacity, by region and year from Arora and Gambardella (2004).

8. Women's Employment as a Barometer of 'Inclusive Growth': How Well is India Doing?

*Elizabeth Hill**

The 21st century has been labeled the 'Asian Century.' In most cases, this epithet is used to refer to the rise of the Chinese economy and how it is fundamentally restructuring the world economy and geopolitics. But China is not the only economic giant demanding recognition. India is also emerging as a new and important economic force on the global stage. Soon to overtake China as the world's most populous country, the potential of the Indian economy is closely observed by business leaders in OECD economies, who are seeking new markets for production, distribution and investment. Like China, India has achieved double digit rates of growth, albeit briefly. But India also has a large proportion of its population living in poverty. This makes sustained economic growth that delivers human development the most pressing challenge facing Indian governments.

Official concern about the connection between growth and development is evident in India's key planning documents, the Five-Year Plans. The title of the Eleventh Plan, 'Inclusive Growth' (2007–2012), signifies the government's commitment to the need for economic growth that benefits all citizens. However growing anxiety about the government's capacity to deliver inclusive growth is captured in the title of the Twelfth Plan: 'Faster, More Inclusive and Sustainable Growth' (2013). In both Plan documents, the generation of productive and decent employment is identified as a fundamental pathway to 'inclusive growth.' The critical assumption in this conception of inclusive growth is that there is a strong linear relationship between GDP growth and the creation of productive, decent work which

*Elizabeth.hill@sydney.edu.au

will deliver households a standard of living that allows them to achieve key determinants of well-being. However, recent evaluations conclude that the era of strong economic growth has not produced productive and decent employment adequate to the needs of a burgeoning working age population (Unni and Raveebdran, 2007; Harriss, 2011; Himanshu, 2011).

This chapter evaluates the concept of inclusive development from the perspective of women's employment experience during the era of strong economic growth. Historically Indian women have had very low rates of workforce participation and when they do work it has been primarily in lowquality, poorly paid and unregulated work. How much, and in what ways, women's employment experience has changed during the high-growth decades provides a useful barometer of the inclusive growth agenda. An examination of the trends in women's labor market participation, access to quality work and employment status provides the basis for this evaluation. In the final part of the chapter, two industry sectors that have expanded significantly and become highly feminized in the high-growth era — information and technology-enabled services and business process outsourcing (ITES & BPO) and domestic service — will be discussed. A short analysis of these sectors will highlight the poor and uneven impact of economic growth on women's employment experience in India.

1. High Growth, Poverty and Inequality

The New Economic Policy introduced as a result of the current account crisis of 1991 fundamentally changed India's economy. After decades of low growth and an introverted economy, the 1991 reforms set India's economic course resolutely on the pathway of market liberalization and global integration. Some of these reforms had begun to be made during the late 1980s under Rajiv Gandhi's prime ministership (Hill, 2009). But it was the extension of these reforms in the 1990s that led to sustained rates of economic growth which peaked in 2007 at 10% (see Figure 1). Global economic crises and the emergence of a number of unresolved domestic issues have seen growth weaken since 2007.[1]

---

[1]Growth declined to 8.4% in 2009–2010 in the aftermath of the global economic crisis and is expected to slow still further in the current fiscal year 2011–2012 to around 7% on account of the European debt crisis and a number of domestic issues (Ministry of Finance, 2011).

Figure 1: GDP growth (annual %).

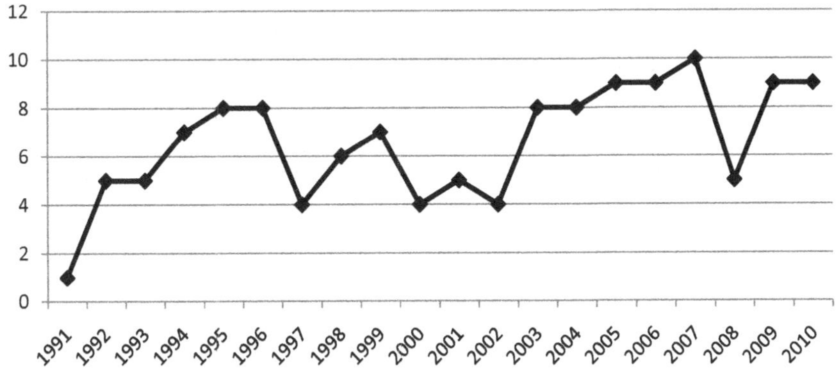

Source: World Development Indicators, World Bank.[2]

Sustained rates of high growth have delivered an exponential rise in gross national income which by 2010 was five times greater than its value in 1991 (World Development Indicators). However, headline-grabbing national growth and income figures belie the pervasive poverty and rising inequality that define the daily lives of hundreds of millions of citizens living in the 'new India.' Poverty rates are on the decline in India: the proportion of people living on less than US$1.25 fell from 51% in 1990 to 42% by 2005. However, this positive development is overshadowed by growth in the absolute headcount number which has risen, on account of population growth, with the total number of poor living on less than US$1.25 a day increasing from 435.5 million in 1990 to 456 million in 2005 (Chen and Ravallion, 2010, pp. 1603–1605).[3]

Population growth may slow any positive impact that economic growth may be expected to have on poverty rates. But the pattern of inequality that has developed alongside the years of high GDP growth suggest there are dynamics apart from population growth hampering the distribution of economic prosperity in India. Over the past two decades, inequality in earnings has doubled. In 1990, the top 10% of Indian wage earners earned six times more than the bottom 10%. In 2010, they earned 12 times as

---

[2]See http://data.worldbank.org/data-catalog/world-development-indicators.

[3]Provisional results from the 2011 National census puts India's total population at over 1.2 Billion (1, 210, 193, 422). An increase of more than 181 million over the decade. Population growth is expected to continue — and to reach around 1.4 billion by 2026 (GOI, 2006).

much (OECD, 2011, p. 58). The highly skewed nature of income distribution is accentuated by the pattern of earnings across the middle of the income spectrum: the top 10% of wage earners make almost five times more than the median 10%, but the median 10% makes just 0.4 times more than the bottom 10% (OECD, 2011, p. 58). This means there are a small number of very high income earners and a large majority who earn very low wages. Such widespread poverty and inequality in the context of strong GDP growth raises important questions about the structure of economic growth and its capacity to deliver human development.

2. Inclusive Growth: The Importance of Employment

Economic policy since 2007 has identified 'inclusive growth' as a national priority. This concept is developed in the 11th Five-Year Plan (2007–2012) and the 12th Five-Year Plan (2013–2017). The Plan documents talk about a number of drivers of inclusive growth. However the most explicit argument focuses on the role that decent employment plays in driving inclusive growth. In the Forward to the 11th Plan, growth, it is argued, '... must be inclusive in the broadest sense... It must generate sufficient volumes of high quality employment to provide the means for uplift of large numbers of our population from the low income, low quality occupations in which too many of them have been traditionally locked' (GOI, 2008, p. iii). In highlighting decent work as a defining feature of inclusive growth, the 11th Plan acknowledges the shortcomings of current employment opportunities and the demographic challenge of a burgeoning working-age population: 'The generation of productive and gainful employment, with decent working conditions, on a sufficient scale to absorb our growing labour force must form a critical element in the strategy for achieving inclusive growth' (GOI, 2008, Chapter 4:4.1, p. 63). The premise that the creation of productive and decent employment is the foundation upon which economic success will enhance well-being and reduce poverty remains a central concern of the 12th Plan: 'For growth to be inclusive it must create adequate livelihood opportunities and add to decent employment commensurate with the expectations of a growing labour force' (GOI, 2011, p. 9).

Employment plays a critical role in defining women's economic and social security. Extreme forms of poverty, social and political vulnerability were first linked to disadvantage in the labor market in the 1988 Report by the National Commission on Self Employed Women and Women in the Informal Sector, *Shramshakti* (GOI, 1988). Many studies and reports released since then show that women have continued to experience multiple forms of disadvantage in the labor market. Whether women's employment situation has improved during the high-growth decades is evaluated in the following section.

2.1. *Women's participation in the labor market*

Indian women have traditionally had a very low official rate of labor market participation. World Bank data reports Indian women's labor market participation at only 29%, lower than the average rate of 32% for women across South Asia, much lower than the 37% participation rate for women in other lower-middle income countries and half the East Asian and Pacific average (see Table 1).[4] Low participation rates mean that women only make up about a quarter of the total Indian labor market.

Women's workforce participation varies significantly across the urban–rural divide.[5] Urban women have the lowest average workforce participation rates, oscillating between 16.6% and 13.8% over the past 15 years (see Figure 2). Rural women participate in paid employment at twice the rate

Table 1: Women's labor force participation 2010: Indian comparison.

	Labor force participation for women[6]	% of total labor force who are women
India	29	25
South Asia	32	27
Lower-middle income countries	37	31
East Asia and Pacific (developing only)	65	44

Source: World Development Indicators, World Bank.

---

[4]India is classified by the World Bank as a lower middle-income country. These are countries with US$1,006–US$3,975 GNI/capita 2010.

[5]Workforce participation rates are based upon the number of employed people as a proportion of the total population. This is different from labor force figures which include employed and unemployed people looking for work as a proportion of the total population.

[6]Aged 15 years and above.

Figure 2: Workforce participation rate according to usual status (ps + ss) as a percentage in NSS rounds.

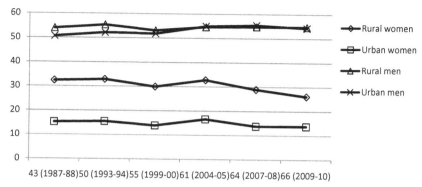

NSS Round

Source: Government of India, Employment and Unemployment Situation in India, NSS 64th & 66th Rounds, Ministry of Statistics and Program Implementation, GOI (2010, 2011).

of urban women within a band of 32.8–26.1%.[7] Men, both urban and rural, have much higher workforce participation rates than women. The largest gap in participation is between urban men and urban women, with men almost four times as likely to be in the workforce (54.3%) compared with their female counterparts (13.8%) in 2009–2010.

A comparison of women's absolute and comparative workforce participation rates since the pre-reform years (NSS Round 43) through to the high growth era (NSS Rounds 50–66) shows that overall women's workforce participation has been relatively unresponsive to high rates of economic growth. Workforce participation has remained relatively flat from the late 1980s to 2010, with some upward movement around 2004–2005,[8] before returning to trend by 2007–2008, when rates stabilized for urban women and declined for rural women in the 2009–2010 data. Women's participation has also not changed very much relative to that of men. The large gap in participation rates between men and women throughout the period of high

---

[7]Figures are for 'usual status.' This is the most generous measure of workforce participation and includes primary plus subsidiary workforce status.

[8]Studies of women's workforce participation in the first decade of the 21st century have concluded that the improvement in women's participation in the 2004–2005 data is most probably 'distress employment' (see Unni and Raveebdran, 2007; Harriss, 2011; Himanshu, 2011).

growth has remained relatively constant, although widening slightly since 2000 on account of a small improvement in men's urban participation and a decline in women's rural and urban participation. This is reflected in the decline in the total number of women employed, from 148.6 million in 2004–2005 to 127.3 million in 2009–2010, while the size of the workforce remained quite stable at 458.4 million (457.4 million in 2004–2005). Sustained high growth rates do not appear to have generated an increase in women's workforce participation.

The modest decline in women's participation within the context of a high-growth economy locates India's experience outside the norm. In most developing economies, periods of strong economic growth have led to a substantial increase in women's labor force participation (Elson and Pearson, 1981; Standing 1989, 1999). In the East Asian export-led development model, rapid economic growth produced a feminization of the labor force as women left their rural villages and moved to urban environments for work in new factories (Lim, 1990). The Indian growth story has produced neither significant urbanization nor wide-scale feminization of labor (Mazumdar, 2007). Instead the vast majority of Indian women continue to be employed in agriculture.[9]

3. The Quality of Women's Employment

Participation is one dimension of the employment story. Another is the quality of work available — its productivity, security of tenure, conditions and wages. The 11th Plan identifies low-quality work that delivers a low income as an obstacle to inclusive growth. This is a significant problem for India as the economy is highly informal — much more than most other developing economies — and most employment is of very low quality. Accurate data on the size, value and contribution of the informal economy are difficult to obtain due to the inadequacy of official statistics and the hidden nature of much informal work. Mindful of these problems, scholars have made a variety of estimates, most of which conclude that informal labor constitutes between 90% and 93% of the total workforce — depending on the definition and method of data collection. One of the most common methodologies

---

[9]Women's employment in agriculture has been on the decline since the early 1990s, when around 75% of employed women were found in agriculture. But it remains high, currently 65% of working women are found in agriculture (World Development Indicators, 2010).

for calculating informal employment in India uses data collected on the 'organized' and the 'unorganized' sectors. Indian statistics and law make a formal distinction between these two parts of the economy. The 'organized sector' includes public sector establishments and non-agricultural establishments employing 10 or more people in the private sector. The 'unorganised sector' comprises establishments in the non-agricultural sector employing less than 10 persons. The organized sector overlaps significantly with what scholars define as formal employment on account of the labor regulations, social security provisions and decent work conditions that accrue to this part of the labor force. Lack of regulation in the unorganized sector means work is highly informal and precarious.

The informal economy is where most women find employment. The National Commission for Enterprises in the Unorganised Sector recently reported that 91.3% of working women are employed in the informal/ unorganized economy (GOI, 2009, p. 23). For most women employed in the informal economy their work is unregulated, they are not protected by labor law and have limited or no access to social security provisions. Their informal status makes them vulnerable to exploitation by middle-men and officials. Work is insecure, defined by low productivity and very low wages. Informal work is highly heterogeneous — including small scale producers, vendors, daily laborers and industrial outworkers — and located across all industry sectors. What is common to all informal workers is the experience of economic insecurity (Hill, 2010).

The dominance of the informal economy and the conditions of pervasive insecurity that define informal work highlight how significant the quality of employment is to the notion of inclusive growth. High-quality employment not only delivers a decent wage that can move a household out of poverty, it can also facilitate long-term well-being through investments in education, health and housing. The quality of employment generated during the decades of high growth and women's employment experience is therefore of interest to our evaluation of inclusive growth.

Numerous studies on the structure of employment since the 1991 reforms show that total employment growth has been heavily weighted toward the informal or unorganized sector. This trend is clearly reflected in employment data released by the National Commission for Enterprises in the Unorganized Sector (GOI, 2009). Between 1999–2000 and 2004–2005, the number of workers employed in the vulnerable unorganized sector of the economy increased by 16.8% to equal a total of 422.61 million workers (see

Table 2: Growth in unorganized employment.

	1999–2000	2004–2005	Percentage change
Total employment/workforce	396.76 m	457.46 m	+15.3
Unorganized sector workers	342.64 m	394.9 m	+15.3
Unorganized workers in the organized sector	20.46 m	29.14 m	+42.0
TOTAL unorganized workers	**361.74**	**422.61**	**+16.8**
Unorganized workers as a percentage of all workers	91.2%	92.4%	+1.3
TOTAL Organized workers	35 m	34.9 m	−0.9
Organized workers as a percentage of all workers	**8.8%**	**7.6%**	**−13.6**

Source: Government of India (2008b) Tables 4.1, 3.2 and 3.4.

Table 2). The growth in the unorganized workforce was not only on account of growth in the overall workforce, which grew at 15.3% over the period. The proportion of the workforce employed in the unorganized sector also grew on account of jobs in the organized sector becoming informalized. This downgrading of employment quality occurred at a rapid rate over the time period which saw a 42% increase in the number of unorganized jobs located within the organized sector. This produced a decline in the overall proportion of formally employed workers.

The informalization of employment is now a long established trend that is reflected across a variety of indicators. Figures released by Manpower company TeamLease showed that between 1991 and 2001, the number of workers in the organized sector increased at an annualized growth rate of only 0.38% compared with the unorganized sector, in which the number of workers grew at an annualized rate of 2.68% (TeamLease, 2006, p. 24). Government data on employment elasticity for the period 1999–2000 to 2004–2005 also reflects the ongoing trend toward informalization, with employment elasticity in the unorganized sector equal to 0.71, almost double the 0.36 reported for the organized sector (GOI, 2008b). These indicators all point to the same conclusion: that the majority of new jobs are in the unorganized/informal economy where job quality is poor and employment is defined by extreme forms of exploitation, insecurity and low wages.

4. Women's Employment Status

A more nuanced way of assessing one aspect of the quality of women's employment experience during the high-growth era is to track changes in the wage–labor relationship and its link to economic security. The National Sample Survey (NSS) Oganisation collects data on the distribution and earnings of workers for three types of wage–labor relationships: Self-employment, regular wage/salaried employee and casual workers.

The majority of women workers, 41% of urban women workers and 55% of rural women workers, are self-employed (see Table 3). Self-employed workers are highly heterogeneous and found in most industries and occupations. They are engaged as small-scale producers in dairy and forestry, as small farmers and in manufacturing. They work as traders, street vendors and transport workers. For some, self-employment can signify entrepreneurship, innovation and economic dynamism. For many, it is a form of distress employment taken up when no other options are available and income must be earned. Self-employment is often insecure, seasonal and unregulated. In the context of widespread economic informality, the category of self-employment often conceals the deeply dependent production, distribution and wage relations that structure self-employed women's work lives and makes them vulnerable to the vagaries of local markets, officials and contractors (Hill, 2010). The inadequacy of income earned through self-employment is reflected in NSS data on workers' levels of satisfaction with their remuneration. Data from the 2004–2005 NSS 61st Round reports that only half of all self-employed women (rural and urban) rate their earnings

Table 3: Distribution (per 1000) of usually employed (ps + ss) women by status of employment, all-India.

	Self-employed		Regular wage/ salaried		Casual labor	
	urban	rural	urban	rural	urban	rural
1993/1994	448	586	292	27	261	387
1999/2000	453	573	333	31	214	396
2004/2005	477	637	356	37	167	326
2007/2008	423	583	379	41	199	376
2009/2010	411	557	393	44	196	399

Source: Government of India (2010 and 2011). Employment and Unemployment Situation in India, NSS 64th and 66th Round.

Table 4: Number of self-employed persons according to usual status (ps + ss) reporting their earning from self-employment as remunerative per 1000 of self-employed persons and their per 1000 distribution by amount (Rs) regarded as remunerative.

	No. per 1000 of self-employed persons reporting earnings as remunerative	Per 1000 distribution of self-employed persons reporting earning as remunerative by amount (Rs.) regarded as remunerative					
		1– 1000	1001– 1500	1501– 2000	2001– 2500	2501– 3000	More than Rs 3000
Rural male	511	129	175	165	114	129	273
Rural female	514	342	235	154	89	72	99
Urban male	609	49	82	99	72	122	565
Urban female	509	328	202	126	77	81	183

Source: Government of India (2006). Employment and Unemployment Situation in India 2004–2005, NSS 61st Round, Statement 5.12, p. 94.

as remunerative (see Table 4). When asked what level of monthly income self-employed women rate as 'remunerative,' around one third of women said they considered less than Rs. 1000 per month remunerative and another fifth considered it to be an income of Rs. 1000–1500 per month (see Table 4). These figures suggest that most self-employed women have very low expectations of the income they can earn from self-employment and that most receive very low wages (Sahu, 2011). Men have much higher expectation of what a remunerative income is.

Regular wage/salaried work can be a more stable form of employment. In urban areas, 39% of working women are engaged in jobs that deliver a regular wage or salary. In rural areas, the proportion is only around 4.5% (see Table 3). Regularity of wage payment is of considerable benefit to women workers and is one criterion of decent work. Women workers counted in this category include women engaged in formal employment who receive relatively decent conditions and wages. However, receipt of a regular wage does not mean that the wage is necessarily of a decent level or that work conditions are good. Domestic service workers, for example, are paid regularly but typically earn very low wages (Sahu, 2011). But even these wages are higher than those received by casual workers. This is unsurprising, given the highly volatile and insecure nature of casual labor. Data from the NSS 66th Round show a large gap in earnings between regular wage/salaried employees and casual workers. On an average, an urban worker receiving a

Table 5: Employment status and daily wages.

	Wage/salaried employee		Casual employees[10]	
	Urban	Rural	Urban	Rural
Average/day	Rs 365	Rs 232	Rs 122	Rs 93
Women	Rs 309	Rs 156	Rs 77	Rs 69
Men	Rs 377	Rs 249	Rs 132	Rs 102
Gender-Wage ratio	0.82	0.63	0.58	0.67

Source: Government of India (2011). Employment and Unemployment situation in India, NSS 66th Round.

regular wage/salary will earn three times as much as their casually employed counterpart. The gap for rural workers is a little less with rural wage/salary workers earning about 2.5 times more than casual workers (see Table 5). The biggest differential, however, is between urban women workers: those engaged in regular wage/salary work earn, on average, four times as much as those in casual employment. Wages are more highly differentiated in urban centers, particularly between men and women: female urban casual workers earn on average only 58% of the male wage while women in regular wage/salary work earn 82% of the average male wage.

The large disparity in wages between regular wage/salaried employees and casual workers, and 'non remunerative' self-employment means that employment status is an important determinant of economic prosperity and associated well-being. The NSS data for the five rounds since 1991 shows that the composition of women's employment status has changed in the high growth era (see Table 3). Women remain predominantly self-employed, although there has been a fall of 3.7 percentage points in the proportion of urban women engaged in self-employment from almost 45% to 41% during the period from 1993–1994 to 2007–2010. Rural women's engagement in self-employment is also down 3 percentage points, from almost 59% to almost 56%. Alongside the small decline in self-employment for women, we find that urban and rural women experienced a strong increase in access to regular wage/salaried employment: an increase of 10 percentage points for urban women up to 39% from 29%, and a small but steady rise up to 4.4% for rural women from 2.7%. By comparison, casual labor is clearly on the

---

[10] For those engaged in works other than public works.

decline for urban women but remains a regular form of employment for rural women.[11]

The shift in the distribution of women workers between employment types is relatively subtle. Self-employment remains the dominant form of women's employment, although the pattern is different for rural and urban women. Throughout the high-growth years, rural women have remained primarily in self-employment and casual labor. Urban women, however, have experienced some significant changes in employment status during the high-growth era and are increasingly finding employment in regular wage/salaried work.

4.1. *Urban women in regular wage/salary work*

Access to a regular wage contributes to women's well-being and security because of the reliability of delivery and reduction in many direct forms of economic exploitation associated with casual labor and self-employment. However not all regular wage/salaried jobs are the same. Some are located within the formal sector of the economy, where wage rates are high and employees enjoy security of tenure, career development opportunities, decent social security provisions and the benefit of protective labor laws. Others are located in the informal economy, where even a regular wage can be very low and the lack of employment protection and social security leaves workers highly vulnerable and insecure. This final section investigates the structure of regular wage/salaried work in two industries in which urban women have found increasing amounts of employment during the era of high growth: the information and technology enabled services and business process outsourcing sector (ITES-BPO) and domestic service. Women's employment experience in these two feminised sectors highlights the uneven structure of 'inclusive growth'.

4.1.1. *ITES-BPO sector*

The stellar rates of economic growth that have defined the post-reform era are in part being driven by entrepreneurship and innovation in the private sector and especially in information and knowledge-based services

---

[11]Male employment shows a different trend: self-employment for rural men is declining, and increasingly in a small way for urban men. Both rural and urban men are experiencing significant decline in opportunities for regular wage/salaried jobs, and casual labour is a growing form of male employment (R: 38%; U: 17%).

industries. The services sector currently accounts for approximately 30% of total exports and is a major driver of GDP growth. India has established itself as a global leader in the ITES-BPO sector, able to provide back-office support and software development services to some of the world's largest and most prestigious companies. Software services are growing rapidly: in the 1990s software services made up 20% of service exports. They currently account for more than half (Cagliarini and Baker, 2010). The sector is making a growing contribution to GDP — ICT services alone contributed 3% of GDP in 2000–2001, doubling to 6% in 2007–2008 (GOI, 2010). The ITES-BPO sector has had a profound impact on the Indian economy and, in many cases, changed the nature of work and production in many OECD economies. It has also generated new forms of employment for an increasingly aspirational workforce. Industry sources claim the Indian ITES-BPO industry is the largest private sector employer in the country, with direct employment of 2.23 million professionals and indirect employment of more than 8 million people (NASSCOM Mercer, 2009). Many of these new workers are women.

Female employment has been a defining feature of employment in the ITES-BPO sector (Palit, 2008). Firms committed to building their competitive advantage in the global market place have harnessed the resources of a highly educated, skilled and English-speaking local labor force. Increasingly, these workers are young, highly skilled women with prestigious degrees and robust career aspirations. The growing employment of women is an intentional and coordinated strategy by the sector to maintain global competitiveness. The peak industry body for the ITES-BPO sector, the National Association of Software and Services Companies (NASSCOM) reported that, in 2008, women constituted 30% of employees in the sector: 671,000 out of 2.23 million workers. The industry is committed to recruiting women and expects that, by 2020, women will make up 50% of the total ITES-BPO workforce (NASSCOM, 2009). Self-reporting by individual companies appears to confirm this trend with 40% of workers at Bangalore-based global IT company, WIPRO, and 50% of their 14,000 new recruits in 2008 reported to be women (NASSCOM Mercer, 2009).

Women are employed across the ITES-BPO sector in low-end domestic call centers and data processing units, and in the high-end export-orientated software development industry. In call centers, women are often preferred because they are assumed to be stable employees. Flexible time schedules also suit many women who fit work in between childcare and school routines.

At the elite end of the market, a shortage of skilled labor makes highly educated women as competitive as their male counterparts in the 'war for talent' that dominates individual company strategies (Hewlett *et al.*, 2010). Efforts to retain skilled staff in a competitive global industry has driven many companies to create policies aimed at developing the careers of women workers and supporting them during times of peak care responsibilities such as at the birth of a baby (Hill, 2009). Common policy initiatives in the sector are around sexual harassment, flexible working hours and flexible leave. The provision of childcare — either onsite, offsite or through company supported childcare search services — remain less common but is on the rise (NASSCOM Mercer, 2009). In its deliberate employment of women workers and intentional support for them in the workplace, the ITES-BPO sector runs counter to the mainstream economy forming a small industrial enclave in which work is rapidly becoming feminized.

The nature and quality of employment varies across the ITES-BPO sector and includes simple data entry and record keeping, highly skilled software development, research, modeling and project management. Call centers, in particular, have attracted much criticism about the terms of employment and labor process. However, most scholars conclude that, while aspects of call center work can be highly problematic for women workers, these jobs are often far better than the alternatives and more highly paid (Patel, 2010; van den Broek, 2004). At the elite end of the ITES-BPO market, women workers are extremely well renumerated and enjoy many of the benefits that accrue to global economy workers in Europe and the US.

Rapid growth in the ITES-BPO sector is directly linked to economic reform in the broader Indian economy and the new, and often decent, employment opportunities that have become available reflect the concept of 'inclusive growth' as it is defined in the 11th and 12th Plan documents. However, the ITES-BPO sector provides employment for only a tiny proportion of the total workforce, and even if the industry target of half all employees are women, this would only equate to jobs for 0.01% of total female workforce.[12] This means inclusive growth is only a reality for very few women. The vast majority of women continue to be engaged in highly informalised, low paid jobs with poor conditions such as household domestic work.

---

[12]The 66th NSS Round reports total workforce of 460.2 million, of which 127.7 million are women (PS + SS).

4.1.2. *Domestic work*

Engagement in the global economy and liberalization of the domestic economy post-1991 has delivered new forms of wealth and increased incomes for the urban middle-classes and rural elites (Jayadev, Motiram and Vakulabharanam, 2011). One reflection of growing economic prosperity has been the burgeoning of a servant-employing middle class (Palriwala and Neetha, 2009). The dynamics driving this trend derive from the macroeconomic and social changes that have developed in response to India's globalizing and liberalizing economy. The expansion in opportunities for domestic work in private households has been, for the most part, driven by the sudden increase in the wealth of urban households and the emergence of dual-earner family structures. With an increasing number of women spending their days occupied in non-household work, a domestic work deficit has emerged. This work is increasingly being outsourced to paid domestic service workers many of whom are migrants from the rural areas (Kaur, 2006). Widespread agrarian distress (Palit and Singh, 2011) along with industrial restructuring and the loss of jobs in the organized industrial sector by male household heads have pushed women into taking up employment as domestic workers.

Rapid growth in the numbers of women employed in private domestic households as housekeepers, cooks, cleaners and child carers is reflected in numerous studies on domestic service workers. Official data only began to be collected by the National Sample Survey in 1999–2000, and while there is some debate over the accuracy of the data after only two rounds of collection, there is evidence that domestic work is growing as a major form of women's employment and is now the dominant form of urban women's employment (Chandrasekhar and Ghosh, 2007). Palriwala and Neetha's work on the Indian care economy includes analysis of domestic service workers based on unit-level NSS employment and unemployment data. This shows a significant surge in women employed as domestic service workers in private households, from 447,100 workers in 1999–2000 to more than 2.5 million in 2004–2005 (see Table 6). Given systemic problems with counting women's informal employment and the private location of domestic work, it is reasonable to assume the total number of women employed in this sector is significantly greater than what has been captured in official data. Some economists have estimated the number to be more than 3 million (Chandrasekhar and Ghosh, 2007). On all accounts, women are rapidly being absorbed into the domestic labor market, which now accounts for around 1.8% of the total female labor force (Neetha and

Table 6: Growth of domestic workers.

	1999–2000			2004–2005		
	No. of workers	Percentage of total female employment	Female share	No. of workers	Percentage of total female employment	Female share
Housemaid/servant	438,200	0.4	80.4	2,381,100	1.6	87.4
Cook	6,400	0.0	72.6	96,600	0.1	73.9
Babysitter/ayah	2,600	0.0	76.4	69,600	0.0	74.2
Total	447,100	0.4	63.4	2,547,400	1.8	71.6

Source: Neetha and Palriwala (2011, p. 102).

Palriwala, 2011). Domestic work is also increasingly feminized, with the total share of paid domestic work performed by women increasing from around 63% in 1999–2000 to almost 72% by 2004–2005.

Domestic service work typically draws a regular wage or salary. However, lack of regulation in the sector means wages are highly variable and differ according to the type of employment (full-time, part-time, live-in, live-out), the tasks performed, the size of the household, the location of the work premises and the socio-economic status of the employer with householders residing in wealthier colonies paying more than those in more middle-class locations. A woman's experience also informs the wage rate with experience attracting a premium. A 2009 study of live-in domestic workers in Delhi by the Institute of Social Studies Trust, Delhi (ISST), reported the average wage received by live-in domestic workers was around Rs 4500 per month (Bhattacharya, 2009). Workers also received board and food as well as other in-kind payments. Live-out workers, some part-time and some full-time, reported much lower average wages of around Rs 1875 per month.

The conditions of work also vary widely amongst domestic workers. The paucity of formal regulation means that domestic workers typically experience very long and unpredictable hours of work. Live-in domestic workers are prone to overwork and often treated as permanently 'on call.' Many do not have regular days off or paid holiday time. Live-out workers, especially part-time and piece-rate workers who perform designated tasks in a number of houses each day sometimes have more control over excessive work requests from employers, but they also do not have paid leave days or holidays. Domestic workers of all kinds are not covered by protective labor laws, experience low levels of employment security, limited social security and are often vulnerable to personal harassment and violence on account of the private and hidden nature of the workplace (Palriwala and Neetha, 2009). Economic growth has delivered new forms of wealth to the servant employing middle classes, but the women who find work in their homes experience unfavorable terms of employment, which leave them personally vulnerable and economically insecure.

5. Discussion

New employment opportunities in the ITES-BPO sector and in domestic service highlight the uneven structure of 'inclusive growth' and the varied terms of employment that shape women's work experience in the high-growth era. Employment in domestic service and the ITES-BPO sector typically deliver women a regular wage or salary. But regular wage/salaried jobs are not intrinsically 'decent' and do not necessarily represent the type of productive and gainful employment with decent working conditions that the 11th and 12th Plan identify as pivotal to the process of inclusive growth. The daily experience of domestic workers demonstrates that wages are not the only determinant of decent work. Minimum standards around work conditions, security of tenure, social security provisions and freedom of association are also important attributes of high-quality work. Domestic workers have historically been sidelined by protective labor laws such as minimum wages schedules, although several states, such as Tamil Nadu, Maharashtra, Kanartaka and Kerala have recently initiated measures to protect some rights of domestic workers (Neetha and Parliwala, 2011, p. 115). Where social security provisions have been available, they have been applied on an ad hoc basis and only in some states. The privatized and personalized nature of domestic work typically performed by women of low caste and class with limited social and political voice, with no union representation means most laws are ignored by employers and government. The inclusion of domestic workers in the 2008 Unorganised Workers Social Security Act, is an important development, but the capacity of the Act to deliver substantive benefits to domestic workers is contested by scholars and activists (Neetha and Palriwala, 2011, p. 116). In response to the growth in the domestic labor force and recognition of the exploitation and economic insecurity that shape the work-life experience of these workers, two draft bills have been developed: The National Commission for Women's 2008 Domestic Workers (Registration, Social Security and Welfare) Bill; and, the National Campaign Committee of Unorganised Sector Workers' 2008 Domestic Workers (Regulation of Employment, Conditions of work, social security and welfare) Bill. Pressure is building on the government to address the need for regulation in the domestic service sector, however, so far, neither Bill has been passed by the Parliament.

The feminization of employment in the ITES-BPO sector provides a contrasting case to domestic work. Rapid growth in the sector and new employment opportunities for women are directly linked to India's economic reform agenda and increased integration into the global economy. Employment in ITES-BPO jobs is of a relatively higher quality than that normally available to women, although long hours and a hostile attitude to union organization are also a feature of this sector (Sandhu, 2006; Singh and Pandey, 2005). Wages are comparatively good across the sector with call-center workers earning from Rs 5000–8000 for low-skilled work and up to Rs 20,000 for high-end graduate employees (Nandi, 2009). Highly skilled software development workers with post-graduate degrees earn very high wages on par with global corporate standards and enjoy excellent conditions and robust career prospects. In many respects, the conditions of women's employment in the ITES-BPO sector is an example of inclusive growth. However it is inclusive growth for the few. The tiny elite that are able to access these new jobs underscores the overwhelming evidence that the majority of women have not been the beneficiaries of a positive link between macroeconomic growth and the generation of productive and gainful employment, with decent working conditions'.

6. Conclusion

The employment dynamics outlined in this chapter show that women's employment experience in the post-1991, high-growth era has not been inclusive and has failed to deliver quality employment opportunities that promote well-being and prosperity amongst the majority poor. Indian women are not increasing their participation in the labor market, and for most women who do work, employment remains informal, precarious, insecure, poorly paid and unprotected. The unevenness of women's employment experience, illustrated in the ITES-BPO sector and domestic service work, shows that economic growth linked to globalization can deliver decent work for those with skills that are highly valued in the global market place. However, the inequality that is being driven by globalization, industrial restructuring and informalization also generates low-quality employment opportunities defined by poor conditions and low wages.

Women's labor market experience in the high-growth era does not reflect the aspirations of the inclusive growth agenda outlined in the 11th and 12th Plan documents. Instead, strong economic growth has so far generated increasing inequality in the labor market, where a few women are able to access new decent employment opportunities and many are forced to perform insecure and precarious forms of informal work. Women's employment experience is not unique in this respect (Unni and Raveebdran, 2007; Harriss, 2011; Himanshu, 2011). Unfortunately, it merely reflects the widespread failure of economic growth to deliver adequate decent work for the entire Indian working-age population.

References

Bhattacharya, S. (2009). "Key Findings from Case Studies of Live in Domestic Workers in NCT of Delhi' & Findings from Survey of Live-Out Domestic workers in NCT of Delhi," ISST Workshop Notes, New Delhi, 4 November (Unpublished).

Cagliarini, A. and M. Baker (2010). "Economic Change in India," _Reserve Bank of Australia Bulletin_ — September Quarter 2010. Available at: http://www.rba.gov.au/publications/bulletin/2010/sep/3.html [accessed on 10 June 2011].

Chandrasekhar, C. P. and J. Ghosh (2007). "Women Workers in Urban India," February 6. Available at: http://www.macroscan.net/fet/feb07/fet060207 Women_Workers.htm [accessed on 17 July 2012].

Chen, S. and M. Ravallion (2010). "The Developing World Is Poorer Than We Thought, but No Less Successful in the Fight Against Poverty," _The Quarterly Journal of Economics_, Vol. 125, No. 4, pp. 1577–1625.

Elson, D. and R. Pearson (1981). "Nimble Fingers make Cheap Workers: An Analysis of Women's Employment in Third World Export Manufacturing," _Feminist Review_, Vol. 7, 87–107.

Government of India (GOI) (1988). _'Shramshakti': Report of the National Commission on Self-Employed Women and Women in the Informal Sector_, New Delhi: Jain Books.

Government of India. Office of the Registrar General (2006). "Population Projections for India and States 2001–2026," Report of the Technical Group on

Population Projections, constituted by the National Commission on Population, May.

Government of India, National Sample Survey Office, Ministry of Statistics and Program Implementation (2006). "Employment and Unemployment Situation in India 2004–2005: NSS 61st Round," Part 1, Report no. 515.

Government of India, Planning Commission (2008). *Eleventh Five Year Plan 2007–12: Volume 1: Inclusive Growth*, Oxford University Press, New Delhi.

Government of India, National Commission for Enterprises in the Unorganized Sector (2008b). *Task Force Report on Definitional and Statistical Issues*, New Delhi, September.

Government of India (2009). *The Challenge of Employment in India: Report of the National Commission for Enterprises in the Unorganised Sector*, Academic Foundation of India, New Delhi.

Government of India, Ministry of Statistics and Program Implementation (2010). *Value Addition and Employment Generation in the ICT Sector in India*, New Delhi.

Government of India, National Sample Survey Office, Ministry of Statistics and Program Implementation (2010). "Employment and Unemployment Situation in India, NSS 64th Round."

Government of India, (2011). Ministry of Finance, "Annual Report 2011–12." Available at: http://finmin.nic.in/reports/annualreport.asp [accessed on 6 June 2012].

Government of India, Planning Commission (2011). "Faster, Sustainable and More Inclusive Growth: An Approach to 12th five year plan," August. Available at: http://planningcommission.nic.in/plans/planrel/12appdrft/12appdrft.htm [accessed on 10 September 2011].

Government of India, National Sample Survey Office Ministry of Statistics and Program Implementation (2011). "Employment and Unemployment Situation in India: NSS 66th. Round." Available at: http://164.100.34.62/index.php/ catalog/18/overview [accessed on 10 October 2011].

Harriss, J. (2011). "Inclusive Growth: How is India Doing?" ISAS Working Paper No. 137, 29 November.

Hewlett, S. A., R. Rashid, L. Leader-Chivee and C. Fredman (2010). *The Battle for Female Talent in India*, New York: Centre for Work-Life Policy.

Hill, E. (2009). "The Indian Industrial Relations System: Struggling to Address the Dynamics of a Globalising Economy," *Journal of Industrial Relations*, Vol. 51, No. 3, pp. 395–410.

Hill, E. (2009). "Waking up to Work and Care: Emerging Policy Frameworks in the Formal Labour Market," Paper Presented at Who Cares for the Child? Gender and the Care Regime in India, UNICEF/ISST Conference, 7–9 December, New Delhi.

Hill, E. (2010). *Worker Identity, Agency and Economic Development: Women's Empowerment in the Indian Informal Economy*, London: Routledge.

Himanshu (2011). "Employment Trends in India: A Re-examination," *Economic and Political Weekly*, Vol. 46, No. 37, pp. 43–56.

Jayadev, A., S. Motiram, and V. Vakulabharanam (2011). "Patterns of Wealth Disparities in India 1991–2002," in *Understanding India's New Political Economy*, S. Ruparelia, S. Reddy, J. Harriss, and S. Corbridge (eds.), London: Routledge, pp. 81–100.

Kaur, R. (2006). "Migrating for Work: Rewriting Gender Relations," in *Poverty, Gender and Migration*, S. Arya and A. Roy (eds.), Vol. 2, New Delhi: Sage, 192–213.

Lim, L. (1990). "Women's Work in Export Factories: The Politics of a Cause," in *Persistent Inequalities: Women and World Development*, I. Tinker (ed.), Oxford: Oxford University Press.

Mazumdar, I. (2007). *Women Workers and Globalisation: Emergent Contradictions in India*, Centre for Women's Development Studies, New Delhi.

Nandi, R. (2009). "Urban Poor Livelihoods in the NCT of Delhi: Emerging Trends in Low-end IT and ITES Workers: Summary of Findings." Paper Presented at ISST Workshop on ITES Workers, New Delhi, 5 November.

NASSCOM (2009). "Perspective 2020: Transform Business, Transform India," NASSCOM, New Delhi. Available at: http://www.nasscom.in/NASSCOM-PERSPECTIVE-2020-Outlines-Transformation-Roadmap-for-The-Indian-Technology-and-Business-Services-Industries-56269 [accessed on 10 July 2012].

NASSCOM Mercer (2009). *Gender Inclusivity in India: Building Empowered Organisations*, NASSCOM, Mercer, New Delhi.

NASSCOM (2011). The IT BPO Sector in India: Strategic Review 2011. Executive Summary. Available at: http://nasscom.in/upload/Publications/Research/140211/Executive_ Summary.pdf [accessed on 16 June 2011].

Neetha, N. and R. Palriwala (2011). "The Absence of State Law: Domestic Workers in India," *Canadian Journal of Women and the Law*, Vol. 23, pp. 97–119.

OECD (2011). *Divided We Stand: Why Inequality Keeps Rising*, OECD, December 2011. Available at: http://www.oecd.org/document/10/0,3746, en_ 2649_33933_49147827_1_1_1_1,00.html [accessed on 16 June 2012].

Palit, A. (2008). *Evolution of Global Production Systems and Their Impact on Employment in India*. ILO Asia-Pacific Working Paper Series, ILO New Delhi.

Palit, A. and P. Singh (2011). "Suicides in India: The Economics at Work," Institute of South Asian Studies, Insights No. 131, 25 August, University of Singapore.

Palriwala, R. and N. Neetha (2009). *Paid Care Workers in India: Domestic Workers and Anganwadi Workers, Research Report 4*, UNRISD, Geneva.

Patel, R. (2010). *Working the Night Shift: Women in the Indian Call Centre Industry*, California: Stanford University Press.

Planning Commission (Government of India) (2013). *Twelfth Five Year Plan (2012–2017) Faster, More Inclusive and Sustainable Growth*, India: SAGE Publications. Available at: http://planningcommission.gov.in/plans/planrel/12thplan/pdf/vol_1.pdf [accessed on 5 September 2013].

Sandhu, A. (2006) "Why Unions Fail in Organising India's BPO-ITES Industry," *Economic and Political Weekly*, Vol. 41, No. 41, 14 October.

Sahu, P. P. (2011). "Is there an Earning Penalty for Self-Employed Workers? Evidence from India," in *Value of Work: Updates on Old Issues*, V. Cuzzocrea and J. Laws (eds.), Oxford, UK: Inter-Disciplinary Press, pp. 113–120.

Singh, P and A. Pandey (2005). "Women in Call Centres," *Economic and Political Weekly*, Vol. 40, No. 07, 12 February.

Standing, G. (1989). "Global Feminisation Through Flexible Labour," *World Development*, Vol. 17, No. 7, pp. 1077–1095.

Standing, G. (1999). "Global Feminization through Flexible Labor: A Theme Revisited," *World Development*, Vol. 27, No. 3, pp. 1077–1095.

TeamLease (2006). *India Labour Report 2006: A Ranking of Indian States by their Labour Econosystem*," A Report by TeamLease Services. Available at: http://www.teamlease.com/tl_reports.htm [accessed on 16 December 2008].

Unni, J. and G. Raveebdran (2007). "Growth of employment (1993–94 to 2004–05): Illusion of inclusiveness," *Economic and Political Weekly*, Vol. 42, No. 3, pp. 196–199.

van den Broek, D. (2004). "Globalising Call Centre Capital: Gender, Culture and Work Identity," *Labour & Industry*, Vol. 14, No. 3, pp. 59–75.

World Bank, World Development Indicators. Available at: http://data.worldbank.org/data-catalog/world-development-indicators [accessed on 10 July 2012].

9. Initiatives for Inclusive Growth at the State Level: Challenges for Andhra Pradesh

Meera Lal*

1. Introduction

Social and economic exclusion is essentially related to the exclusion of groups, wholly or partially, from full participation in society in which they live. Inclusive growth here needs to be expanded to include inclusive development. Being participative in the growth percentage alone is not adequate. Inclusiveness requires each and every person to be part and parcel of the development process and reaping the benefits of all around development. Nobel laureate Amartya Sen (2007) is focused on *capabilities: what people can do, and be.* It is these capabilities, rather than the income or goods that they receive (as in the Basic Needs approach), that determine their well-being. This core idea also underlies the construction of the Human Development Index, a human-focused measure of development pioneered by the UNDP in its Human Development Report. Sen's (2007) influential book, *Development as Freedom*, added an important ethical side to Development Economics.

Inclusive growth refers to *growth coupled with equal opportunities.* This has become increasingly relevant and imperative in the context of globalization, structural transformation and the need for a more regional balanced growth within a country. The Indian economy may have recently achieved rapid economic growth, but equitable sharing of the fruits of development is yet to be achieved. The trickle-down effect has not really taken place in a big way and the only alternative is for the government to introduce innovative schemes and new initiatives to achieve all round inclusive growth. In fact, the goal of all round inclusion has remained elusive. Education,

*Corresponding author: lalmeera@yahoo.com.

health care and microfinance initiatives are all part of inclusive growth. Convergence of quality education and delivery of health care services at an affordable cost to the vast section of the disadvantaged and low-income groups is still a distant dream. Some deliberate initiatives at the state level have been implemented for minimizing exclusion to a large extent.

2. Gross State Domestic Product and Regional Disparities

Andhra Pradesh (AP) is one of the relatively large states in India. It accounts for 8.4% of India's total geographical area and 7.1% of population, ranking fourth in terms of geographical area and fifth in terms of population among the Indian states. The density of population, at 308 per square km, is lower than the density 382 at all-India level. The Scheduled Castes and Scheduled Tribes (SCs and STs) account respectively for 16.2% and 6.6% of the total population in the state. About one-tenth of the state population is belonging to religious minority community.[1] Population belonging to disadvantaged castes and minority communities together accounts for about one-third of the state population. About another one-third of the state population is living in urban areas and the rest in the rural areas of the state. Rural AP is predominantly agricultural, with more than three-fourths of its workforce engaged directly in the agriculture sector. AP has the third largest economy in India in terms of GSDP (see Table 1). AP's economic growth path has been commendable, especially during the last three decades. Starting from a relatively lower per capita income, AP

Table 1: States with GSDP, per capita and growth rate (2010–2011).

Sl. No.	State	GSDP at current prices (2010–2011)	GSDP growth rate (2004–2005)	Per capita (2010–2011)	Population (2011)
1	Maharashtra	1029621	10.47	83471	112372972
2	Uttar Pradesh	595055	7.86	26355	199581477
3	Andhra Pradesh	588963	9.96	62912	84665533
4	Tamil Nadu	547267	11.74	72993	72138958
5	Gujarat	513173	10.47	75115	60383628

Source: Central Statistical Office, Government of India.

---

[1] See "Andhra Pradesh at 50."

has surpassed the national average about a decade ago. Although the state's performance is impressive in terms of economic growth when compared to its past and when compared to rest of the states in India, its overall development is judged as moderate. Its performance in terms of social sector indicators such as literacy and skills has not been impressive enough on a comparative scale.

The challenges faced by AP in this regard have been many, but one cannot deny the pioneering efforts of this state to achieve inclusive growth for its rural population, be it in the form of self-help groups (SHGs), Development of Women and Children in Rural Areas (DWCRA) Schemes, National Rural Employment Guarantee Act (NREGA) and the more recent AADHAR Unique Identification (UID). This chapter attempts to understand the inclusive growth with reference to all these efforts in AP and aims to study the strategies and initiatives adopted by the state. This study's descriptive research design is based on both primary and secondary data. Much recourse has been taken from Draft Approach to 12th Five-Year Plan for AP prepared by the Centre for Economic and Social Studies, Hyderabad.[2]

The growth experience of AP in the recent past is commendable. When compared to previous decades, the last decade's (i.e., 2000s) average growth rate of the state economy is substantially higher. The economy has been growing at an average rate of 8.2% during the last decade (2002–2012). The last two year's average growth is at 8.4% which is even higher. It is noteworthy that the state growth performance was better than that of national average during both the 10th and the 11th Plan periods particularly in agricultural and industrial sectors. Agricultural sector grew at 4.6%, while industry and service sectors grew at 9.5% and 9.3% respectively during this period (Table 2). AP's economic growth has been impressive particularly from 2003–2004 onward. The average growth rate of the GSDP in the 10th Plan was 8.1% as against the national average of 7.6%. Global recession and drought brought down the GSDP growth from 12.0% in 2007–2008 to about 6.9% during 2008–2009 and to 6.0% during 2009–2010.

The higher growth of GSDP and faster decline in the state's rate of population growth raised the level of per capita income. As a result, the per capita income of state rose to 10% higher than the national average.

---

[2]Draft for Discussion — Approach to the 12th Five-Year Plan Andhra Pradesh.

Table 2: Growth in real gross domestic product of AP and all India by major sectors.

Period	Andhra Pradesh				All India			
	AGRI	IND	SER	GSDP	AGRI	IND	SER	GDP
2000–2001	12.7	2.9	7.6	7.9	0.0	6.0	5.1	4.1
2001–2002	−1.7	4.5	7.4	4.1	6.0	2.6	6.6	5.4
2002–2003	−7.2	8.2	6.1	2.9	−6.6	7.2	6.7	3.9
2003–2004	14.3	6.1	7.8	9.0	9.0	7.3	7.9	8.0
2004–2005	4.2	12.3	7.9	8.0	0.2	9.8	8.3	7.1
2005–2006	6.1	10.1	11.0	9.6	5.1	9.7	10.9	9.5
2006–2007	2.0	17.6	12.5	11.2	4.2	12.2	10.1	9.6
2007–2008	17.4	10.9	10.3	12.0	5.8	9.7	10.3	9.3
2008–2009 (R)	0.8	7.1	9.5	6.9	0.1	4.4	10.0	6.7
2009–2010 (P)	1.3	6.4	7.7	6.0	1.0	8.4	10.5	8.4
2010–2011 (Q)	9.0	9.2	10.7	10.0	7.0	7.2	9.3	8.4
2011–2012 (A)	−1.5	7.3	9.8	6.8	2.5	3.9	9.4	6.9
10th Plan (2002–2007) Average	3.9	10.9	9.1	8.1	2.4	9.2	8.8	7.6
11th Plan (2007–2012) Average	5.4	8.2	9.6	8.3	3.3	6.7	9.9	7.9
Decadal Average (2002–2012)	4.6	9.5	9.3	8.2	2.8	8.0	9.3	7.8

Source: Publications of Central Statistical Office, Govt. India and Directorate of Economics Statistics, Govt. of AP.

One of the important elements of inclusive growth is reduction in regional disparities.[3] The Directorate of Economics and Statistics provides domestic product for each district in the state. Growth rates in district domestic product (DDP) and per capita DDP shows that seven districts of Telangana (Ranga Reddy, Nizamabad, Khammam, Hyderabad, Mahbubnagar, Warangal and Medak) and two districts of North Coastal (Visakhapatnam and Srikakulam) record higher growth rates than that of state average. On the other hand, all the districts in South Coastal and Rayalaseema and three districts of Telangana and one district of North Coastal show lower growth than that of state average. In terms of per capita income, the disparity between the poorest four districts and the richest four districts has increased during the pre-reform and post-reform period. Thus it is clear that, within state, there are variations in the level of economic

---

[3]Draft for Discussion (2012).

development across districts. For example, Srikakulam and Mahaboobnagar are at the bottom end by the average per capita income during 2007–2010, while Hyderabad and Visakhapatnam are at the top end. The growth of per capita income in districts with low level of per capita income in the base year has shown a better improvement during the last decade. However, the inter-district variations as measured by co-efficient of variation indicates continuous increasing trend although at a slower pace in the recent past. Whereas Table 3 shows growth rates of Real Gross Domestic product in AP by Major Sectors, Table 4 shows the glaring disparities in per capita income between several districts within AP.

It may also be noted that the quality of growth is important. Some of the Telangana districts like Ranga Reddy may be showing higher per capita incomes, but one is not sure about the quality of growth. One is also not sure whether it is inclusive growth in this region or whether regional disparities in the levels of development are still significant.

Table 3: Real GSDP growth in AP, 1961 to 2012.

Period	Agriculture	Industry	Services	GSDP Total
1961–1979	1.75	5.83	4.42	3.02
1980–1989	3.79	6.32	8.99	6.16
1990–1999	2.36	8.05	5.93	5.05
2000–2012	4.8	8.6	9.0	7.9
Average 2000–2005	4.45	6.82	7.36	6.38
Average 2005–2012	5.00	9.80	10.23	8.91

Source: DES.

Table 4: District per capita incomes (in Rs.): 2009–2010.

Sl. No.	District	2009–2010
1	Hyderabad	86897
2	Ranga Reddy	74970
3	Visakhapatnam	72512
4	Krishna	63202
5	Medak	61596
6	Prakasam	56345
7	East Godavari	55661

Source: Directorate of Economics and Statistics (DES), Hyderabad and CSO, New Delhi.

3. Urban Challenges

The latest 2011 Census has shown that, in AP, about one-third of the population is located in urban topography. Although urbanization is considered as a part of development, the pattern of urbanization shows a disturbing trend. Rapid urbanization increases the pressure on urban infrastructure and civic amenities and then creates environmental problems unless precautionary measures are taken. Most of the urban population in the state is getting concentrated in its three larger cities: Hyderabad, Visakhpatnam and Vijayawada. Lack of physical infrastructure and other civic amenities in the small and medium towns is leading to movement of people from these towns to large cities. As a result, many of small and medium towns in the state are getting declassified. The recent 2011 Census indicates the number of statutory and Census towns have increased over the previous 2001 Census as indicated in Table 5. It shows the increasing burden on urban development authorities in terms of allocation of resources and provision of infrastructure and civic amenities in these emerging urban centers.

Table 5: Trends in urbanization in AP: 1961–2011.

Census year	Total number of UAs/towns	Total population (in millions)	Urban population (in millions)	Urban population (%)	Growth of urban population (%)
1961	223 (1 UA)	36.0	6.3	17.4	1.5
1971	224 (4 UAs)	43.5	8.4	19.3	3.0
1981	252 (4 UAs)	53.5	12.5	23.3	4.0
1991	264 (15 UAs)	66.5	17.9	26.9	3.7
2001	210 (37 UAs)	75.7	20.5	27.1	1.4
2011	353 (x UAs)	84.7	28.4	33.5	3.1

Note: UA — Urban Agglomeration.
Source: Census of India.

4. Agricultural Growth

The state of agriculture has improved after experiencing long-term stagnation during the period from mid-1990s to mid-2000s. Although the global recession and drought affected the growth during 2008–2009 and 2009–2010, this sector picked up considerably during 2010–2011. The sector recorded higher growth rate during 2000–2010. There are wide fluctuations in the

Table 6: Trend growth of overall GSDP and that of agriculture, non-agriculture and per capita GSDP.

Item	1960–1961	1970–1971	1980–1981	1990–1991	2000–2001	2009–2010
GSDP	1.81	2.8	4.9	5.2	5.9	7.38
Agriculture	1.61	0.7	2.1	0.9	2.76	3.69
Non-Agri	4.8	4.6	6.6	6.4	7.4	7.76
Per capita GSDP	0.03	0.8	2.8	3.9	4.1	4.32

Source: Department of Economics and Statistics, Government of AP, Hyderabad.

growth of crop and fisheries in the agricultural sector.[4] Livestock sector recorded a substantial growth while forestry and logging showed a moderate improvement. There are, however, considerable differences across the districts in their contribution to the GSDP from agriculture. For about half of the districts, each one contributes less than 4% to the state GSDP from agriculture. This is evident from Table 6.

AP is the second largest producer of horticulture crops. It contributes 4% to the GSDP. It covers an area of 1.6 million hectares which accounts for 13% of total cropped area. It occupies one-fifth share of agriculture and allied crops economy of the state. There has been a perceptible change in the consumption pattern characterized by declining share of food grains and the increasing share of non-food grain items in the consumption baskets particularly fruits and vegetables — a three-tier approach is desirable for the development of horticulture sector *viz.*, infrastructure at Producer Groups/SHG level in clusters of 20–30 villages; need-based collection centers or aggregation centers for these clusters and development of food parks or central processing units with transportation facility. Involvement of marginal and small farmers in crop diversification and food security are hence important aspects to be addressed in accelerating crop diversification in the state.

Exclusion has thus continued in terms of low agriculture growth, with increasing visibility in farmers' suicides, low-quality employment growth, inadequate development of women and children, concentration of poverty and low human development, both geographically and in terms of social categories, increase in rural/urban divides and regional disparities (Dev, 2006).

Trends in crop production have been mixed. Maize productivity has persistently improved, followed by rice productivity. But productivity of

---

[4]Subrahmaniam (2007).

Figure 1: Trends in crop productivity in AP.

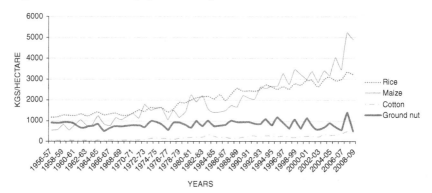

ground nut and cotton has been stagnant (Figure 1). There are four major concerns in the production sector with regard to the major crops, *viz.* considerable variations across the districts within the state; cost of production is relatively high in AP as compared to other states; dearth of new seed technology to enhance productivity and post-harvest related issues.

5.   Industrial Growth

The performance of industry during the first four years of the 11th Plan has been slow except for electricity/gas/water supply (Figure 2). Construction sector is maintaining steady growth of 9.95%. The mining and quarrying

Figure 2: Average annual growth rate (%) of GSDP from industries for AP (2004–2005 prices).

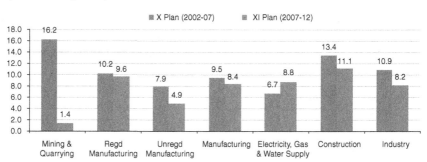

Note: Industry including all the sub-sectors.
Source: DES.

sector experienced a huge slump during this period.[5] The manufacturing sector, which contributes 50% of SDP from industry and 10% to the GSDP is growing at 8% against the targeted growth of 10–11%. The AP Government came up with a policy framework for special economic zones (SEZs) in 2002. The state stands in first position among the other developed states in terms of number of SEZs. Out of total 75 notified SEZs in the state, 27 are in operation and created 10% of targeted employment of 8.5 lakhs. The state is contributing almost 100% of exports from trading SEZs in the country.

However, issues such as forcible acquisition of multiple cropping lands, rehabilitation and resettlement have to be taken seriously. The information communication technology (ICT) has been performing consistently well in the last two decades in the state. AP occupies the fourth position in the country with a share of 15% of national IT exports. There is a scope for its exports expansion to Asia-Pacific countries. The ICT sector is heavily concentrated around the Hyderabad city and unable to move to tier-II and

Table 7: Key industrial sectors of growth in AP.

Industry	Current size in AP (Rs. in crore)	Projected size of industry in 2015 (Rs. in crore)	Drivers of growth
Drugs and Pharma	17,400	55,000	Accounts for about one-third of the bulk drugs and pharmaceuticals produced in India
Textiles	10,750	41,000	Leading producer of cotton
Engineering	11,000	38,000	Strong presence of engineering industry with large number of civil and defence research establishments
Agro and Food Processing	9,300	22,300	Leading producer of many fruits and vegetables
Mines and Minerals	7,800	21,000	2nd largest storehouse of mineral resources in India and around 48 minerals are available
Chemicals and Festilisers	8,400	17,000	Ranked 3rd in India in the production of chemicals
Paper	2,400	4,700	Leading producer of paper in India
Biotechnology	560	4,100	Growing industry

Source: CII.

---

[5]Dev and Ravi (2003).

Table 8: Number of SEZs in AP and other developed states (as on 31.3.2010).

State	Formal approvals	In-principle approvals	Notified	Total
Andhra Pradesh	109	5	75	180
Maharashtra	104	14	63	181
Tamil Nadu	71	5	57	133
Karnataka	58	1	36	95
Haryana	46	3	35	84
Gujarat	45	5	29	79
India	**585**	**42**	**381**	**1,008**

Source: India SEZ Report.

tier-III cities. The drivers of growth of manufacturing sector are identified as textiles, drugs and pharmaceuticals, engineering goods, food processing, minerals and metals, chemicals and fertilizers, paper and bio-technology. Tables 7 and 8 indicate the industrial growth drivers as well as the increase in number of SEZ units in the state.

6. Employment: Trends and Challenges

Expanding productive employment is central for sustained poverty reduction as labor is the main asset for majority of the poor. The long term total (rural + urban) employment growth in AP was around 1.8–2% per annum from 1983 to 2008–2009. The growth of employment in AP has declined from 2.72% in pre-reform to 0.95% in post-reform period. It declined both in rural and urban areas. In the post-reform period, growth in employment in urban areas was almost twice that of rural areas. However, within the post-reform period, we see marked fluctuations in employment growth. Some of the districts have shown some employment generation and investments in SME units (see Table 10). Table 9 gives a general idea of labor's net value added in factories of AP *vis-à-vis* 4 other Indian states.

7. Power Sector

In AP, power/electricity is an important sector that gained policy attention and hence priority in resource allocation during 1950s to 1970s. The state has pioneered in the generation of hydroelectric power among Indian

Table 9: Percentage contribution shares of major Indian states.

States	No. of factories			Persons employed in lakhs			Net value added		
	1977–1978	1988–1989	2004–2005	1977–1978	1988–1989	2004–2005	1977–1978	1988–1989	2004–2005
Tamil Nadu	10.41	12.59	15.44	9.54	11.59	15.86	10.09	10.86	8.30
Maharashtra	17.35	14.53	13.87	17.78	15.67	12.34	24.93	23.72	19.74
Andhra Pradesh	7.84	13.73	11.42	7.09	9.38	11.88	4.76	5.26	6.31
Gujarat	10.04	10.67	9.97	8.31	8.72	9.20	10.04	9.78	13.86
Uttar Pradesh	9.68	9.04	7.03	9.97	9.77	6.86	6.38	8.59	5.50

Source: Department of Economics and Statistics, Government of AP, Hyderabad.

Table 10: District-wise SME units and investments with employment generated for AP (2009).

Sl. No.	District	Units	Investment (crores)	Employment
1.	Hyderabad	15,477	374.68	125,329
2	Ranga Reddy	21,551	2,961.44	232,175
3	Visakhapatnam	10,746	646.87	94,067
4	Krishna	9,246	657.11	92,919
5	Medak	5,159	1,008.83	69,976
6	Prakasam	5,868	374.35	61,028
7	East Godavari	8,582	549.48	82,659
	Total	**158,173**	**10,504.31**	**1,532,015**

Source: CIL.

Table 11: Pattern of electricity consumption in AP — from 2001–2002 to 2008–2009 (%).

Year	Domestic	Non-domestic	Non-agriculture	Industrial	Railways	Others	Total (MU)
2001–2002	22.89	4.78	41.53	14.91	3.28	12.61	29402.21
2002–2003	22.18	4.98	39.31	17.27	3.41	12.85	31,319.30
2003–2004	21.12	4.87	37.39	20.15	3.31	13.15	34,084.09
2004–2005	20.71	4.87	36.18	22.33	3.12	12.79	37,617.65
2005–2006	22.49	5.44	35.82	26.07	3.25	6.92	37,617.65
2006–2007	20.46	5.12	35.31	25.70	2.85	10.55	44,850.21
2007–2008	21.45	5.56	31.04	28.65	2.92	10.37	47,914.46
2008–2009	21.57	5.66	31.95	28.91	1.79	10.12	53,335.13
CGR (%)	7.96	11.54	4.87	19.58	−0.12	5.51	8.88

Source: DES.

states. Most of the power generation in the state is through thermal and hydro-electric plants. The state has also taken up initiatives in renewable energy resources in particular wind and solar energy to supplement the fuel fossils. In terms of performance the power sector is the best in AP. The pattern of electricity consumption in AP can be seen from Table 11.

8. Poverty

Divergence of per-capita expenditure is seen across states with the already better-off states (southern and western regions) growing more rapidly than the poorer states in the north and east (Deaton and Dreze, 2002, pp. 3729–3748).

Table 12: Poverty ratios in AP and for all-India level.

	Poverty head count ratio			% Change/annum	
	1993–1994	2004–2005	2009–2010	1993–2004	2004–2010
Andhra Pradesh					
Rural	48.1	32.3	20.7	−1.44	−2.33
Urban	35.2	23.4	14.9	−1.07	−1.70
All	44.6	29.9	19.0	−1.34	−2.17
All India					
Rural	50.1	41.8	36.4	−0.75	−1.07
Urban	31.8	25.7	20.8	−0.56	−0.99
All	45.3	37.2	32.2	−0.74	−1.00

Source: Planning Commission.

The performance of AP in reducing income poverty has been impressive, particularly in rural areas. Estimates based on National Sample Survey (NSS) household consumption data indicate that poverty in AP has always been lower than the national average and also that its pace of reduction is faster than that of all India. AP presents a unique case of poverty reduction between 1970–1971 and 1987–1988 which is understandable because of high agricultural growth in AP. As could be seen from Table 12, the poverty head count ratio declined from 44.6% to 29.9% during 1993–1994 to 2004–2005 at a rate of 1.3 percentage points per annum. During the same period, all India poverty ratio fell from 45.3 to 37.2% at a rate of 0.7 percentage points per annum. There has been acceleration in the pace of reduction of poverty especially in AP between 2004–2005 and 2009–2010. Estimates for 2009–2010 indicate a further decline in poverty to 19% in AP from 30% in 2004–2005 in AP, while it fell to 32% from 37% at the all-India level during the same period which is evident from Tables 12 and 13. Rural poverty in the state has reduced by more than half, i.e., from 48% in 1993–1994 to 21% in 2009–2010.[6] Similarly, the urban poverty in the state has declined considerably to 15% in 2009–2010 from 35% in 1993–1994. During this period, rural poverty at the all-India level declined from 50% to 36% and urban poverty from 32% to 21%. Sen includes the relative price of cereals in a regressive equation for the proportion of rural population living below the poverty line and finds a highly significant positive

---

[6]Radhakrishna (1990).

Table 13: Number of poor in AP and in India.

State/sector	Number of poor (millions)		
	1993–1994	2004–2005	2009–2010
Andhra Pradesh			
Rural	24.3	18.0	11.6
Urban	6.6	5.5	4.1
All	30.8	23.7	15.9
All India			
Rural	330.1	324.2	292.6
Urban	74.9	81.9	71.8
All	405.1	407.0	369.9

Source: Computed.

Figure 3: Share of AP in number of poor at all-India level.

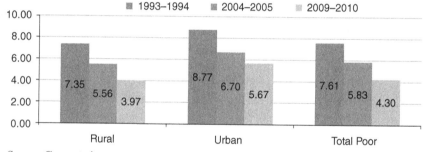

Source: Computed.

co-efficient.' Vol. 35, No. 10, pp. 823–825. Thus, AP's growth process seems to be widespread enough to benefit the poor.[7]

Although the share of poverty has shown a decline in recent years (Figure 3), it is difficult to completely remove poverty with 60% of workers in agriculture. Need for development of rural non-farm sector is obvious.[8] Agricultural growth of around 4% and manufacturing growth of more than 10% are necessary for this purpose. Another challenge is to provide livelihood and security to the vast low-productive and low-wage informal/

---

[7]Deshpande *et al.* (2004).
[8]Dev and Mahendra (2006).

unorganized sector.[9] For improving their productivity and reduce risk and vulnerability, cluster approach, training and skill improvement, credit and technology and social security are needed. The problem of 'working poor' is the major problem in AP. Inclusive growth also should frame appropriate policies to improve the conditions of socially disadvantaged sections like Scheduled Castes and Scheduled Tribes.

9. Social Sector

9.1. *Education*

Education is one of the critical aspects of the social and economic progress at the individual as well as at the national level. On the lines of international movement toward *Education for All* (EFA) especially since the early 1990s, the Government of India has also been committed to it. The EFA encompasses six goals of early childhood care and education, universal elementary education, adult literacy, adolescent and life skill education, gender equality and the quality of education. Aspects of elementary education are included in another global initiative of the *Millenium Development Goals* (MDGs), and India, being part of the initiative, has committed to the goals.[10]

AP is committed to both EFA and MDGs, and thus making efforts toward achieving these goals. In order to achieve inclusive growth, the Centrally Sponsored Schemes for elementary education have been streamlined and rationalized through a zero-based budgeting exercise. All the schemes have been converged under five major schemes: District Primary Education programme (DPEP), and the subsequent Sarva Shiksha Abhiyan (SSA) launched in 2001; National programme for Nutritional Support to Primary Education (Mid-Day Meals Scheme); Teachers Education Programme; Kasturba Gandhi Balika Vidyalaya (KGBV); and Mahila Samakhya — most of these activities under the National Literacy Mission as well as special programs for promotion of Early Childhood Care and Education, Inclusive Education etc.

At the elementary level, which is foundation of the pyramid in the formal education system, the state has made some kind of breakthrough,

---

[9]Working Group Report of the *Development of Education of SC/ST/Minorities/Girls and other Disadvantaged Groups for 11th Five-Year Plan (2007–2012)*.
[10]Mehta (2005).

especially during the last two decades, under DPEP and SSA. However, the goal of universalization of elementary education is yet to be achieved. Moreover, now it is realized that, in an emerging knowledge-based economy, a mere eight years of elementary education would be grossly inadequate for the young children to acquire necessary skills that industry demands and hence to compete in the job market. Therefore, there is need for universalization of secondary education, which is a goal of Rashtriya Madhyamik Shiksha Abhiyan (RMSA) — a scheme launched by Government of India in 2009. AP has to make efforts toward achieving this goal. Besides, the higher and technical education is also important, especially in its contribution to the economic growth point of view. When the performance of the state with respect to education can be seen in terms of access, enrolment, retention, equity and quality, there has been a substantial progress over time, but it is not substantial enough in terms of goals, especially with respect to elementary and secondary education.[11] Table 14 shows the literacy rate of AP, which is comparable to the all-India figure.

Although the attendance rate has increased in the recent years, there is nevertheless a humungous problem and grave concern for the state of adult literacy (Table 15). The latest 2011 Census has shown that only two-thirds of the state population has become literates. Due to the poor performance of the state with respect to the literacy rate, AP is in the group of states with moderate human development ranking in India. In fact, the problem

Table 14: Literacy rate (%) in AP and India.

| Year | Andhra Pradesh | | | All-India | | |
| | Person | Male | Female | Person | Male | Female |
1	2	3	4	5	6	7
1961	21	30	12	28	40	15
1971	25	33	16	34	46	22
1981	30	39	20	44	56	30
1991	44	55	33	52	64	39
2001	61	71	51	65	76	54
2011[$]	67.66	75.56	59.74	74.04	82.14	65.46

Note: 1 [$] Provisional Figures; 2 Literacy is for 5 + age population till 1981, thereafter it is for 7 + age population.
Source: 1 Census of India.

---

[11]Rao (2007).

Table 15: Attendance rates in educational institutions across age groups in AP compared to all-India rates.

		Andhra Pradesh			All-India		
Sl. No.	Age Groups	1995–1996	2007–2008	2009–2010	1995–1996	2007–2008	2009–2010
1	2	3	4	5	6	7	8
1	5 to 9	76.0	93.7	95.3	64.7	85.1	86.7
2	10 to 14	60.2	85.8	93.7	69.8	85.3	90.8
3	5 to 14	68.2	89.7	94.5	67.2	85.2	88.8
4	15 to 19	28.5	45.5	59.3	37.2	48.3	58.8
5	20 to 24	5.7	10.1	17.8	9.1	12.0	18.1
6	25 to 29	0.2	0.8	2.2	0.5	1.2	2.7

Note: Attendance rale refers attendance in educational institutions such as schools, colleges, institutes, centres, research institutes.
Source: Using NSS 52nd (1995–1996) and 64th (2007–2008) Rounds Literacy and Participation in Education Survey (Sch. 25) and 66th (2009–2010) Employment and Unemployment Survey unit record data.

of illiteracy and absence of formal education is affecting the quality of labor force in the state. This is one main reason why most of the workforce in the state is engaged in the elementary occupations, such as agricultural activity, which requires no specialized skills. Even among those engaged in the non-agriculture activities, most of them are engaged in those occupations which require only elementary skills. Therefore, improving quality of the labor force through skill development initiatives needs to be considered a crucial policy concern.

There seems to be an unspoken belief that the problem is with the 'people' and not the existing 'system'. The 1990s saw renewed interest to improve access to primary and upper primary schools in India through the mobilization of national and international resources. Although by 2003, 86.96% of habitations had a school within 1 km, and 78.11% had an upper primary school within a 3-km radius, significant inter-state differences yet persist. This is evident from the Figure 4. The attendance rates as shown in Figure 5 are also a cause of concern.

Also, while expansion of schooling led to tremendous increase in enrolment across the country, it did not address the needs of all children of the school-going age. Even though the total number of girls and SC children who enrolled in schools rose substantially, several girls and children from deprived communities (working children, residents of far-flung habitations,

Figure 4: Access to schooling in AP — Percentage of population by their nearest distance to school 2007–2008.

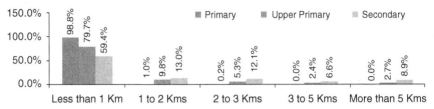

Note: Refers to Schools with primary, middle and secondary classes.
Source: Based on NSS 64th (2007–2008) Round Survey on Literacy and Participation Education (Sch 25.0) unit record data.

Figure 5: Attendance rate (%) pre-school age (3–6 years) in AP 2009–2010.

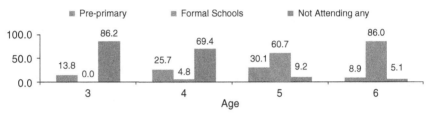

Note: 1. Rural and urban combined; 2. Pre-primary including those attending nursery/kindergarten etc.
Source: Estimated using NSS 66th (2009–2010) round employment and unemployment survey unit record data.

SCs/STs and nomadic groups) never enrolled. Severe social barriers to meaningful participation of children from some communities continue to exist. In AP, the Education department is responsible for providing education to all children, including children of weaker sections. Social Welfare, Tribal, Backward classes, Minorities, Women and Child welfare departments have all been implementing several educational programmes like hostels, scholarships, residential bridge schools etc., while allocating a major portion of their departmental budget provisions toward education of weaker sections. Tables 16 and 17 provide a macroanalysis of drop-out rates among SC and ST boys and Girls in AP and overall in India.

From the above tables, it is clear that AP ranks highest in drop-out rates in all categories of SC/ST children, with girls being greater victims in all classes. In most of the cases, the axe falls on the girl child. With meager income, many parents with four or five school-going children, on an average, find it difficult to spend equally for the schooling needs of all

Table 16: I–XII Class (All) and SC dropouts.

Year	All dropouts			SC dropouts		
	Boys	Girls	Total	Boys	Girls	Total
2001–2002	71.62	73.28	72.37	76.44	79.87	77.96
2005–2006	62.24	65.2	63.67	68.41	72.2	70.24
2006–2007	62.99	65.33	64.13	68.27	71.43	69.82
2007–2008	62.3	64	63.13	68.12	70.09	69.09

Source: http://ssa.ap.nic.in/ (Sarva Shiksha Abhiayan Andhra Pradesh).

Table 17: I–XII class (All) and ST dropouts in AP.

Year	General dropouts			ST dropouts		
	Boys	Girls	Total	Boys	Girls	Total
2001–2002	71.62	73.28	72.37	83.45	88.98	85.71
2005–2006	62.24	65.2	63.67	80.05	83.88	81.76
2006–2007	62.99	65.33	64.13	80.19	84.08	81.96
2007–2008	62.3	64.0	63.13	81.08	83.61	82.26

Source: http://ssa.ap.nic.in/ (Sarva Shiksha Abhiayan Andhra Pradesh).

children. So the variations of choices emerge, namely educate one child, withdraw the girl child, push the better performing child to another level or let the girls continue in government schools and move the boys to hostels. These are the extra costs among all the factors that deter the poorest from accessing schools even if they are in the same village.

9.2. Health care status in AP

Health is an important aspect in AP that needs the policy attention. The state's performance in faster demographic transition owing to fertility decline and the resultant faster decline in population growth is remarkable, owing to efforts of family planning initiatives. AP has emerged as one of those states with the lowest fertility rate and second lowest rate of growth in population. Nevertheless, its performance in other health indicators, such as infant mortality, malnutrition and HIV/AIDS is not much impressive. In comparison with other states, AP is found to be a moderately performing state in the health sector, although its performance of the state seen over its past record appears to be better. While AP has been emerging as one of the destinations of "Health Tourism," owing to its emerging private entrepreneurs in the health care sector, with the adoption of appropriate technology and development in health care sector, the status of health of its own population is not impressive. The growing private health care sector in the state is not affordable to large sections of economically poor and middle classes in the state. Therefore there is need for improving and strengthening public health care system in AP.

With respect to the health outcomes, the most important is the infant/child mortality rate. It reflects its health status, socio-economic development and the quality of life, which are crucial aspects of human development in a country/state/region. In this respect, AP has shown a remarkable performance over its past. The infant mortality rate (IMR) in the state in the recent period had declined to less than half of that of the base level — from 106 in the early 1970s to 46 in 2010 (see Table 18). The recent IMR estimate (46 in 2010) implies that one infant death occurs every seven minutes in the state. The declining trend shows that during the last four decades the rate of reduction in IMR in the state was 2.2% per annum. The rate of reduction (3.2% per annum) is sharpest in the recent period (2001–2010) and it was very minimal (0.7% per annum) during the 1990s. However, AP performance is lagging behind when compared to the other states in India, especially the southern ones. The progress and targets for select health indicators is apparent from Table 18.

Two initiative specific to AP in health sector are noteworthy. The state pioneered the promotion of Public–Private Partnership (PPP) in health care (*Arogyashree* and fee reimbursement for medical students of both private and government colleges). AP also pioneered the mobile emergency pre-hospital health care services. The Emergency Management Research Institute (EMRI) is managing the mobile emergency health services, popularly known as 108 services, by providing timely emergency health services aid to the accident victims or other emergency-related cases.

The performance of AP in the health indicators is better when compared that in its past, but not very impressive when compared with the other states in India, especially its southern sisters. AP has one-third of its children as malnourished, while the ratio is 40% at the national level. In the case of full vaccination and safe deliveries, the performances of the state are 68% and 95.6%, respectively, which are better than the all-India figures. However, there are regional variations, and this performance is not in line with the growth of the economy. The major constraint in the health sector

Table 18: Progress and targets for selected health indicators.

Indicator	Year	Progress and targets
Infant Mortality Rate	2002	62
	2010	46
	2020 — Target	10
Maternal Mortality Rate	1997	220
	2007–2009	134
	2020 — Target	50
Total Fertility Rate	1992–1993	2.29
	2005–2006	1.79
	2020 — Target	1.5
Child Malnutrition	1992–1993	42.9
	2009	29.8
Full Vaccination	1992–1993	72.3
	2009	68.0
Safe Deliveries	1992–1993	77.8
	2009	95.6

Source: NRHM, Andhra Pradesh.

is public health care (PHC) facilities, especially in rural AP. Although each Mandal headquarter is equipped with PHC facilities, inadequate infrastructure and human resources and then the malfunctioning of these facilities are a cause of concern.

Thirty-eight per cent of children (0–3 years) in AP are underweight compared to the national average of 47 per cent. The percentage of stunted children in same age group in Andhra Pradesh is 39 per cent compared to 46 per cent across India. The combined indicator of inadequacy of weight-for-height for the state is nine per cent, considerably lower than the all-India average of 16 per cent. There are wide rural/urban and gender disparities with respect to child nutritional indicators within Andhra Pradesh as well as for all-India. The proportion of underweight children in rural Andhra Pradesh is 41 per cent compared to 29 per cent in urban areas, with the corresponding rates for stunting being 42 per cent and 30 per cent respectively. Moderate to severe malnutrition is higher among rural children than urban children, and this holds among Hindus and Muslims, among scheduled castes and scheduled tribes in India. Only 32 per cent of children who belong to scheduled castes/tribes are fully immunized compared to 49 per cent of others (UNICEF, 2011).

Among the morbidity factors, anemia is more common among girls than boys, and boys are more likely to show wasting than girls. Besides this, access to a health care facility is far from satisfactory, even though

Figure 6: Water supply coverage in AP.

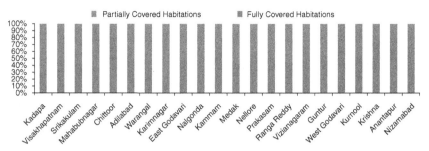

Source: www.indiawater.gov.in 2011.

the population covered by primary health care in AP is higher than the all-India average.

There are disparities in the availability of health care services, particularly among the weaker sections in rural areas. The health status of the tribals of AP is a serious cause of concern. In respect of several indicators of health status, the tribals in AP are badly placed. As per the NFHS-II, 1998–1999, IMR among the tribals was the highest at 103.6 (per thousand live births) relative to for instance the rate of 47.1 for 'others.' In respect of the tetanus-TT injections administered to ST pregnant women, the statistics was worst, with as many as 31.9% receiving none. The Maternal Mortality Rate was again the highest as compared at 652 (per hundred thousand) compared to 516 for others. The vicious circle of hunger–disease–low productivity–low wages–indebtedness–reduced consumption levels–persistent morbidity–disease haunts the tribals, and the development process has not helped them to break free of the cycle. It has also been observed that female ST children are found more among the nutritional categories "moderate" and "very severe." On the assumption that both male and female children are of the same nutritional status when born, it thus means that neglect of the female child sets in very early, even before the girl child reaches 7 months of age. Also, most often the parents rely only on mid-day meals scheme at school; hence all food at home is stopped for the children further leading to the woes of malnutrition and inadequate food for the children. Even drinking water is available to only 50% of the tribal habitations. And even where it is available, neither is it dependable nor is its quality good. Figure 6 shows the water supply coverage of AP with partially and fully covered habitations.

The same is true for sanitation. Sanitation facilities are only partially covered. There are a large number of individual households where sanitation

Figure 7: District-wise partially covered and fully covered status.

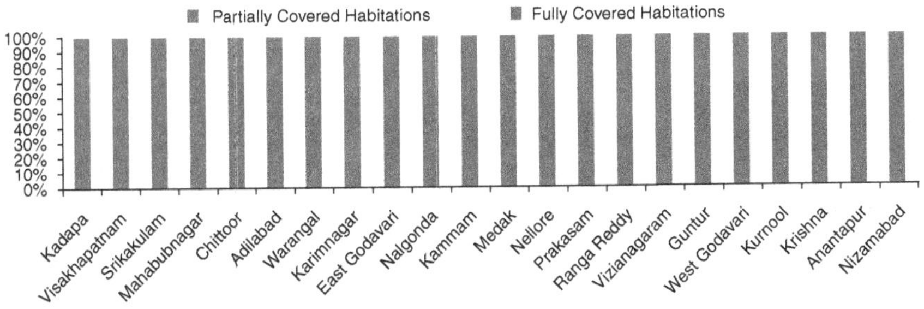

Source: www.indiawater.gov.in 2011.

remains uncovered in many parts of districts in Andhra Pradesh as obvious from Fig. 7.

To bring in the desired changes for a better health care sector, a well-defined partnership between the government and the private sector is essential. To catalyze desired changes in the health care industry, the Federation of Indian Chambers of Commerce and Industry (FICCI) has a Health Services Committee, with representatives from the industry. The purpose of the Committee is to develop an agenda for Health Services Reforms and recommend a framework for PPP to enhance quality health care in our country.

10. Microfinance and Financial Inclusion

Microfinance 'AP is regarded as 'Mecca' of Indian microfinance; home for more than half the cumulative number of SHG groups financed by the banks. EPW, Vol. 42, No. 13, pp. 1176–1184.

Microfinance is the provision of financial services to low-income clients, including consumers and the self-employed, who traditionally lack access to banking and related services. Microfinance in India has served over 40 million Indians through its two major channels — SHGs linkage and Micro-Finance Institutions (MFIs). Four out of five microfinance clients in India are women. The microcredit portfolio of India Microfinance amounts to more than Rs. 22,000 crore. About 75% are accounted for by SHGs Linkage, 20% by large MFIs and 5% by medium and small MFIs. SHGs' linkage reports of over Rs. 3,500 crore savings, whereas KBS Bank[12] — a local microfinance bank — reports only about Rs. 40 crore of savings portfolio.

10.1. *Financial inclusion*

Financial inclusion is integral to the inclusive growth process and sustainable development of the country. However, the financial inclusion models that banks come up with should be replicable and viable across the country. Although the banking network has rapidly expanded over the years, the key challenge would be to extend the banking coverage to include the large population living in 600,000 villages in the country. In AP, the use of SHGs to implement poverty alleviation programs can be seen as an evolution over time of governmental initiatives, national and state as well as NGO efforts.[13] The evolution goes back to 1979, with the national implementation of the Integrated Rural Development Program (IRDP) that targeted the poorest of the poor. Under IRDP in 1982–1983, the Government of India (GOI) started the Development of Women and Children in Rural Areas program (DWCRA) as a sub-component. Each of the Village Organizations (VOs) comprises of the SHGs of a village (8–10 groups) and its task is to address the common issues of the groups. *Mahila Mandal Samakhyas* (MMSs) are the highest federated entities, which bring the VOs together. This three-tier edifice is an attempt to construct a structure that can stand up against the existing monoliths like the state, private sector, banking sector, etc.

An important project, *Velugu*, is promoting the use of animators to provide facilitation support to members and leaders and develop linkages with banks and other institutions. The project has conducted several training

---

[12]Krishna Bhima Samruddhi (KBS) Local Area Bank is a Bank promoted by Basix, a group known for its pioneering work in microfinance in India. KBS Bank was set up in 2001, after receiving its licence from the Reserve Bank of India, as a local area bank with its operations in Mahabubnagar district of AP (where its headquarters are located) and the neighboring districts of Gulbarga (which was subsequently split to form the district of Yadgir) and Raichur in Karnataka. KBS Bank is one of the four local area banks operating in the country today. The Bank currently operates in over 1700 villages in these four districts serving a population of over 175,000 customers. While the Bank has 14 branches, it has extended its reach by using the services of business correspondent (BC), thus totally reaching out to 73 locations within the operating area (*Source: Wikipedia*).

[13]Himanshu (2007).

programs for District Program Managers (Dpms), Community Coordinators and trainers of support organizations in seven districts. A total of 292 of the proposed 460 *Mandal Velugu* training centers have been set up. The overall national economic environment has played a pivotal role in the spread of microcredit to the rural poor.

The AP Government has facilitated the organization of the below-poverty-line households into SHGs to advance their economic advancement, especially by linking these groups with the banking network for their financial inclusion. It is often the case that these SHGs are exploited by private MFIs through usurious interest rates and coercive means of recovery, resulting in their impoverishment and, in some cases, leading to suicides. It is, therefore, expedient to make provisions for protecting the interests of the SHGs, by regulating the money-lending MFIs in order to achieve greater transparency in their transactions in AP. The *Andhra Pradesh Microfinance Institutions (regulation of money lending) Ordinance 2010* is has been designed to protect the women SHGs from exploitation by MFIs in AP.

11. Toward an Inclusive Growth

In AP, one noteworthy observation is that there have been linkages established between different approaches to identify economic indicators of poverty. It is, however, not enough to merely address the economic indicators of poverty. Social poverty needs to be highlighted and woven into empowerment programs. Social poverty manifests in the presence of corrosive evils like caste taboos, norms of dowry and adherence to other vices such as alcohol and drugs as well. Needs have to be voiced and vigilance have to be maintained for making sure that people do not succumb to short-lived sops. There is no doubt that the state, implementing agencies and service providers have to be accountable to the people. The flip side of accountability is responsibility. It is only when people themselves are also seen as accountable toward their own lives and THE development of their regions, that it becomes their responsibility to participate in the decision-making processes.

11.1. *Good governance initiatives*

Using the emerging ICT, there are many good governance initiatives in the service delivery stream of governance. During the last two decades, many such initiatives have been put in place. These include Best Practices in school education, *Neeru-Meeru* Programme,[14] Power and Public Sector Reforms, Property Tax Reforms, Services Outsourcing, Single Window System (SWS), e-Governance Initiatives (e-Seva, e-Procurement, Online performance tracking), Citizen Charters, Rythu Bazars, e-Panchayats, etc. Some of the initiatives (including e-Seva centers, Rythu Bazars, e-Procurement and electricity reforms) have gained instant popularity and appreciation. The success of e-Seva centers is reflected in their adoption across the country. The Rythu Bazar is rated as one of 10 best practices in the country and are immensely popular among all sections of the population.[15] The performance of the AP Electricity Board has been rated as the best in country for two years in a row after the reforms. Similarly, the continuation of e-Procurement approach by the present government is an indication of its effectiveness. Most important has been the implementation of the recent centrally sponsored scheme Mahatma Gandhi National Rural Employment Guarantee Scheme (MGNREGS) in the state using ICT and social audit methods. The good governance initiatives have helped in curtailing red tape and rent-seeking in some cases. Though the attempt to eliminate intermediaries has brought the people in contact with the line departments, some of these initiatives suffer from proper implementation rather than improper design.[16]

11.2. *Key challenges*

Despite the initiatives and their practice, there are key challenges which remain.

➤ Integration of parallel institution with democratic institutions (PRIs)
➤ Red-tapism and corruption
➤ Lack of convergence across line departments
➤ Deficit in decentralization
➤ Accountability
➤ Transparency

---

[14]The Government of Andhra Pradesh has constituted Water Conservation mission to focus attention on conservation of water in a big way by taking large scale water conservation measures under Neeru–Meeru Programme.
[15]Rao (2007).
[16]Sen (1996).

Thus, although economic growth has increased in AP, inclusive growth has yet to be achieved and needs to be improved.

To conclude, the economy of AP seems to be on a relatively high-growth path. The fiscal performance is also satisfactory. The success of the IT sector is well known. Population growth also declined significantly in the state. The growth prospects for AP are promising, given its past trend, especially during the last 10 years. A pre-condition required for better overall growth is the growth of the agriculture sector, which is affected by weather conditions and natural calamities, such as frequent droughts and floods. For industrial growth, although an industry-friendly policy environment is in place, the preconditions of industrial growth, such as infrastructure, roads and transportation, power and access to finance are still acting as impediments in materializing potential of high industrial growth in the state.

On the social sector front, school education at elementary as well as at secondary state performance is better over its past, there is a possibility of universalization of school education (elementary and secondary education) as efforts are being made rigorously. The state's achievement in higher education is also better, but the quality of education is a matter of concern. In the health sector, the state's performance in family planning is remarkable, which resulted in one of the least fertility rates in India and thereby faster demographic transition. However, the performance in other health parameters such as infant mortality and malnutrition is still lagging behind. Similarly, there are other social sector aspects such drinking water, urban development, development of disadvantaged castes and minority communities that need more attention.

Total inclusive growth is important to reduce existing poverty and various types of inequalities in the state, the economy and society. Structural transformation in terms of workers shifting from agriculture to non-agriculture is also important for poverty alleviation. As discussed earlier, there are many challenges for achieving inclusive growth even if the economy records high growth of 7–8% per annum in GDP. This could be the result of improvement in technology to bring this high growth rate and surveys are being conducted by Department of Science and Technology (DST) to find a positive co-relation between technology and SGDP in various districts.[17] In other words, achieving inclusive growth is much more challenging than

---

[17]Institute of Public Enterprise (2012).

achieving 7–8% growth in GDP. The post-reform witnesses increase in disparities across regions and social groups and between rural and urban areas. There is certainly a need for a broad-based and inclusive growth to benefit all sections of the society. Improving decentralization and governance should also be a part and parcel for inclusive growth. Therefore, focused government interventions and enlightened civil society, including NGOs, are important for the success of macro policies, sectoral interventions, targeted poverty alleviation programmes and even for going beyond MDGs.

Acknowledgments

The author would like to acknowledge that some of the data used in this chapter have been collected from a survey report and Draft Approach to 12th Five-Year Plan conducted by the Centre for Economic and Social Studies (CESS) at Hyderabad.

References

Annual Reports of MFIs in Hyderabad — BASIX, APMAS, SHARE, and SKS.

"Common School Education System: 2007," — A Report by Expert Committee under the Chairmanship of Professor Muchkund Dubey on schools in Bihar.

District Elementary Education Report Card 2005–06, *Sarva Siksha Abhiyan*, Government of India 2010.

Deaton, A. and J. Dreze (2002). "Poverty and Inequality in India: A Reexamination," *Economic and Political Weekly*, Vol. 37, No. 36.

Deshpande, L. K., A. N. Sharma, A. K. Karan, and S. Sarka (2004). *Liberalisation and Labour: Labour Flexibility in Indian Manufacturing*, New Delhi: Institute of Human Development.

Dev, S. M. and C. Ravi (2003). "Macroeconomic Performance: Performance and Policies," in *Andhra Pradesh Development: Economic Reforms and Challenges Ahead*, in C. H. H. Rao and S. Dev (eds.), Hyderabad: Mahendra Centre for Economic and Social Studies (CESS).

Dev, S. M. and C. Ravi (2007). "Poverty and Inequality for all India and Major States: 1983 to 2004-05," *Economic and Political Weekly*, Vol. XLV, No. 26, pp. 519–520.

Dev, S. M. (2006). "Inclusive Growth in India: Performance, Issues and Challenges," First Dr. P. R. Dubashi Lecture, Gokhale Institute of Politics and Economics, November 29; GOI (2006). "Report of the XI Plan Working Group on Poverty Elimination Programmes," Planning Commission.

Draft for Discussion (2012). *Approach to the 12th Five Year Plan Andhra Pradesh*, Hyderabad: Centre for Economic and Social Studies (CESS), June.

Ghate, P. (2006). *Microfinance in India — A State of the Sector Report*, New Delhi: Microfinance India.

Government of India. "Andhra Pradesh at 50: A Data Based Analysis, A Data News Features," Annual Report 2006–07, Ministry of Rural Development, Government of India 2008.

Himanshu, R. (2007). "Recent Trends in Poverty and Inequality: Some Preliminary Results," *Economic and Political Weekly*.

Institute of Public Enterprise (2012). Workshop on "Research Methodology for Evaluating Co-Relationship Between Technology and Increased SGDP, October, Hyderabad: DST.

Mehta, A. C. (2005), *Elementary Education in India-Where do we stand?* State Report Cards. NIEPA, New Delhi.

NSS 59th Round Sch. 33: 2003, NSSO, Ministry of Statistics, Government of India.

Parthasarathy, G. (1995). "Public Intervention and Rural Poverty: Case of Non Sustainable Reduction in Andhra Pradesh," *Economic and Political Weekly*, Vol. 30.

Radhakrishna, R. (1990). "Poverty in Andhra Pradesh, Underpinnings and Policy Intervention," in *Andhra Pradesh Economy in Transition' Proceedings of Seminar held Feb. 1989*, K. Mukund (ed.), Vol. 7, Centre for Economic and Social Studies, Hyderabad and Book Links Corp.

Rao, B. (2007). "Minimal Visible Inequality is Human Development," in *India's Economic and Social Development, CESS Silver Jubilee Lectures*, S. M. Dev and K. S. Babu (eds.), New Delhi: Academic Foundation.

Rao, C. H. H. and S. M. Dev (2003). *Andhra Pradesh Development: Economic Reforms and Challenges Ahead*, Hyderabad: Centre for Economic and Social Studies.

Rao, C. H. H. (2007). "Statehood for Telangana: New Imperatives," *The Hindu*, 8 January.

Sen, A. (1996). 'Economic Reforms, Employment and Poverty: Trends and Options," *Economic and Political Weekly*, Vol. 31, No. 35/37.

Sen, A. (2007). *Development as Freedom*, London: Oxford University Press.

Subrahmaniam, S. (2007). "Agricultural Crisis in Andhra Pradesh: Causes and Remedies," *mimeo*, Hyderabad: Centre for Economic and Social Studies.

UNICEF Annual Report, 2011, www.unicef-org/files.

Working Group Report, *Development of Education of SC/ST/Minorities/Girls and other Disadvantaged Groups for 11th Five-Year Plan (2007–2012)*, Government of India, Planning Commission, New Delhi 2007.

Index

Printed in the United States
By Bookmasters